# THE DOCTOR LOOKS AT LITERATURE

## PSYCHOLOGICAL STUDIES OF LIFE AND LETTERS

BY

JOSEPH COLLINS

KENNIKAT PRESS
Port Washington, N. Y./London

THE DOCTOR LOOKS AT LITERATURE

Copyright 1923 by George H. Doran Company
Reissued in 1972 by Kennikat Press by
arrangement with Doubleday & Company, Inc.
Library of Congress Catalog Card No: 79-153245
ISBN 0-8046-1498-9

Manufactured by Taylor Publishing Company      Dallas, Texas

ESSAY AND GENERAL LITERATURE INDEX REPRINT SERIES

*In Memoriam*

## PEARCE BAILEY

DEVOTED COLLEAGUE
LOYAL COADJUTOR
INDULGENT FRIEND

# ACKNOWLEDGMENT

The author wishes to express his thanks to the editors of the *North American Review,* the *New York Times* and the *Literary Digest International Book Review* for permission to elaborate material used by them into certain chapters of this volume.

# CONTENTS

# ILLUSTRATIONS

# THE DOCTOR LOOKS
# AT LITERATURE

# THE DOCTOR LOOKS AT LITERATURE

## CHAPTER I

### PSYCHOLOGY AND FICTION

FEW words attract us like the word psychology. It has the call of the unknown, the lure of the mysterious. It is used and heard so frequently that it has come to have a definite connotation, but the individual who is asked to say what it is finds it difficult either to be exact or exhaustive. Psychologists themselves experience similar difficulty. Psychology means the science of the soul, but we have no clearer conception of the soul today than Aristotle had when he wrote his treatise on it.

Professor Palmer states that William James once said that psychology was "a nasty little subject," and that "all one cares to know lies outside." Doubtless many who have far less knowledge of it have often felt the same way. The present fate of psychology, or the science of mental life, is to be handled either as a department of metaphysics, or as subsidiary to so-called intelligence testing. The few remaining true psychologists are the physiological psychologists and a small group of behaviourists. In this country Woodworth, who takes the ground of utilising the best in the arsenal of both the introspectionists and the behaviourists, and calls the result "dynamic psychology,"leads the former; and Watson the latter.

Psychology has no interest in the nature of the soul, its origin or destiny, or in the reality of ideas. Nor does it concern itself with explanation of mental phenomena in terms of forces which can neither be experienced nor inferred from experience. It is concerned with the facts of mental life and with describing, analysing, and classifying them.  When it has done this it hands the results over to the logician who occupies himself with them from a purposeful rather than a causal point of view; and he makes what he may of them, or he puts them at the disposal of fellow scientists who use them to support conjectures or to give foundation to theories.

It is universally admitted that when we want to get a true picture of human life: behaviour, manners, customs, aspirations, indulgences, vices, virtues, it is to the novelist and historian that we turn, not to the psychologist or the physiologist. The novelists gather materials more abundantly than the psychologists, who for the most part have a parsimonious outfit in anything but morbid psychology.  Psychologists are the most indolent of scientists in collecting and ordering materials, James and Stanley Hall being outstanding exceptions.

Fiction writers should not attempt to carry over the results of psychological inquiries as the warp and woof of their work. They should study psychology to sharpen and discipline their wits, but after that the sooner they forget it the better.  The best thing that fiction writers can do is to depict the problematic in life in all its intensity and perplexity, and put it up to the psychologists as a challenge.

In the fifty years that psychology has had its claims as a science begrudgingly allowed, there have arisen many different schools, the most important of which are:   (1) Those that claim that psychology is the science of mental states, mental processes, mental contents, mental functions.  They are the "Functionalists."  There is an alternative to the consciousness psychology—the psychology of habit—touched on its edges by Professor Dewey in "Habit and Conduct."  And (2) those that claim the true subject matter of psychology is not mind or consciousness, but behaviour.  They refuse to occupy themselves with "consciousness," and for introspection they substitute experiment and observation of behaviour. Their theoretical goal is the prediction and control of behaviour. They are the "Behaviourists." The literature infused with interest in psychological problems—fiction, criticism, and to a small extent social economics—has little connection with the older psychology based on subjectivities, except as it takes over the vagaries of technique and terminology of the psychoanalysts. The literature of greatest merit seems to avail itself most profitably of definite psychological materials when it turns to the behaviourist type. Indeed, it is with this school that the novelist most closely allies himself. Or it was, until the "New Psychology" seduced him.

This last school claims that consciousness and all it implies is a barren field for the psychologist to till. If he is to gather a crop that will be an earnest of his effort, he must turn to the unconscious, which we have with us so conspicuously eight hours out of every twenty-four that even the most benighted recognise it, and which is inconspicuously with us always, looking out for our self- and species-preservation, conditioning our ends, and shaping our destinies.

The New Psychology, which is by no means synonymous with the teachings of Dr. Sigmund Freud of Vienna, regards the human mind as an intricate and complex mechanism which has gradually evolved through the ages to suit the needs of its possessor. The adaptation has, however, not been perfect, and the imperfections reveal themselves in frequent, startling, and embarrassing lapses from the kind of mind which would best enable its possessor to adjust himself to the conditions and demands of modern civilisation. It recognises that it deals with a mind which sometimes insists upon behaving like a savage, but which is nevertheless the main engine of the human machinery, human personality, from which society expects and exacts behaviour consistent with the ideals of advanced civilisation. The practical psychologist realises that he has to cope with this wayward mind, and if he is to be of service in effecting a reconciliation between it and the requirements of civilisation, he cannot ignore it, spank it, or coerce it by calling it bad names. He must understand it first; then he may train it. The trouble with the New Psychology, whether it is "New Thought" or one of the mutually antagonistic schools of psychoanalysis, is that it almost inevitably runs off into what James terms "bitch-philosophy."

Through this tangled web of vagaries there is a thin thread of work that is not only fiction, but literature; and this is usually characterised by obvious parade of psychological technique.

Just as civilised man's body has been evolved gradually from more primitive species and has changed through the various stages of evolution to meet the changing conditions of the environment and necessities, so has his mind. In this advance and transformation the body has not lost the fundamental functions necessary for the preservation of the physical being. Neither has the mind. But both the body and the mind, or the physical and psychical planes of the individual, have been slowly developed by environment and life in such a way that these fundamental functions and instincts have been brought more and more into harmony with the changing demands of life. This process, outwardly in man's circumstances and his acts, inwardly in his ability to shape one and perform the other, constitutes civilisation. It is doubtful if the instincts are quite as definite as some of our professors, McDougall and his followers, claim, and they lack utility when used as a basis for social interpretation either in essays or fiction.

Dr. Loeb's forced movements as a basis for a structure of interests is far more plausible. It is the interplay of interests, rather than of instincts, which is the clay our practical activities are pottered from, and should be the reliable source of materials for literature. Whenever fiction cuts itself down to instincts it becomes ephemeral as literature.

The two fundamental and primitive instincts of all living

organisms, civilised man included, are the nutritional urge and the creative urge, or the instinct of self-preservation and that of the preservation of the species. To these there is added, even in the most primitive savages, the herd instinct, which leads men to form groups or tribes, to fight and labour for the preservation of them, and to conform to certain standards or symbols of identification with the tribe. The Freudians do not recognise the herd instinct as anything but sublimated bi-sexuality, attributing the tendency to regard the opinion of one's associates to the psychic censor, instead of to an instinct. These three instincts are recognised in their commonest and most normal expression today as the tendency to provide for oneself and one's family; the tendency to marry and rear children under the best conditions known; and the tendency to regard the opinion of one's associates and to be a consistent member of the social order to which one acknowledges adherence.

It is small wonder, then, that the realist and the romanticist, whose arsenal consists of observation and imagination, find in narration of dominancy and display of these instincts and tendencies the way to the goal for which they strive: viz., interest of others, possibly edification. Certain novelists, Mr. D. H. Lawrence for instance, pursue discussion of the fundamental ones with such assiduity and vehemence that the unsophisticated reader might well suspect that life was made up of the display and vagaries of these essences of all living beings. But without cant or piety it may be said there is such a thing as higher life, spiritual life, and readers of psycho-analytic novels must keep in mind the fact that the Freudian psychology denies the reality of any such higher life, accounting for the evidences of it which are unescapable in terms of "subliminations," such as "taboos." Though these three instincts form the basis upon which the whole of man's mental activity is built, they by no means form its boundary. At some prehistoric period it is possible that they did, but during countless ages man's mind has been subject to experiences which called for other mental activity than the direct and primitive expression of these urges, and he has had to use his mental machinery as best he could to meet these demands. He had no choice. He could not scrap his old machinery and supply his mind with a new equipment better fitted to do the complex work civilisation demanded.

The result is that the working of these instincts on the experience presented to the mind has brought about innumerable complications. These are known in the New Psychology as mental complexes. They have been to some modern novelists what the miraculous food given to Israel in the Wilderness was—their sole nutriment. Complexes, or conflicts resulting from adaptation of the primitive mental machinery to more intricate and varied processes than those with which it was originally intended to cope, determine much of man's mental life.

To understand the workings of a mind is like trying to unravel a tangled skein of thread. The two main difficulties are: (1) That up to this time our mental training, our perceptions, our consciousness, our reason, have been exercised for the specific purpose of maintaining ourselves in the world. They have not been concerned with helping us to understand ourselves; (2) That there are parts of our minds whose existence we do not recognise, either because we will not or because we cannot, for the reason that they have come to be regarded as being in conflict with other parts which we have long admitted as having the first claim to recognition. In other words, not having known how to adapt certain parts of our mental machinery to the newer purposes for which we needed them, we have tried to suppress them or ignore them. In doing so we have only deceived ourselves, because they are still connected up with the main engine and influence all of the latter's output, harmoniously or jarringly—sometimes to the extent of interfering seriously with its working.

The work of the practical psychologist is to learn how to overcome these two difficulties and to teach others how to use the knowledge. This is the task novelists frequently set themselves, and some, Willa Cather in "Paul's Case" and Booth Tarkington in "Alice Adams," accomplish it admirably. Like the teacher and the priest, they have learned that surplus energy of the mind may be diverted from the biologically necessary activities into other fields of useful and elevating effort. They have learned that the second difficulty can be best overcome by facing the truth about our minds, however unpleasant and unflattering it may at first sight appear to be. Recognition of the existence of the two primitive urges, the instincts of self-preservation and of the preservation of the race, is the first step toward appreciation of their reasonable limitations and the extent to which they may be brought into harmony with the requirements of a well-balanced life.

This leads us to refer for a moment to a tremendous force which, in any discussion of the working of the instincts, cannot be ignored. It is a constant effort or tendency, lying behind all instincts, to attain and maintain mental, emotional, and spiritual equilibrium. The tendency is expressed by the interaction, usually automatic and unconscious, which goes on between complexes and tends to establish the equilibrium. At the same time the working of individual instincts tends to upset it. Whenever the automatic process is suspended to any great degree, as by the cutting off from the rest of the mind of one complex, the result is a one-sided development which causes mental disturbances and often eventually mental derangement. As the instincts and complexes incline to war among themselves, there is a stabilising influence at work tending to hold us in mental equilibrium and thus to keep us balanced or sane. No one in the domain of letters has understood this force and its potentialities like Dostoievsky. "The Possessed" is a chart of that sea so subject to storm and agitation. The effort toward integration is perhaps a true instinct, and rests on a sound physiological basis, so well described by Sherrington. It furnishes a genuine theme for description of life's activities, and well-wrought studies of integration and disintegration take highest rank in fiction.

With all their prolixity, the Victorian novelists managed to depict progress in one direction or another. This is more than can be said of most modern novelists, who are exhausted when they have succeeded in a single analysis, and commit the crass literary error of seeking to explain, when all that the most acute psychologist could possibly do would be to catch at a pattern, a direction, and an outcome, as mere description—problem rather than explanation being the dramatic motive.

While the novelist's business is to see life and his aspiration is to understand what he sees, many novelists of today are, by their work, claiming to understand life in a sense that is not humanly possible. Human conduct affords the best raw material for the novelist. If he represents this in such a way that it seems to reflect life faithfully he is an artist; but the psychological novelist goes further and feels bound to account for what he represents. Ordinarily he accounts for it in one of three ways: (1) by the inscrutability of Providence—as many of the older novelists did; (2) by theories of his own; (3) by the theories of those whose profession to understand life and conduct he accepts. In short, he must have a philosophy of life. The mistake many novelists are making is to confuse such a philosophy of life with an explanation of mental processes and a formula for regulating them. Neither philosophy nor psychology is an exact science. If a novelist wishes to describe an operation for appendicitis or a death from a gastric ulcer, he can easily get the data necessary for making the description true to fact. But if he aspires to depict the conduct, under stress, of a person who has for years been a prey to conflicting fear and aspiration, or jealousy and remorse, or hatred and conscience, what psychologist can give him a formula for the correct procedure? Who can predict the reactions of his closest friend under unusual conditions?

With our earnest realistic novelist ready to sit at the feet of science and avail himself of its investigations—prepared, as Shaw would say, to base his work on a genuinely scientific natural history—there is danger of his basing it, too, upon psychology which is not "genuinely scientific," because its claims cannot be substantiated by experience. While the novelist is in such a receptive state along comes a scientist, hedged also with that special authority which physicians possess in the eyes of many laymen, and offers the complete outfit of knowledge and (as he assures the novelist) inductively derived theory that the novelist has been sighing for. This is Freud. He or his disciples can explain anything in the character and conduct line while you wait. If you want to know why a given person is what he is, or why he acts as he does, Freud can tell you. His outfit is not, ostensibly, "metaphysical," like much of the older psychology that our novelist encountered in college days. It is human, concrete, and surprisingly easy to understand. A child can grasp the main principles. Our novelist tests out a few of them on life as he has known it and finds that they seem to work. If he is not completely carried off his feet, he may grin at some of the formulas as he might at a smutty joke, but his own observations concerning the excessively mothered boy and his reading of some of the great dramas of the world are to him sufficient evidence of their soundness; and he bases the behaviour of his characters upon them with the same assurance of their accuracy that he would have in basing the account of a surgical operation and its results upon the data supplied him by a surgeon who had successfully performed hundreds of exactly similar operations and watched their after effects.

One of the rudimentary instincts of human nature is curiosity, an urge to investigate the unknown, the mysterious. It is mystery that constitutes romance. It is the unknown that makes romance of one's future, fate, fortune, mind—at least that part of the mind which we do not understand and which is always taking us by surprise and playing us tricks. Curiosity is forced movement developed along the lines of interest. It is quite likely to follow the line of least resistance, and just now there is little resistance to sex curiosity. Those who find fascination in the New Psychology today found the old psychology of a quarter of a century ago a stupid bore. The old psychology dealt exclusively with what is now called the "conscious mind:" with analysing the concept of directed thought, with measuring the processes of the mind which we harnessed, or believed we harnessed, and drove subject to our wills to do our work. The old psychology was academic, dry, as proper and conventional as the C Major scale, without mystery, without thrills, and therefore without interest, except to the psychologist.

The New Psychology is different. And this "difference" is exactly why it has proved to be almost as effective bait to the feminine angler after romance which may serve her as caviar to the prosaic diet of every-day existence as are spiritualism and the many other cults and new religions whose attraction and apparent potency are now explainable by what we understand of this very psychology—or the science of the mind. There is no reason to suppose that the current doctrines of the subconscious will do more for civilisation or art than the older doctrines of consciousness. The fact that they seize the popular fancy and are espoused with enthusiasm is of no particular significance, since the very same attitude was an accompaniment of the older doctrines.

It would be difficult to exaggerate the prevalent interest in psychology. I shall cite three indications of it: The pastor of one of the large and influential churches in New York asked me a short time ago if I would give a talk on Psychology before the Girls' Club of his church. When I suggested that some other subject might be more fitting and helpful, he replied that all the girls were reading books on psychology, that he was sure none or few of them understood what they read, and that he was convinced that their indulgence was unhealthy. Should one go into any large general book-shop in New York or elsewhere and survey the display, he will find that a conspicuous department is devoted to "Books on Advanced Thinking," and upon inquiry he will find that it is the most popular department of the store. The most uniform information that a psychiatrist elicits from the families of youths whose minds have undergone dissolution is that for some time previous to the onset of symptoms they displayed a great interest in books on philosophy and psychology, and many of them had taken up psychoanalysis, or whatever passes under that name; joined some League of the Higher Illumination; or gone in for "mental fancy work" of some kind.

Before taking up specific illustrations of psychology in modern fiction, I wish to say to amateurs interested in the study of psychology, that frank recognition of their own unconscious minds or of the part of their instinctive life or memories which may have been intentionally or automatically pushed out of consciousness, does not call for digging into the unconscious through elaborate processes of introspection or through invoking the symbolism of dreams. Even were it done, the result would probably reveal nothing more startling than would a faithful account of the undirected thoughts which float uninvited through the mind during any idle hour. For most normal persons such thoughts need neither to be proclaimed nor denied. The involuntary effort toward equilibrium of a normal mind will take adequate care of them. The study of such mental conditions and processes in abnormal individuals, however, is often of great service to the psychologist and facilitates understanding of the workings of both the normal and the unbalanced mind.

I also desire to call attention to the value of an objective mental attitude if one would conserve mental equilibrium and keep the working mind at its highest point of health and productivity.   One of the greatest safeguards of mental equilibrium is the desire for objective truth.   This is an indication that the mind is seeking for harmony between itself and the external world, and it has a biological basis in the fact that such harmony between the organism and the external world makes for security.   The desire for objective truth is a straight pathway between the ego-complex and the ideal of a rational unified self.   Parallel with this rational self there is an ethical self which has freed itself from the complexes caused by the conflict between the egoistic instincts and the external moral codes, and uses the rational self to secure harmony of thought and action based on self-knowledge.   These two ideals may be pursued consciously and may be made the main support of that complete and enlightened self-consciousness which is essential for the most highly developed harmonious personality.

For a time it seemed to the casual observer that the New Psychology was so steeped in pruriency that it could not be investigated without armour and gas mask.   Happily such belief is passing, and many now see in it something more than the dominancy and vagaries of the libido, which convention has insisted shall veil its face and which expediency has suggested shall sit at the foot of the table rather than at the head. It has awakened a new interest in the life of the spirit, which is in part or in whole outside consciousness, and it has finally challenged the statement of the father of modern psychology, Descartes: "I think, therefore I am."

The religionist advises us to "Get right with God."   At least he is bidding for integration of interests.   The humanist in literature who tries to get life going right with its memories is doing the same thing.   To be on good terms with memory is happiness; to be on bad terms with it is tragedy.   Both are fields for literary workmanship.   The more the individual works up his memories in contact with his experiences, the more objective he becomes.   On "Main Street" everybody remembers everything about everybody else and thinking becomes objective, with aspects no finer than the daily experiences of the thinkers. There is no chance for romance and adventure because the memories of the few who erred by embarking on adventurous ways are so vivid in the minds of their neighbours, and so often rehearsed by them, as to inhibit the venturesome. Instead of mental equilibrium between vital and struggling interests, there is only inertia. This makes a good theme for a sporadic novel, but it is not a basis for a school of novelists. Mr. Lewis set himself a task that he could perform. On a level where life is richer and memories are crowded out by sensational experiences the task is harder.

It is a mistake to think that psychology is all introspection and conjecture of the unconscious. Mental life in the broadest sense is behaviour, instinctive and intelligent. Few have shown themselves more competent to observe, estimate, and describe such behaviour than the author of "Main Street." That novel was a study of temperament, a portrayal of environment, and an attempt to estimate their interaction and to state the result. It was recognised by those who had encountered or experienced the temperament and who had lived, voluntarily or compulsorily, in the environment, to be a true cross-section of life focussed beneath a microscopic lens, and anyone who examined it had before him an accurate representation of the conscious experiences of at least two individuals, and a suggestion of their unconscious experiences as well. This permitted the reader, even suggested to him, to compare them with his own sensations and ideas. Thus it was that emotions, sentiments, and judgments were engendered which, given expression, constituted something akin to public opinion. The result was a beneficence to American literature, for the purpose of the writer was known, and it was obvious to the knowing that he had accomplished it.

In "Babbitt" Mr. Lewis set himself a much more limited task. The picture is life in a Middle Western city of the

U. S. A. It is as accurate as if it had been reflected from a giant mirror or reproduced from a photographic plate. George F. Babbitt is signalled by his fellow townsmen as an enviable success from a financial and familiar point of view. Nevertheless he grows more discontent with life as prosperity overtakes him. The burden of his complaint is that he has never done a single thing he wanted to in his whole life. It is hard to square his words with his actions, but he convinces himself. So having run the gamut of prosperity, paternity, applause, wine, women, and song—in his case it is dance, not song—without appeasement, he finally gets it vicariously through observing his son who not only knows what he wants to do, but does it. He summarises what life has taught him in a few words: "Don't be scared of the family. No, nor of all Zenith. Nor of yourself, the way I've been. Go ahead, old man! The world is yours!"

Mr. Lewis' purpose was to describe the behaviour of a certain type of man in a certain kind of city, of which the world is full. He gives the former a definite heredity, an education with an amalgam of sentiment, a vague belief that material success spells happiness, that vulgar contact with one's fellows constitutes companionship, and that Pisgah sights of life are to be had by gaining a social elevation just beyond the one occupied. Then he thwarts his ambition to become a lawyer with an incontrovertible outburst of sex and sentimentality, and all his life he hears a bell tolling the echoes of his thwarted ambition. He feels that he has been tricked by circumstance and environment, and that display of chivalry to his wife and loyalty to his chum were wasted. They were indeed, for they had been offered, like the prayers of the hypocrites, in clubs and in corners of the street, and displayed for his own glory.

Materialism was Babbitt's undoing. It destroyed the framework on which man slings happiness and contentment, and which is called morality and idealism. When that went he became a creature of Mr. Karel Capek's creation. Mr. Babbitt, in common with countless benighted parents, cherished a delusion. He believed that filial love, so-called, is an integral part of an offspring's make-up. It is an artefact, an acquisition, a convention: it is a thing like patriotism and creed. One is born with a certain slant toward it and as soon as he becomes a cognisant, sentient organism he realises that it is proper to have it and to display it. In fact he is made to do so during his formative years; thus it becomes second nature. And that is just what it is—second nature. Parental love is first nature. If this were a disquisition on love, instead of on novelists, I should contend that there are two kinds of love: a parent's love for its child, especially the mother's; and a believer's love for God. When Mr. Babbitt wallows in the trough of the waves of emotion because he doesn't get the affection and recognition from his children which is his due, he alienates our sympathy and Mr. Lewis reveals the vulnerable tendon of his own psychology.

Were I the dispenser of eugenic licenses to marry, I should insist that everyone contemplating parenthood should have read the life history of the spider, especially the female of the species, who is devoured by her offspring. All novelists should study spiders first-hand. Filial love, or the delusion of it, furnishes the material for some of the finest ironies and deepest tragedies of life, and as Mr. Lewis adopts it as a medium for characterisation quite free from the teaching of the Freudians who would make it a fundamental instinct, the reader is entitled to expect from him a more reasonable treatment of the subject.

Babbitt's tragedy in the failure of his children's affection is the tragedy of millions of parents the world over. There is hardly a note that would be more sure of wide appeal. But it cannot be explained by the mere fact that, despite the Decalogue, no person of reason will ever "honour" where honour is not merited. It is hard to pity Babbitt because he could not commandeer the filial respect and honour which he had failed to inspire. If this were all, the situation would be simple. But, like countless other deluded parents, Babbitt believes that merely by bringing children into the world he has staked out a claim on their love, just as the child has a claim on the love of those who brought him into the world. And in this belief lies the irony and the tragedy: in the disparity between tradition and fact; between reason and instinct. The tradition or convention that filial love corresponds to parental love probably had its origin in the mind of the parent who would have liked to supply the child with such reciprocal instinct—a love that would transcend reason and survive when respect and honour had failed—but nature has not kept pact with the parental wish. In the realisation and acceptance of the truth lies the Gethsemane that each parent must face who would mount to higher heights of parenthood than the planes of instinct. Hence the universal appeal: the reason why the reader sympathises with Babbitt even while condemning him. He has forfeited the right to what he might have claimed—honour and affection—to fall back upon more elemental rights which were a figment of the imagination. Mr. Lewis' psychology would have struck a truer note if he had differentiated more clearly between the universal parent tragedy and Babbitt's own failure as a parent.

With the regeneration or civic orientation of Babbitt I am not concerned—that is in the field of ethics. But, as a student of literary art and craftsmanship, it seems to me the sawdust in Mr. Lewis' last doll.

To depict the display of Babbitt's consciousness as Mr. Lewis has done is to make a contribution to behaviourism, to make a psychological chart of mental activity. One may call it realism if one likes, because it narrates facts, but it is first and foremost a narrative of the activities and operation of the human mind.

"Babbitt" may be construed as the American intelligence of

Mr. Lewis' generation turning on its taskmaster. All men who live by writing, and have any regard for fine art and "belles lettres," or any ideals for which, in extremity, they might be willing to get out alone with no support from cheering multitudes and do a little dying on barricades, live and work with the Babbitt iron in their souls. Mr. Lewis probably had his full dose of it. He had been an advertising copy-writer, selling goods by his skill with a pen, to Babbitts, and for Babbitts. He had been sub-editor for a time of one of those magazines which are owned and published by Babbitts and tricked out and bedizened for a "mass circulation" of Babbitts. He hated Babbitt. When he saw the favourable opportunity he meant to turn Babbitt inside out and hold him up to scorn. But Mr. Lewis is not savage enough, and his talent is not swinging and extravagant enough, and he has not humour enough, to make him a satirist. He is a photographic artist with an incomparable capacity for the lingo of "one hundred per cent Americans." As he gets deeper and deeper into the odious and contemptible Babbitt, he begins to be sorry for him, and at the end he is rather fond of him—faithfully telling the facts about him all the while. He pities Babbitt in Babbitt's sense of frustration by social environment and circumstances, and admires him for telling his son not to let himself be similarly frustrated.

To call such a book "an exceedingly clever satire" and its leading character "an exceedingly clever caricature" is, it seems to me, to confess unacquaintance with one's countrymen or unfamiliarity with the conventional meaning of the words "satire" and "caricature." Such admission on the part of the distinguished educator and critic who has recently applied these terms to it is most improbable.

If a photograph of a man is caricature and a phonographic record of his internal and externalised speech constitutes satire, then "Babbitt" is what the learned professor says it is.

There is a type of novel much in evidence at present called

mated it justly, Mr. Harry Dounce. Yet "Bunker Bean" is one of the few really meritorious American psychological novels of the present generation. It is done with a lightness of touch worthy of Anthony Hope at his best; with an insight of motives, impulses, aspirations, and determinations equal to the creator of "Mr. Polly"; and with a knowledge of child psychology that would be creditable to Professor Watson.

There are few more vivid descriptions of the  workings of the child mind than that given by Mr. Harry Leon Wilson in the account of Bunker's visit to "Granper" and "Grammer," and the seduction of his early childhood by the shell from the sea. Dickens never portrayed infantile emotions and reactions with greater verisimilitude than Mr. Wilson when knowledge of the two inevitables of life—birth and death—came, nearly simultaneously, to Bunker's budding mind.

If journals whose purpose is to orient and guide unsophisticated readers, and to illuminate the road that prospective readers must travel, would give the "once over" to books when they are published and the review ten years later, it would mark a great advance on the present method. If such a plan were in operation at the present time "Bunker Bean" would be a best seller and "If Winter Comes" would be substituting in the coal famine.

Force or energy in a new form has come into fictional literature within the past decade, and I propose to consider it as it is displayed in the writings of those who are mostly responsible for it: James Joyce, Dorothy Richardson, Marcel Proust, and to consider some of the younger English novelists from the point of view of psychology.

# CHAPTER II

"The supreme question about a work ·of art is out of
how deep a life does it spring."—STEPHEN DÆDALUS.

IRELAND has had the attention of the world focussed on
her with much constancy the past ten years. She has
weathered her storms; she has calmed her tempests; and she
is fast repairing the devastations of her tornadoes. None but
defamers and ill-wishers contend that she will not bring her
ship of state successfully to port and that it will not find
safe and secure anchorage. During her perilous voyage one
of her rebellious sons has been violently rocking the boat of
literature. His name is James Joyce and his craft has had
various names: first "The Dubliners," and last "Ulysses."

A few intuitive sensitive visionaries may understand and
comprehend "Ulysses," James Joyce's mammoth volume, without previous training or instruction, but the average intelligent reader will glean little or nothing from it, save bewilder-
ment and disgust. It should be companioned with a key and a
glossary like the Berlitz books. Then the attentive and diligent reader might get some comprehension of Mr. Joyce's
message, which is to tell of the people whom he has encountered in his forty years of sentiency; to describe their behaviour and speech; to analyse their motives; and to charac-
terise their conduct. He is determined that we shall know
the effect the "world," sordid, turbulent, disorderly, steeped
in alcohol and saturated with jesuitry, had upon an emotional
Celt, an egocentric genius whose chief diversion has been
blasphemy and keenest pleasure self-exaltation, and whose

life-long important occupation has been keeping a note-book
in which he has recorded incident encountered and speech
heard with photographic accuracy and Boswellian fidelity.
Moreover, he is determined to tell them in a new way, not in
straightforward, narrative fashion with a certain sequentiality
of idea, fact, occurrence; in sentence, phrase, and paragraph
that is comprehensible to a person of education and culture;
but in parodies of classic prose and current slang, in perversions of sacred literature, in carefully metred prose with studied
incoherence, in symbols so occult and mystic that only the
initiated and profoundly versed can understand; in short, by
means of every trick and illusion that a master artificer, or
even magician, can play with the English language.

It has been said of the writings of Tertullian, one of the
two greatest church writers, that they are rich in thought, and
destitute of form, passionate and hair-splitting, elegant and
pithy in expression, energetic and condensed to the point of
obscurity.  Mr. Joyce was devoted to Tertullian in his youth.
Dostoievsky also intrigued him.  From him he learned what
he knows of *mise en scene,* and particularly to disregard the
time element.  Ibsen and Hauptmann he called master after he
had weaned himself from Aristotle and St. Thomas Aquinas.
But he calls no one master now; even Homer he calls *comare.*
It is related that "A.E." once said to him, "I'm afraid you have
not enough chaos in you to make a world."  The poet was a
poor prophet.  Mr. Joyce has made a world, and a chaotic one
in which no decent person wants to live.

It is likely that there is no one writing English today who
could parallel his feat, and it is also likely that few would
care to do it were they capable.  This statement requires that
it be said at once that Mr. Joyce has seen fit to use words and
phrases which the entire world has covenanted not to use and
which people in general, cultured and uncultured, civilised and
savage, believer and heathen, have agreed shall not be used
because they are vulgar, vicious, and vile.  Mr. Joyce's reply

JAMES JOYCE

to this is: "This race and this country and this life produced me—I shall express myself as I am."

An endurance test should always be preceded by training. It requires real endurance to finish "Ulysses." The best training for it is careful perusal or reperusal of "A Portrait of the Artist as a Young Man," the volume published six or seven years ago which revealed Mr. Joyce's capacity to externalise his consciousness, to set it down in words. It is the story of his own life before he exiled himself from his native land, told with uncommon candour and extraordinary revelations of thought, impulse, and action, many of them of a nature and texture which most persons do not feel free to reveal, or which they do not feel it is decent and proper to confide to the world.

The facts of Mr. Joyce's life with which the reader who seeks to comprehend his writings should be familiar are: He was one of many children of South Ireland Catholic parents. In his early childhood his father had not yet dissipated their small fortune and he was sent to Clongowes Wood, a renowned Jesuit College near Dublin, and remained there until it seemed to his teachers and his parents that he should decide whether or not he had a vocation; that is whether he felt within himself, in his soul, a desire to join the order. Meanwhile he had experienced the profoundly disturbing impulses of pubescence; the incoming waves of genesic potency had swept over him, submerged him, and carried him into a deep trough of sin, from which, however, he was extricated, resuscitated, and purged by confession, penitence, and prayer. But the state of grace would not endure. He lost his faith, and soon his patriotism, and he held those with whom he formerly worshipped up to ridicule, and his country and her aspirations up to contumely. He continued his studies in the Old Royal University of Dublin, notwithstanding the abject poverty of his family. He was reputed to be a poet then, and many of the poems in "Chamber Music" were composed at this period.

He had no hesitation in admitting the reputation, even contending for it. "I have written the most perfect lyric since Shakespeare," he said to Padraic Colum; and to Yeats, "We have met too late; you are too old to be influenced by me." If belief in his own greatness has ever forsaken him in the years of trial and distress that have elapsed between then and now, no one, save possibly one, has heard of it. Mr. William Hohenzollern in his sanguine moments was never as sure of himself as Mr. James Joyce in his hours of despair.

After graduation he decided to study medicine, and, in fact, he did pursue the study for two or three years, one of them in the medical school of the University of Paris. Eventually he became convinced that medicine was not his vocation, even though funds were available for him to continue his studies, and he decided to take up singing as a profession, "having a phenomenally beautiful tenor voice." These three novitiates furnished him with all the material he has used in the four volumes that he has published. Matrimony, parentage, ill-health, and a number of other factors put an end to his musical ambitions. He taught for a brief time in Dublin and wrote the stories that are in "Dubliners," which his countrymen baptised with fire; and began the "Portrait." But he couldn't tolerate "a place fettered by the reformed conscience, a country in which the symbol of its art was the cracked looking-glass of a servant," so he betook himself to a country in the last explosive crisis of paretic grandeur. In Trieste he gained his daily bread by teaching Austrians English and Italian, having a mastery of the latter language that would flatter a Padovian professor. The war drove him to the haven of the expatriate, Switzerland, and for four years he taught German, Italian, French, English, to anyone in Zurich who had time, ambition, and money to acquire a new language. Since the Armistice he has lived in Paris, first finishing the book which is his *magnum opus* and which he says and believes represents everything that he has to say or will have to say, and he is now enjoying the fame and the infamy which its publication and three editions within two years have brought him.

As a boy Mr. Joyce's cherished hero was Odysseus. He approved of his subterfuge for evading military service; he envied him the companionship of Penelope; and all his latent vengeance was vicariously satisfied by reading of the way in which he revenged himself on Palamedes. The craftiness and resourcefulness of the final artificer of the siege of Troy made him permanently big with envy and admiration. But it was the ten years of his hero's life after he had eaten of the lotus plant, that wholly seduced Mr. Joyce and appeased his emotional soul. As years went by he realised that his own experiences were not unlike those of the slayer of Polyphemus and the favourite of Pallas-Athene, and after careful deliberation and planning he decided to write an Odyssey. In early childhood Mr. Joyce had identified himself with Dædalus, the Athenian architect, sculptor, and magician, and in all his writings he carries on in the name of Stephen Dædalus. Like the original Dædalus, his genius is great, his vanity is greater, and he can brook no rival. Like his prototype, he was exiled from his native land after he had made a great contribution to the world. Like him, he was received kindly in exile, and like him, also, having ingeniously contrived wings for himself and used them successfully, he is now enjoying a period of tranquillity after his sufferings and his labour.

"Ulysses" is the record of the thoughts, antics, vagaries, and actions—more particularly the thoughts—of Stephen Dædalus, an Irishman, of artistic temperament; of Leopold Bloom, an Irish-Hungarian Jew, of scientific temperament and perverted instincts; and of his wife, Marion Tweedy, daughter of an Irish major of the Royal Dublin Fusiliers stationed in Gibraltar, and a Jewish girl. Marion was a concert singer given to coprophilly, especially in her involutional stages, spiritual and physical. Bloom's acquired perversion he attempted to conceal by canvassing for advertisements for *The Freeman*.

Dublin is the scene of action. The events—those that can be mentioned—and their sequence are:

"The preparation for breakfast, intestinal congestion, the bath, the funeral, the advertisement of Alexander Keyes, the unsubstantial lunch, the visit to Museum and National Library, the book-hunt along Bedford Row, Merchants' Arch, Wellington Quay, the music in the Ormond Hotel, the altercation with a truculent troglodyte, in Bernard Kierman's premises, a blank period of time including a car-drive, a visit to a house of mourning, a leave-taking, . . . the prolonged delivery of Mrs. Nina Purefoy, the visit to a disorderly house . . . and subsequent brawl and chance medley in Beaver Street, nocturnal perambulation to and from the cabman's shelter, Butt Bridge."

And these are some of the things they thought and talked of:

"Music, literature, Ireland, Dublin, Paris, friendship, woman, prostitution, diet, the influence of gaslight or the light of arc and glowlamps on the growth of adjoining paraheliotropic trees, exposed corporation emergency dustbuckets, the Roman catholic church, ecclesiastical celibacy, the Irish nation, jesuit education, careers, the study of medicine, the past day, the maleficent influence of the presabbath, Stephen's collapse."

Mr. Joyce is an alert, keen-witted, educated man who has made it a life-long habit to jot down every thought that he has had, drunk or sober, depressed or exalted, despairing or hopeful, hungry or satiated, in brothel or in sanctuary, and likewise to put down what he has seen or heard others do or say —and rhythm has from infancy been an enchantment of the heart. It is not unlikely that every thought he has had, every experience he has ever encountered, every person he has ever met, one might say everything he has ever read in sacred or profane literature, is to be encountered in the ob-

scurities and in the franknesses of "Ulysses." If personality
is the sum total of all one's experiences, all one's thoughts and
emotions, inhibitions and liberations, acquisitions and inheri-
tances, then it may truthfully be said that "Ulysses" comes
nearer to being the perfect revelation of a personality than any
book I know.

He sets down every thought that comes into consciousness.
Decency, propriety, pertinency are not considered.  He does
not seek to give them orderliness, sequence, or conclusiveness.
His literary output would seem to substantiate some of Freud's
contentions.  The majority of writers, practically all, transfer
their conscious, deliberate thought to paper.  Mr. Joyce trans-
fers the product of his unconscious mind to paper without
submitting it to the conscious mind, or if he submits it, it is
to receive approval and encouragement, perhaps even praise.
He holds with Freud that the unconscious mind represents the
real man, the man of Nature, and the conscious mind the
artificed man, the man of convention, of expediency, the slave
of Mrs. Grundy, the sycophant of the Church, the plastic
puppet of Society and State.  For him the movements which
work revolutions in the world are born out of the dreams and
visions in a peasant's heart on the hillside.  "Peasant's heart"
psychologically is the unconscious mind.  When a master
technician of words and phrases set himself the task of revealing the product of the unconscious mind of a moral monster, a pervert and an invert, an apostate to his race and his
religion, the simulacrum of a man who has neither cultural
background nor personal self-respect, who can neither be
taught by experience nor lessoned by example, as Mr. Joyce
did in drawing the picture of Leopold Bloom, he undoubtedly knew full well what he was undertaking, how unac-
ceptable the vile contents of that unconscious mind would be
to ninety-nine out of a hundred readers, and how incensed
they would be at having the disgusting product thrown in their
faces.  But that has nothing to do with the question: has the

job been done well; is it a work of art? The answer is in the affirmative.

The proceedings of the council of the gods, with which the book opens, are tame. Stephen Dædalus, the Telemachus of this Odyssey, is seen chafing beneath his sin—refusal to kneel down at the bedside of his dying mother and pray for her—while having an *al fresco* breakfast in a semi-abandoned turret with his friend Buck Mulligan (now an esteemed physician of Dublin), and a ponderous Saxon from Oxford whose father "made his tin by selling jalap to the Zulus," who applauds Stephen's sarcasms and witticisms. Stephen has a grouch because Buck Mulligan has referred to him, "O, it's only Dædalus whose mother is beastly dead." This Stephen construes to be an offense to him, not to his mother. Persecutory ideas are dear to Stephen Dædalus. In his moody brooding this is how he welds words:

"Woodshadows floated silently by through the morning peace from the stairhead seaward where he gazed. Inshore and farther out the mirror of water whitened, spurned by lightshod hurrying feet. White breast of the dim sea. The twining stresses, two by two. A hand plucking the harpstrings merging their twining chords. Wavewhite wedded words shimmering on the dim tide."

Meanwhile his sin pursues him as "the Russian gentleman of a particular kind" pursued Ivan Karamazov when delirium began to overtake him. He recalls his mother, her secrets, her illness, her last appeals. While breakfasting Buck and Stephen plan a glorious drunk to astonish the druidy druids, with the latter's wage of schoolmaster which he will receive that day. Later Buck goes in the sea while Stephen animadverts on Ireland's two masters, the Pope of Rome and the King of England, and recites blasphemous poetry.

Stephen spends the forenoon in school, then takes leave of the pedantic proprietor, who gives him his salary and a paper on foot and mouth disease. Telemachus embarks on his voyage, and the goddess who sails with him communes with him as follows:

"Ineluctable modality of the visible; at least that if no more, thought through my eyes. Signatures of all things I am here to read, seaspawn and seawrack, the nearing tide, that rusty boot. Snotgreen, bluesilver, rust: coloured signs. Limits of the diaphane. But he adds: in bodies. Then he was aware of them bodies before of them coloured. How? By knocking his sconce against them, sure. Go easy. Bald he was and a millionaire, *maestro di color che sanno*. Limit of the diaphane in. Why in? Diaphane, adiaphane. If you can put your five fingers through it, it is a gate, if not a door. Shut your eyes and see."

This is the first specimen of the saltatory, flitting, fugitive, on-the-surface purposeless thought that Stephen produces as he walks Sandymount Strand. From this point the book teems with it and with Bloom's autistic thoughts. It is quite impossible to give a synopsis or summary of them. It must suffice to say that in the fifteen pages Mr. Joyce devotes to the first leg of the voyage that will give him news of Ulysses, an hour's duration, a film picture has been thrown on the screen of his visual cortex for which he writes legends as fast as the machine reels them off. It is Mr. Joyce's life that is thus remembered: his thoughts, ambitions, aspirations, failures, and disappointments; the record of his contacts and their engenderment—what was and what might have been. On casual examination, such record transformed into print looks like gibberish, and is meaningless. So does shorthand. It is full of meaning for anyone who knows how to read it.

The next fifty pages are devoted to displaying the reel of Mr. Leopold Bloom's mind, the workings of his psycho-physical machinery, autonomic and heteronomic, the idle and purposeful thoughts of the most obnoxious wretch of all mankind, as Eolus called the real Ulysses. While he forages for his wife's breakfast, prepares and serves it, his thoughts and reflections are answers to the question "Digman, how camest thou into the realms of darkness?" for no burial honours yet had Irish Elpenor received.

Then follows a picture of Dublin before the revolution, its newspapers, and the men who made them, with comment and characterisation by Stephen Dædalus, · interpolations and solicitations by Leopold Bloom.   Naturally the reader who knew or knew of William Brayden, Esquire, of Oakland, Sandymount, Mr. J. J. Smolley whose speech reminds of Edmund Burke's writings, or Mr. Myles Crawford whose witticisms are founded on Pietro Aretino, would find this chapter more illuminating, though not more entertaining, than one who had heard of Dublin for the first time in 1914.   Nor does it facilitate understanding of the conversation there to know the geography of an isle afloat where lived the son of Hippotas, his six daughters, and six blooming sons.

Bloom continues his apparently purposeless and obviously purposeful thoughts after the Irish Læstrygonians had stoned him, for another fifty pages.   Everything he sees and everyone he encounters generate them.   They are connected, yet they are disparate.   I choose one of the simplest and easiest to quote:

"A procession of whitesmocked men marched slowly towards him along the gutter, scarlet sashes across their boards.   Bargains.   Like that priest they are this morning: we have sinned. we have suffered.   He read the scarlet letters on their five tall white hats: H. E. L. Y. S.   Wisdom Hely's.   Y lagging behind drew a chunk of bread from under his foreboard, crammed it into his mouth and munched as he walked.   Our staple food.   Three bob a day, walking along the gutters, street after street.   Just keep skin and bone together, bread and skilly.   They are not Boyl: no: M'Glade's men.   Doesn't bring in any business either.   I suggested to him about a transparent show cart with two smart girls sitting inside writing letters, copybooks, envelopes, blotting paper.   I bet that would have caught on.   Smart girls writing something catch the eye at once.   Everyone dying to know what she's writing. Get twenty of them round you if you stare at nothing. Have a finger in the pie. Women too. Curiosity. Pillar of salt. Wouldn't have it of course because he didn't think of it himself first. Or the inkbottle I suggested with a false stain of black celluloid. His ideas for ads like Plumtree's potted under the obituaries, cold meat department. You can't like 'em. What? Our envelops. Hello! Jones, where are you going? Can't stop, Robinson, I am hastening to purchase the only reliable inkeraser *Kansell*, sold by Hely's Ltd, 85 Dame Street. Well out of that ruck I am. Devil of a job it was collecting accounts of those convents. Tranquilla convent. That was a nice nun there, really sweet face. Wimple suited her small head. Sister? Sister? I am sure she was crossed in love by her eyes. Very hard to bargain with that sort of a woman. I disturbed her at her devotions that morning. But glad to communicate with the outside world. Our great day, she said, Feast of Our Lady of Mount Carmel. Sweet name too: caramel. She knew, I think she knew by the way she. If she had married she would have changed. I suppose they really were short of money. Fried everything in the best butter all the same. No lard for them. My heart's broke eating dripping. They like buttering themselves in and out. Molly tasting it, her veil up. Sister? Pat Claffey, the pawnbroker's daughter. It was a nun they say invented barbed wire."

Man may not think like this, but it is up to the psychologist to prove it. So far as I know he does. Lunatics do, in manic "flights"; and flights of ideas are but accentuations of normal mental activity.

The following is a specimen of what psychologists call "flight of ideas." To the uninitiated reader it means nothing. To the initiated it is like the writing on the wall.

"Bloom. Flood of warm jimjam lickitup secretness flowed to flow in music out, in desire, dark to lick flow, invading. Tipping her tepping her tapping her topping her. Tup. Pores to dilate dilating. Tup. The joy the feel the warm the. Tup. To pour o'er sluices pouring gushes. Flood, gush, flow, joygush, tupthrop. Now! Language of love."

In the next section Stephen holds forth on ideals and literature and gives the world that which Mr. Joyce gave his fellow students in Dublin to satiety, viz. his views of Shakespeare, and particularly his conception of Hamlet. "Shakespeare is the happy hunting ground of all minds that have lost their balance," one of his cronies remarked. Even in those days Mr. Joyce's ideas of grandeur suggested to a student of psychiatry who heard him talk that he had the mental disease with which that symptom is most constantly associated, and to another of his auditors that he had an *idée fixe,* and that "the moral idea seems lacking, the sense of destiny, of retribution." They never hurt Mr. Joyce—such views as these. The armour of his *amour propre* has never been pierced; the belief in his destiny has never wavered. The meeting in the National Library twenty years ago gives him opportunity to display philosophic erudition, dialectic skill, and artistic feeling in his talk with the young men and their elders. It would be interesting to know from any of them, or from Mr. T. S. Eliot, if the following is the sort of grist that is brought to the free-verse miller, and can poetry be made from it.

"Yogibogeybox in Dawson chambers. *Isis Unveiled.* Their Pali book we tried to pawn. Crosslegged under an umbrel umbershoot he thrones an Aztec logos, functioning on astral levels, their oversoul, mahamahatma. The faithful hermetists await the light, ripe for chelaship, ringroundabout him. Louis H. Victory. T. Caulfield Irwin. Lotus ladies tend them i' the eyes, their pineal glands aglow. Filled with his god he thrones, Buddh under plantain. Gulfer of souls, engulfer. He souls, she souls, shoals of souls. Engulfed with wailing creecries, whirled, whirling, they bewail."

In contrast with this take the following description of the drowned man in Dublin Bay as a specimen of masterly realism:

"Five fathoms out there. Full fathom five thy father lies. At one he said. Found drowned. High water at Dublin Bar.

Driving before it a loose drift of rubble, fanshoals of fishes, silly shells. A corpse rising saltwhite from the undertow, bobbing landward, a pace a pace a porpoise. There he is. Hook it quick. Sunk though he be beneath the watery floor. We have him. Easy now. Bag of corpsegas sopping in foul brine. . . . Dead breaths I living breathe, tread dead dust. . . . Hauled stark over the gunwale he breathes upward the stench of his green grave, his leprous nosehole snorting to the sun."

There are so many "specimens" of writing in the volume that it is quite impossible to give examples of them. Frankness compels me to state that he goes out of his way to scoff at God and to besmirch convention, but that's to show he is not afraid, like the man who defied God to kill him at 9.48 p.m.

"The playwright who wrote the folio of this world and wrote it badly (He gave us light first and the sun two days later), the lord of things as they are whom the most Roman of catholics call *bio boia*, hangman god, is doubtless all in all in all of us, ostler and butcher, and would be bawd and cuckold too but that in the economy of heaven, foretold by Hamlet, there are no more marriages, glorified man, an androgynous angel, being a wife unto himself."

The Dædalus family and their neighbourhood—their pawnbrokers, shopkeepers, spiritual advisers; the people they despised, those they envied, the Viceroy of Ireland, now come in for consideration. Mr. Dædalus is a sweet-tempered, mealymouthed man given to strong drink and high-grade vagrancy who calls his daughters "an insolent pack of little bitches since your poor mother died." Their appearances and emotional reactions, and their contacts with Stephen and Bloom who are passing the time till they shall begin the orgy which is the high-water mark of the book, are instructive to the student of behaviouristic psychology.

Readers of Dostoievsky rarely fail to note the fact that occurrences of a few hours required hundreds of pages to narrate. The element of time seems to have been eliminated. It is the same in "Ulysses." This enormous volume of seven hundred and thirty-two pages is taken up with thoughts of two men during twelve hours of sobriety and six of drunkenness. I do not know the population of Dublin, but whatever it may be, a vast number of these people come into the ken of Dædalus and Bloom during those hours, and into the readers'; for it is through their eyes and their ears that we see and hear what transpires and is said. And so the trusting reader accompanies one or both of them to the beach, and observes them in revery and in repose; or to a café concert, and observes them in ructions and in ruminations. A countryman of Mr. Joyce, Edmund Burke, said "custom reconciles us to everything," and after we have accompanied these earthly twins, Stephen and Leopold, thus far, we do not baulk at the lying-in hospital or even the red light district, though others more sensitive and less tolerant than myself would surely wish they had deserted the "bark-waggons" when the occupants were invited into the brothel.

The book in reality is a moving picture with picturesque legends, many profane and more vulgar. For a brief time Mr. Joyce was associated with the "movies," and the form in which "Ulysses" was cast may have been suggested by experiences with the Volta Theatre, as his cinematograph enterprise was called.

Mr. Joyce learned from St. Thomas Aquinas what Socrates learned from his mother: how to bring thoughts into the world; and from his boyhood he had a tenderness for rhythm. It crops out frequently in "Ulysses."

"In Inisfail the fair there lies a land, the land of holy Michan. There rises a watchtower beheld of men afar. There sleep the mighty dead as in life they slept, warrior and princes of high renown. A pleasant land it is in sooth of murmuring waters, fishful streams where sport the gunnard, the plaice, the roach, the halibut, the gibbed haddock, the grilse, the dab, the brill, the flounder, the mixed coarse fish generally and other denizens of the aqueous kingdom too numerous to be enumerated.  In the mild breezes of the west and of the east the lofty trees wave in different directions their first class foliage, the wafty sycamore, the Lebanonian cedar, the exalted planetree, the eugenic eucalyptus and other ornaments of the arboreal world with which that region is thoroughly well supplied.  Lovely maidens sit in close proximity to the roots of the lovely trees singing the most lovely songs while they play with all kinds of lovely objects as for example golden ingots, silvery fishes, crans of herrings, drafts of eels, codlings, creels of fingerlings, purple seagems and playful insects.  And heroes voyage from afar to woo them, from Eblana to Slievemargy, the peerless princes of unfettered Munster and of Connacht the just and of smooth sleek Leinster and of Cruachan's land and of Armagh the splendid and of the noble district of Boyle, princes, the sons of kings."

At other times he seems to echo the sonorous phrasing of some forgotten master: Pater or Rabelais, or to paraphrase William Morris or Walt Whitman, or to pilfer from the Reverend William Sunday.

"The figure seated on a large boulder at the foot of a round tower was that of a broadshouldered deepchested stronglimbed frankeyed redhaired freely freckled shaggy-bearded widemouthed largenosed longheaded deepvoiced bare-kneed brawnyhanded hairylegged ruddyfaced, sinewyarmed hero.  From shoulder to shoulder he measured several ells and his rocklike mountainous knees were covered, as was likewise the rest of his body wherever visible, with a strong growth of tawny prickly hair in hue and toughness similar to the mountain gorse (*Ulex Europeus*).  The widewinged nostrils, from which bristles of the same tawny hue projected, were of such capaciousness that within their cavernous obscurity the fieldlark might easily have lodged her nest.  The eyes in which a tear and a smile strove ever for the mastery were of the dimensions of a goodsized cauliflower.  A powerful current of warm breath issued at regular intervals from the profound cavity of his mouth while in rhythmic resonance the loud strong hale reverberations of his formidable heart thundered rumblingly causing the ground, the summit of the lofty tower and the still loftier walls of the cave to vibrate and tremble."

The chapter from which these quotations are taken, when the friends turn into Barney Kiernan's to slake their thirst, shows Mr. Joyce with loosed tongue—the voluble, witty, philosophic Celt, with an extraordinary faculty of words. If an expert stenographer had taken down the ejaculations as they spurted from the mouth of Tom and Jerry, and the deliberations of Alf and Joe, and the other characters of impulsive energy and vivid desire, then accurately transcribed them, interpolating "says" frequently, they would read like this chapter.

Conspicuous amongst Mr. Joyce's possessions is a gift for facile emotional utterance. The reader feels himself affected by his impulses and swept along by his eloquence. He is scathingly sarcastic about Irish cultural and political aspirations; loathsomely lewd about their morals and habits; merciless in his revelations of their temperamental possessions and infirmities; and arbitrary and unyielding in his belief that their degeneration is beyond redemption. Like the buckets on an endless chain of a dredger, the vials of his wrath are poured time after time upon England and the British Empire "on which the sun never rises," but they are never emptied. Finally he embodies his sentiment in paraphrase of the Creed.

"They believe in rod, the scourger almighty, creator of hell upon earth and in Jacky Tar, the son of a gun, who was conceived of unholy boast, born of the fighting navy, suffered under rump and dozen, was scarified, flayed and curried, yelled like bloody hell, the third day he arose again from the bed, steered into haven, sitteth on his beamend till further orders whence he shall come to drudge for a living and be paid."

He recounts his country's former days of fame and fortune, but he doesn't foresee any of the happenings of the past three years.

"Where are our missing twenty millions of Irish should be
here today instead of four, our lost tribes? And our potteries
and textiles, the finest in the whole world! And our wool that
was sold in Rome in the time of Juvenal and our flax and our
damask from the looms of Antrim and our Limerick lace,
our tanneries and our white flint glass down there by Bally-
bough and our Huguenot poplin that we have since Jacquand
de Lyon and our woven silk and our Foxford tweeds and
ivory raised point from the Carmelite convent in New Ross,
nothing like it in the whole wide world. Where are the Greek
merchants that came through the pillars of Hercules, the
Gibraltar now grabbed by the foe of mankind, with gold and
Tyrian purple to sell in Wexford at the fair of Carmen?
Read Tacitus and Ptolemy, even Giraldus Cambrensis, Wine,
peltries, Connemara marble, silver from Tipperary, second to
none, our farfamed horses even today, the Irish hobbies, with
King Philip of Spain offering to pay customs duties for the
right to fish in our waters. What do the yellowjohns of
Anglia owe us for our ruined trade and our ruined hearths?
And the beds of the Barrow and Shannon they won't deepen
with millions of acres of marsh and bog to make us all die of
consumption."

Nowhere is his note-book more evident than in this chapter. Krafft-Ebing, a noted Vienese psychiatrist, said a certain
disease was due to civilisation and syphilisation. Mr. Joyce
made note of it and uses it. The *Slocum* steamboat disaster in
New York, which touched all American hearts twenty years
ago; the prurient details of a scandal in "loop" circles of Chi-
cago; a lynching in the South are referred to as casually by
Lenehan, Wyse *et al* while consuming their two pints, as if
they were family matters.

That the author has succeeded in cutting and holding up
to view a slice of life in this chapter and in the succeeding one
—Bloom amongst the Nurse-girls—it would be idle to deny.
That it is sordid and repulsive need scarcely be said. It has
this in common with the writings of all the naturalists.

The author's familiarity with the Dadaists is best seen in

his chapter on the visit to the Lying-in Hospital. Some of it is done in the pseudostyle of the English and Norse Saga; some in the method adopted by d'Annunzio in his composition of "Nocturne." He wrote thousands and thousands of words on small pieces of paper, then threw them into a basket, and shuffled them thoroughly. With a blank sheet before him and a dripping mucilage brush in one hand, he proceeded to paste them one after another on the sheet. A sample of the result is:

"Universally that person's acumen is esteemed very little perceptive concerning whatsoever matters are being held as most profitably by mortals with sapience endowed to be studied who is ignorant of that which the most in doctrine erudite and certainly by reason of that in them high mind's ornament deserving of veneration constantly maintain when by general consent they affirm that other circumstances being equal by no exterior splendour is the prosperity of a nation more efficaciously asserted than by the measure of how far forward may have progressed the tribute of its solicitude for that proliferent continuance which of evils the original if it be absent when fortunately present constitutes the certain sign of omnipollent nature's incorrupted benefaction."

Tired of this, he paraphrases the Holy Writ.

"And whiles they spake the door of the castle was opened and there nighed them a mickle noise as of many that sat there at meat. And there came against the place as they stood a young learning knight yclept Dixon. And the traveller Leopold was couth to him sithen it had happed that they had had ado each with other in the house of misericord where this learning knight lay by cause the traveller Leopold came there to be healed for he was sore wounded in his breast by a spear wherewith a horrible and dreadful dragon was smitten him for which he did do make a salve of volatile salt and chrism as much as he might suffice. And he said now that he should go into that castle for to make merry with them that were there."

When this palls, he apes a satirist like Rabelais, or a mystic like Bunyan. Weary of this, he turns to a treatise on embryology and a volume of obstetrics and strains them through his mind. One day some serious person, a disciple or a benighted admirer, such as M. Valery Larbaud, will go through "Ulysses" to find references to toxicology, Mosaic law, the Kamustra, eugenics, etc., as such persons and scholars have gone through Shakespeare. Until it is done no one will believe the number of subjects he touches is marvellous, and sometimes even the way he does it. For instance this on birth control:

"Murmur, Sirs, is eke oft among lay folk. Both babe and parent now glorify their Maker, the one limbo gloom, the other in purge fire. But, Gramercy, what of those Godpossibled souls that we nightly impossibilise, which is the sin against the Holy Ghost, Very God, Lord and Giver of Life."

It is worthy of note also that Mr. Joyce defines specifically the sin against the Holy Ghost, which for long has been a stumbling block to priest and physician. He does not agree with the great Scandinavian writer toward whom he looked reverently in his youth. Ella Rentheim says to Borkman, "The Bible speaks of a mysterious sin for which there is no forgiveness. I have never understood what it could be; but now I understand. The great, unpardonable sin is to murder the love-life in a human soul."

The object of it all is to display the thought and erudition of Stephen Dædalus, "a sensitive nature, smarting under the lashes of an undivined and squalid way of life"; and the emotions, perversions, and ambitions of Leopold Bloom, a devotee of applied science, whose inventions were for the purpose of

"rendering obsolete popguns, elastic airbladders, games of hazard, catapults. They comprised astronomical kaleidoscopes, exhibiting the twelve constellations of the Zodiac from

Aries to Pisces, miniature mechanical orreries, arithmetical gelatine lozenges, geometrical to correspond with zoological biscuits, globemap playing balls, historically costumed dolls."

It is particularly in the next chapter, one of the strangest of literature, that Mr. Joyce displays the apogee of his art. Dædalus and Bloom have passed in review on a mystic stage all their intimates and enemies, all their detractors and sycophants, the scum of Dublin, and the spawn of the devil. Mr. Joyce resurrects Saint Walpurgis, galvanises her into life after twelve centuries' death intimacy with Beelzebub, and substituting a squalid section of Dublin for Brocken, proceeds to depict a festival, the devil being host. The guests in the flesh and of the spirit have still many of their distinctive corporeal possessions, but the reactions of life no longer exist. The chapter is replete with wit, humour, satire, philosophy, learning, knowledge of human frailties, and human indulgences, especially with the brakes of morality off. And alcohol or congenital deficiency takes them off for most of the characters. It reeks of lust and filth, but Mr. Joyce says life does, and the morality he depicts is the only one he knows.

In this chapter is compressed all of the author's experiences, all his determinations and unyieldingness, and most of the incidents that gave a persecutory twist to his mind, made him an exile from his native land, and deprived him of the courage to return. He does not hesitate to bring in the ghost of his mother whom he had been accused of killing because he would not kneel down and pray for her when she was dying, and to question her as to the verity of the accusation. But he does not repent even when she returns from the spiritual world. In fact, the capacity for repentence is left out of Mr. Joyce's makeup. It is as impossible to convince Mr. Joyce that he is wrong about anything on which he has made up his mind as it is to convince a paranoiac of the unreality of his false beliefs, or a jealous woman of the groundlessness of her suspicions. It may be said that this chapter does not represent life, but I venture to say that it represents life with photographic accuracy as Mr. Joyce has seen it and lived it; that every scene has come within his gaze; that every speech has been heard or said; and every sentiment experienced or thrust upon him. It is a mirror held up to life—life which we could sincerely wish and devoutly pray that we were spared; for it is life in which happiness is impossible, save when forgetfulness of its existence is brought about by alcohol, and in which mankind is destitute of virtue, deprived of ideals, deserted by love.

To disclaim it is life that countless men and women know would be untrue, absurd, and libellous. I do not know that Mr. Joyce makes any such claim, but I claim that it is life that he has known.

Mr. Joyce had the good fortune to be born with a quality which the world calls genius. Nature exacts a galling income tax from genius, and as a rule she co-endows it with unamenability to law and order. Genius and reverence are antipodal, Galileo being the exception to the rule. Mr. Joyce has no reverence for organised religion, for conventional morality, for literary style or form. He has no conception of the word obedience, and he bends the knee neither to God nor man. It is interesting and important to have the revelations of such a personality, to have them first hand and not dressed up. Heretofore our only avenues of information concerning them led through asylums for the insane, for it was there that revelations were made without reserve. I have spent much time and money in my endeavour to get such revelations, without great success. Mr. Joyce has made it unnecessary for me to pursue the quest. He has supplied the little and big pieces of material from which the mental mosaic is made.

He had the profound misfortune to lose his faith, and he cannot rid himself of the obsession that the Jesuits did it for him. He is trying to get square by saying disagreeable things about them and holding their teachings up to scorn and obloquy. He was so unfortunate as to be born without a sense of duty, of service, of conformity to the State, to the community, to society; and he is convinced he should tell about it, just as some who have experienced a surgical operation feel that they must relate minutely all its details, particularly at dinner parties and to casual acquaintances.

Not ten men or women out of a hundred can read "Ulysses" through, and of the ten who succeed in doing it for five of them it will be a *tour de force*. I am probably the only person aside from the author that has ever read it twice from beginning to end. I read it as a test of Christian fortitude: to see if I could still love my fellow-man after reading a book that depicts such repugnance of humanity, such abhorence of the human body, and such loathsomeness of the possession that links man with God, the creative endowment. Also the author is a psychologist, and I find his empiric knowledge supplements mine acquired by prolonged and sustained effort.

M. Valery Larbaud, a French critic who hailed "Ulysses" with the reverence with which Boccaccio hailed the Divine Comedy, and who has been giving conferences on "Ulysses" in Paris, says the key to the book is Homer's immortal poem. If M. Larbaud has the key he cannot spring the lock of the door of the dark safe in which "Ulysses" rests, metaphorically, for most readers. At least he has not done so up to this writing.

The key is to be found in the antepenultimate chapter of the book; and it isn't a key, it's a combination, a countryman of Mr. Joyce's might say. Anyone who tries at it long enough will succeed in working it, even if he is not of M. Larbaud's cultivated readers who can fully appreciate such authors as Rabelais, Montaigne, and Descartes.

The symbolism of the book is something that concerns only Mr. Joyce, as nuns do, and other animate and inanimate things of which he has fugitive thoughts and systematised beliefs.

After the Cheu-sinese orgy, Bloom takes Stephen home, and

unfortunately they awaken Marion, for she embraces the occasion to purge her mind in soliloquy.   Odo of Cluny never
said anything of a woman's body in life that is so repulsive as
that which Mr. Joyce has said of Marion's mind: a cesspool
of forty years' accumulation.   Into it has drained the inherited
vulgarities of Jew and gentile parent; within it has accumulated the increment of a sordid, dissolute life in two countries,
extending over twenty-five years; in it have been compressed
the putrid exhalations of studied devotion to sense gratification.   Mr. Joyce takes off the lid and opens the sluice-way
simultaneously, and the result is that the reader, even though
his sensitisation has been fortified by reading the book, is
bowled over.   As soon as he regains equilibrium he communes
with himself to the effect that if the world has many Marions
missionaries should be withdrawn from heathen countries and
turned into this field where their work will be praised by man
and rewarded by God.

Mental hygiene takes on a deeper significance to one who
succeeds in reading "Ulysses," and psychology has a larger
ceinture.

Much time has been wasted in conjecturing what Mr.
Joyce's message is.   In another connection he said, "My ancestors threw off their language and took another.   They allowed a handful of foreigners to subject them.   Do you fancy
I am going to pay in my own life and person debts they
made?   No honourable and sincere man has given up his life,
his youth, and his affections to Ireland from the days of Tome
to those of Parnell but the Irish sold him to the enemy or
failed him in need or reviled him and left him for another.
Ireland is the old sow that eats her farrow."

"Ulysses" is in part vendetta.   He will ridicule Gaelic ren-
naissance of literature and language; he will traduce the Irish
people and villify their religion; he will scorn their institutions,
lampoon their morals, pasquinade their customs; he will stun
them with obscene vituperation, wound them with sacrilege and

profanity, immerse them in the vitriolic dripping from the "tank" that he seeks to drive over them; and for what purpose? Revenge. Those dissatisfied with the simile of the fury of a scorned woman should try "Ulysses."

Mr. Joyce has made a contribution to the science of psychology, and he has done it quite unbeknownst to himself, a fellow-countryman might say. He has shown us the process of the transmuting of thought to words. It isn't epoch making like "relativity," but it will give him notoriety, possibly immortality.

> "A man of genius makes no mistakes; his errors are volitional and are the portals of discovery."—STEPHEN DÆDALUS.

# CHAPTER III

A HUNDRED years ago, in Moscow, a being manifested its existence, who in the fullness of extraordinary vision and intellectuality heralded a religious rebirth, became the prophet of a new moral, ethical, and geographical order in the world, and the prototype of a new hero. Time has accorded Feodor Mikhailovitch Dostoievsky the position of one of the greatest writers of the nineteenth century, and as time passes his position becomes more secure. Like the prophet of old, during life he was fastened between two pieces of timber—debts and epilepsy—and sawn asunder by his creditors and his conscience. Posterity links his name with Pushkin and Tolstoi as the three great writers of their times. They are to the Russian Renaissance what Leonardo, Michelangelo, and Raphael were to the Italian Renaissance.

It is appropriate now, the centenary of his birth, to make a brief statement of Dostoievsky's position as a writer or novelist, and in so doing estimate must be made of him as a prophet, preacher, psychologist, pathologist, artist, and individual. Though he was not schooled to speak as expert in any of these fields, yet speak in them he did, and in a way that would have reflected credit upon a professor. It is particularly the field of morbid psychology, usually called psychiatry, that Dostoievsky made uniquely his own. He described many of the nervous and mental disorders, such as mania and depression, the psychoneuroses, hysteria, obsessive states, epilepsy, moral insanity, alcoholism, and that mysterious mental and moral constitution called "degeneracy" (apparently first hand, for there is no evidence or indication that he had access to books on mental medicine), in such a way that alienists recognise in his descriptions masterpieces in the same way that the painter recognises the apogee of his art in Giotto or Velasquez.

Not only did he portray the mental activity and output of the partially and potentially insane, but he described the conduct and reproduced the speech of individuals with personality defects, and with emotional disequilibrium, in a way that has never been excelled in any literature. For instance, it would be difficult to find a more comprehensive account of adult infantilism than the history of Stepan Trofimovitch, a more accurate presentation of the composition of a hypocrite than Rahkitin, of "The Brothers Karamazov." No one save Shakespeare has shown how consuming and overwhelming jealousy may be. That infirmity has a deeper significance for anyone familiar with the story of Katerina Ivanovna. Indeed Dostoievsky is the novelist of passions. He creates his creatures that they may suffer, not that they may enjoy from the reactions of life, though some of them get pleasure in suffering. Such was Lise, the true hysteric, who said, "I should like some one to torture me, marry me and then torture me, deceive me and then go away. I don't want to be happy."

Like Baudelaire and Nietzsche, whom he resembled morally and intellectually, Dostoievsky was an intellectual romantic in rebellion against life. His determination seemed to be to create an individual who should defy life, and when he had defied it to his heart's content "to hand God back his ticket," having no further need of it as the journey of existence was at an end. There is no place to go, nothing to do, everything worth trying has been tried and found valueless, and wherever he turns his gaze he sees the angel standing upon the sea and upon the earth avowing that there shall be time no longer; so he puts a bullet in his temple if his name is Svidrigailov, or soaps a silken cord so that it will support his weight when one end is attached to a large nail and the other to his neck,

FEODOR DOSTOIEVSKY

if it is Stavrogin.  Dostoievsky as a littérateur was obsessed with sin and expiation.  He connived and laboured to invent some new sin; he struggled and fought to augment some old one with which he could inflict one of his creation, and then watch him contend with it, stagger beneath it, or flaunt it in the world's face.  After it has wrought havoc, shipwrecked the possessor's life, and brought inestimable calamity and suffering to others, then he must devise adequate expiation.  Expiation is synonomous with sincere regret, honest request for forgiveness, and genuine determination to sin no more, but Dostoievsky's sinners must do something more; they must make renunciation in keeping with the magnitude of their sins, and as this is beyond human expression they usually kill themselves or go mad.

He had planned for his masterpiece "The Life of a Great Sinner," and the outline of it from his note-book deposited in the Central Archiv Department of the Russian Socialist Federative Soviet Republic, has now been published.  The hero is a composite of the Seven Deadly Sins: pride, covetousness, lust, anger, gluttony, envy, and sloth, plus the sin against the Holy Ghost.  No one has yet succeeded in defining that sin satisfactorily, but it is what Dostoievsky's antinomian heroes were trying to do, especially such an one as Stavrogin.  Another noteworthy feature about them is that they were all sadistic or masochistic: they got pleasure varying from an appreciative glow to voluptuous ecstasy and beyond, from causing pain and inducing humiliation, or having it caused in them by others.

This was a conditioning factor of conduct of all his antinomian heroes, and unless it be kept in mind when reading of them, their antics and their reflections are sometimes difficult of comprehension.  He makes one of them, one of the most intellectual and moral, Ivan Karamazov, say "You know we prefer beating-rods and scourges—that's our national institution. . . . I know for a fact there are people who at every blow are worked up to sensuality, which increases progressively at every blow they inflict."

It is difficult for a psychiatrist, after reading Dostoievsky's novels, to believe that he did not have access to the literature of insanity or have first-hand knowledge of the insane, and the criminologist must wonder where he got his extraordinary knowledge of the relation between suffering and lust. It may be that the habits of the Emperor Cheou-sin Yeow-waug were known to him, just as those of Caligula and Claudius were known to him.

It is not with the passions of the body or of the senses alone that his heroes contend, but with those of the mind. The fire that burns within them is abstraction, and the fuel that replenishes it is thought—thought of whence and whither. By it the possessors are lashed to a conduct that surpasses that of hate, jealousy, lubricity, or any of the baser passions as the light of an incandescent bulb surpasses that of a tallow candle. They are all men of parts, either originally endowed with great intelligence or brought to a certain elevation of intellectuality by education. Their conduct, their actions, their misdeeds, their crimes are the direct result of their argumentation, not of concrete, but of abstract things, and chiefly the nature and existence of God, the varieties of use that an individual may permit his intelligence, freewill, free determination, and of the impositions of dogma founded on faith and inspiration which seem contrary to reason and science.

All his heroes are more or less insane. Herein lies Dostoievsky's strength and his weakness in character creation. None of them could be held fully responsible in a court of justice. Out of the mouth of babes and sucklings the Lord ordained strength, but there is no writing to show that out of the mouths of the insane comes wisdom. Not that insanity is inimical to brilliant, even wise, utterance; but the pragmatic application of wisdom to life calls for sanity.

Dostoievsky himself was abnormal. He was what the physician calls a neuropathic and psychopathic individual. In addition, he had genuine epilepsy, that is, epilepsy not dependent upon some accidental disease, such as infection, injury, or new growth. He was of psychopathic temperament and at different times in his life displayed hallucination, obsession, and hypochondria.

He wrote of them as if he were the professor, not the possessor. The psychopathic constitution displays itself as:

"An unstable balance of the psychic impulses, an overfacile tendency to emotion, an overswift interchange of mental phases, an abnormally violent reaction of the psychic mechanism. The feature most striking to the beholder in the character of such sufferers is its heterogeneous medley of moods and whims, of sympathies and antipathies; of ideas in turn joyous, stern, gloomy, depressed and philosophical; of aspirations at first charged with energy then dying away to nothing. Another feature peculiar to these sufferers is their self-love. They are the most naïve of egoists; they talk exclusively and persistently and absorbedly of themselves; they strive always to attract the general attention, to excite the general interest and to engage everyone in conversation concerning their personality, their ailments and even their vices."

Scores of his characters had such constitution, and in none is it more perfectly delineated than in Katerina Ivanovna, though Lise Hohlakov, of the same novel, had wider display of the hysteria that grew on this fertile soil.

The facts of Dostoievsky's life that are important to the reader who would comprehend his psychopathic creations are that his father, surgeon to the Workhouse Hospital at Moscow, was a stern, suspicious, narrow-minded, gloomy, distrustful man who made a failure of life. "He has lived in the world fifty years and yet he has the same opinions of mankind that he had thirty years ago," wrote Feodor when seventeen years old. His mother was tender-minded, pious, and domestic, and died early of tuberculosis. Although much has been written of his boyhood, there is nothing particularly interesting in it bearing on his career save that he was sensitive, introspective, unsociable, and early displayed a desire to be alone. The hero of the book "Youth" relates that in the lowest classes of the gymnasium he scorned all relations with those of his class who surpassed him in any way in the sciences, physical strength, or in clever repartee. He did not hate such a person nor wish him harm. He simply turned away from him, that being his nature. These characteristics run like a red thread through the entire life of Dostoievsky. A tendency to day-dreaming was apparent in his earliest years, and he gives graphic accounts of hallucination in "An Author's Diary." At the age of sixteen he was admitted to the School of Engineering and remained there six years. During the latter part of his student days he decided upon literature as a career. Before taking it up, however, he had a brief experience with life after he had obtained his commission as engineer, which showed him to be totally incapable of dealing with its everyday eventualities, particularly in relation to money, whose purpose he knew but whose value was ever to remain a secret. It was then that he first displayed inability to subscribe or to submit to ordinary social conventions; indeed, a determination to transgress them.

From his earliest years the misfortunes of others hurt him and distressed him, and in later life the despised and the rejected, the poor and the oppressed, always had his sympathy and his understanding. God and the people, that is the Russian people, were his passion. "The people have a lofty instinct for truth. They may be dirty, degraded, repellent, but without them and in disregard of them nothing useful can be effected." The intellectuals who held themselves aloof from the masses he could not abide, and atheists, and their propaganda socialism, were anathema. He demanded of men who arrogated to themselves a distinction above their fellow men, "who go to the people not to learn to know it, but condescendingly to instruct and patronise it," not only repentance, but expiation by suffering.

His first important literary contribution was entitled "Poor Folk." He was fortunate enough to be praised by his contemporaries and particularly by Bielinsky, an editor and great critic, who saw in the central idea of the story corroboration of his favourite theory, viz.: abnormal social conditions distort and dehumanise mankind to such an extent that they lose the human form and semblance. As the result of this publication, Dostoievsky made the acquaintance of the leading literary lights of St. Petersburg, many of whom praised him too immoderately for his own good, as he produced nothing worthy of his fame until many years after the event in his life which must be looked upon as the beginning of his mental awakenment—banishment and penal servitude in Siberia.

Toward the middle of the nineteenth century the doctrines of the Frenchman, Charles Fourier, were having such acceptance in this country, where the North American Phalanx in New Jersey and the Brook farm in Massachusetts were thriving, as to encourage the disciples of that sentimental but wholly mad socialist in other lands, particularly in Russia, that their hopes of seeing the world dotted with *Phalansteres* might be fulfilled. Dostoievsky later stated most emphatically that he never believed in Fourierism, but nibbling at it nearly cost him his life. In fact, all that stood between him and death was the utterance of the word "Go," which it would seem the lips of the executioner had puckered to utter when the reprieve came. Dostoievsky was suspected of being a Revolutionary. One evening at the Petrashevsky Club he declaimed Pushkin's poem on Solitude:

"My friends, I see the people no longer oppressed,
And slavery fallen by the will of the Czar,
And a dawn breaking over us, glorious and bright,
And our country lighted by freedom's rays."

In discussion he suggested that the emancipation of the peasantry might have to come through a rising. Thus he became suspected. But it was not until he denounced the censorship and reflected on its severity and injustice that he was taken into custody. He and twenty-one others were sentenced to death. He spent four years in a Siberian prison and there became acquainted with misery, suffering, and criminality that beggars description.

"What a number of national types and characters I became familiar with in the prison; I lived into their lives and so I believe I know them really well. Many tramps' and thieves' careers were laid bare to me, and above all the whole wretched existence of the common pople. I learnt to know the Russian people as only a few know them."

After four years he was, through the mediation of powerful friends, transferred for five years to military service in Siberia, chiefly at Semipalatinsk. In 1859 he was permitted to return to St. Petersburg, and in the twenty years that followed he published those books upon which his fame rests; namely, "Crime and Punishment," "The Idiot," "The Possessed," "The Journal of an Author," and "The Brothers Karamazov." In 1867 he was obliged to leave Russia to escape imprisonment for debt, and he remained abroad, chiefly in Switzerland, for four years.

In his appeal to General Todleben to get transferred from the military to the civil service and to be permitted to employ himself in literature, he said:

"Perhaps you have heard something of my arrest, my trial and the supreme ratification of the sentence which was given in the case concerning me in the year 1849. I was guilty and am very conscious of it. I was convicted of the intention (but only the intention) of acting against the Government; I was lawfully and quite justly condemned; the hard and painful experiences of the ensuing years have sobered me and altered my views in many respects, but then while I was still blind I believed in all the theories and Utopias.  For two years before my offense I had suffered from a strange moral disease —I had fallen into hypochondria.  There was a time even when I lost my reason.  I was exaggeratedly irritable, had a morbidly developed sensibility and the power of distorting the most ordinary events into things immeasurable."

While Dostoievsky was in prison his physical health improved very strikingly, but, despite this, his epilepsy, which had previously manifested itself only in vague or minor attacks, became fully developed.  Attempts have been made to prove that prison life and particularly its hardships and inhumanities were responsible in a measure for Dostoievsky's epilepsy; but such allegations are no more acceptable than those which attribute it to his father's alcoholism.  His epilepsy was a part of his general make-up, a part of his constitution.  It was an integral part of him and it became an integral part of his books.

The phenomena of epilepsy may be said to be the epileptic personality and the attack with its warning, its manifestations, and the after-effects.  The disease is veiled in the same mystery today as it was when Hercules was alleged to have had it. Nothing is known of its causation or of its dependency, and all that can truthfully be said of the personality of the epileptic is that it is likely to display psychic disorder, evanescent or fixed.  Attacks are subject to the widest variation both as to frequency and intensity, but the most enigmatic things about the disease are the warnings of the attack, and the phenomena that sometimes appear vicariously of the attack—the epileptic equivalent they are called.  Dostoievsky had these *auræ* and equivalents in an unusual way and with extraordinary intensity, and narration of them as they were displayed in the different characters of his creation who were afflicted with epilepsy, and of their effects and consequences is an important part of every one of his great books.  Dostoievsky would seem to have been of the belief that a brain in which some of the mechanisms are disordered may yet remain superior both intellectually and morally to others less affected, and that the display of such weakness or maladjustment may put the possessor in tune with the Infinite, may permit him to blend momentarily with the Eternal Harmony, to be restored temporarily to the Source of its temporal emanation. Although he describes this in his "Letters," as he experienced it, he elaborates it in his epileptic heroes, and in none so seductively as in "The Idiot." He makes Prince Myshkin say:

"He thought amongst other things how in his epileptic condition there was one stage, just before the actual attack, when suddenly in the midst of sadness, mental darkness and oppression his brain flared up, as it were, and with an unwonted outburst all his vital powers were vivified simultaneously. The sensation of living and of self-consciousness was increased at such moments almost tenfold. They were moments like prolonged lightning. As he thought over this afterward in a normal state he often said to himself that all these flashes and beams of the highest self-realisation, self-consciousness and "highest existence" were nothing but disease, the interruption of the normal state. If this were so, then it was by no means the highest state, but, on the contrary, it must be reckoned as the very lowest. And yet he came at last to the very paradoxical conclusion: What matter if it is a morbid state? What difference can it make that the tension is abnormal, if the result itself, if the moment of sensation when remembered and examined in the healthy state proves to be in the highest degree harmony and beauty, and gives an unheard-of and undreamed-of feeling of completion, of balance, of satisfaction and exultant prayerful fusion with the highest synthesis of life? If at the last moment of consciousness before the attack he had happened to say to himself lucidly and deliberately "for this one moment one might give one's whole life," then certainly that moment would be worth a lifetime. However, he did not stand out for dialectics; obfuscation, mental darkness and idiocy stand before him as the obvious consequences of those loftiest moments."

It is a question for the individual to decide whether one would give his whole life for a moment of perfection and bliss, but it is probable that no one would without assurance that some permanent advantage, some growth of spirit that could be retained, some impress of spirituality that was indelible, such as comes from an understanding reading of "Hamlet" or a comprehended rendering of "Parsifal," would flow from it or follow it. But to have it and then come back to a world that is "just one damn thing after another" it is impossible to believe. Dostoievsky was right when he said that Myshkin could look forward to obfuscation, mental darkness, and im-becility with some certainty, for physicians experienced with epilepsy know empirically that the unfortunates who have panoplied warnings, and especially illusions, are most liable to become demented early. But that all epileptics with such warnings do not suffer this degradation is attested by the life of Dostoievsky, who was in his mental summation when death seized him in his sixtieth year.

Another phenomenon of epilepsy that Dostoievsky makes many of his characters display is detachment of the spirit from the body. They cease to feel their bodies at supreme moments, such as at the moment of condemnation, of pre-meditated murder, or planned crime. In other words, they are thrown into a state of ecstasy similar to that responsible for the mystic utterances of St. Theresa, or of insensibility to obvious agonies such as that of Santa Fina. He not only depicts the phenomena of the epileptic attack, its warnings, and its after-effects in the most masterful way, as they have never been rendered in literature, lay or scientific, but he also describes many varieties of the disease. Before he was exiled, in 1847, he gave a most perfect description of the epileptic con-stitution as it was manifested in Murin, a character in "The Landlady." The disease, as it displays itself in the classical way, is revealed by Nelly in "The Insulted and Injured," but it is in Myshkin, in "The Idiot," that we see epilepsy transforming the individual from adult infantilism, gradually, almost imperceptibly, to imbecility, the victim meantime displaying nobility and tender-mindedness that make the reader's heart go out to him.

The first fruits of Dostoievsky's activities after he had obtained permission to publish were inconsequential. It was not until the appearance of "Letters from a Deadhouse," which revealed his experiences and thoughts while in prison, and the volume called "The Despised and the Rejected," that the literary world of St. Petersburg realised that the brilliant promise which he had given in 1846 was realised. Some of his literary adventures, especially in journalism, got him into financial difficulties, and he began to write under the lash, as he described it, and against time.

In 1865 appeared the novel by which he is widely known, "Crime and Punishment," in which Dostoievsky's first great antinomian hero, Raskolnikov, a repentant nihilist, is introduced to the reader. He believes that he has a special right to live, to rebel against society, to transgress every law and moral precept, and to follow the dictates of his own will and the lead of his own thought. Such a proud, arrogant, intellectual spirit requires to be cleansed, and inasmuch as the verity, the essence of life, lies in humility, Dostoievsky makes his hero murder an old pawnbroker and his sister and then proceeds to put him through the most excrutiating mental agony imaginable. At the same time his mother and sister undergo profound vicarious suffering, while a successor of Mary Magdalene succours him in his increasingly agonised state and finally accompanies him to penal servitude. Many times Raskolnikov appears upon the point of confessing his crime from the torments of his own conscience, but, in reality, Svidrigailov, a strange monster of sin and sentiment, and the police officer, Petrovitch, a forerunner of Sherlock Holmes, suggest the confession to him, and between the effect of their suggestion and the appeal of Sonia, whose love moves him strangely, he confesses but does not repent. He does not repent because he has done no sin. He has committed no crime. The scales have not yet fallen from his eyes. That is reserved for the days and nights of his prison life and is to be mediated by Sonia's sacrificial heroism.

It is interesting to contemplate Dostoievsky at the state of development when he wrote "Crime and Punishment," or rather the state of development of his idea of free will. Raskolnikov has the same relation to Stavrogin of "The Possessed" and to Kirillov, the epileptic of the same book, as one of the trial pictures of the figures in the Last Supper has to Leonardo's masterpiece. Dostoievsky apparently was content to describe a case of moral imbecility in its most attractive way, and then when he had outlined its lineaments, to leave it and not adjust it to the other groupings of the picture that was undertaken. It would seem that his interest had got switched from Raskolnikov to Svidrigailov, who has dared to outrage covenants and conventions, laws and morality, and has measured his will against all things. Svidrigailov knows the difference between good and evil, right and wrong; indeed he realises it with great keenness, and when he finds that he is up against it, as it were, and has no escape, he puts the revolver to his temple and pulls the trigger. Death is the only thing he has not tried, and why wait to see whether eternity·is just one little room like a bathhouse in the country, or whether it is something beyond conception? Why not find out at once as everything has been found out? Svidrigailov is Dostoievsky's symbol of the denial of God, the denial of a will beyond his own.

"If there is a will beyond my own, it must be an evil will because pain exists. Therefore I must will evil to be in harmony with it. If there is no will beyond my own, then I must assert my own will until it is free of all check beyond itself. Therefore I must will evil."

Raskolnikov represents the conflict of will with the element of moral duty and conscience, and Svidrigailov represents its conflict with defined, deliberate passion. This same will in conflict with the will of the people, the State, is represented by Stavrogin and Shatov, while its conflict with metaphysical and religious mystery is represented by Karamazov, Myshkin, and Kirillov. Despite the fact that they pass through the furnace of burning conflicts and the fire of inflaming passions, the force of dominant will is ever supreme. Their human individuality, as represented by their ego, remains definite and concrete. It is untouched, unaltered, undissolved. Though they oppose themselves to the elements that are devouring them, they continue to assert their ego and self-will even when their end is at hand. Myshkin, Aloysha, and Zosima submit to God's will but not to man's.

"Crime and Punishment" and "The Brothers Karamazov" are the books by which Dostoievsky is best known in this country, and the latter, though unfinished, was intended by him to be his great work, "a work that is very dear to me for I have put a great deal of my inmost self into it," and it has been so estimated by the critics. Indeed, it is the summary of all his thoughts, of all his doubts, of all his fancies, and such statement of his faith as he could formulate. It is saturated in mysticism and it is a *vade mecum* of psychiatry. It is the narrative of the life of an egotistic, depraved, sensuous monster, who is a toad, a cynic, a scoffer, a drunkard, and a profligate, the synthesis of which, when combined with moral anæsthesia, constitutes degeneracy; of his three legitimate sons and their mistresses; and of an epileptic bastard son who resulted from the rape of an idiot girl.

The eldest son, Dimitri, grows up unloved, unguided, unappreciated, frankly hostile to his father whom he loathes and despises, particularly when he is convinced that the father has robbed him of his patrimony. He has had a rake's career, but when Katerina Ivanovna puts herself unconditionally in his power to save her father's honour he spares her. Three months later, when betrothed to her, he has become entangled in Circe's toils by Grushenka, for whose favour Fyodor Pavlovitch, his father, is bidding.

The second son, Ivan, half brother to Dimitri, whose mother was driven to insanity by the orgies staged in her own house and by the lusts and cruelties of her husband, is an intellectual and a nihilist. He is in rebellion against life, but he has an unquenchable thirst for life, and he will not accept the world. To love one's neighbours is impossible; even to conceive of it is repugnant. He will not admit that all must suffer to pay for the eternal harmony, and he insists "while I am on earth, I make haste to take my own measures." He does not want forgiveness earned for him vicariously. He wants to do it himself. He wants to avenge his suffering, to satisfy his indignation, even if he is wrong. Too high a price is asked for harmony; it is beyond our means to pay so much to enter on it. "And so," he says to his younger brother, the potential Saint Aloysha, "I hasten to give back my entrance ticket. It's not God that I don't accept, only I most respectfully return Him the ticket."

Dostoievsky speaks oftener out of the mouth of Ivan than of any of his other characters. When some understanding Slav like Myereski shall formulate Dostoievsky's religious beliefs it will likely be found that they do not differ materially from those of Ivan, as stated in the chapter "Pro and Contra" of "The Brothers Karamazov." He sees in Christ the Salvation of mankind, and the woe of the world is that it has not accepted Him.

The third brother, Aloysha, is the prototype of the man's redeemer—a tender-minded, preoccupied youth, chaste and pure, who takes no thought for the morrow and always turns the other cheek, and esteems his neighbour far more than himself. At heart he is a sensualist. "All the Karamazovs are insects to whom God has given sensual lust which will stir up a tempest in your blood," said Ivan to Aloysha when he was attempting to set forth his philosophy of life. But this endowment permits him the more comprehensively to understand the frailties of others and to condone their offences. The monastic life appeals to him, but he is warded off from it by Father Zosima, the prototype of Bishop Tikhon, in "Stavrogin's Confession," whose clay was lovingly moulded by Dostoievsky, but into whose nostrils he did not blow the breath of life. This monk, who had been worldly and who, because of his knowledge, forgives readily and wholly, is a favourite figure of Dostoievsky, and one through whom he frequently expresses his sentiments and describes his visions. His convictions, conduct and teaching may be summarised in his own words:

"Fear nothing and never be afraid; and don't fret. If only your penitence fail not, God will forgive all. There is no sin, and there can be no sin on all the earth, which the Lord will not forgive to the truly repentant! Man cannot commit a sin so great as to exhaust the infinite love of God. Can there be a sin which could exceed the love of God? Think only of repentance, continual repentance, but dismiss fear altogether. Believe that God loves you as you cannot conceive; that He loves you with your sin, in your sin. It has been said of old that over one repentant sinner there is more joy in heaven than over ten righteous men. Go, and fear not. Be not bitter against men. Be not angry if you are wronged. Forgive the dead man in your heart what wrong he did you. Be reconciled with him in truth. If you are penitent, you love. And if you love you are of God. All things are atoned for, all things are saved by love. If I, a sinner, even as you are, am tender with you and have pity on you, how much more will God. Love is such a priceless treasure that you can redeem the whole world by it, and expiate not only your own sins but the sins of others."

Aloysha is Dostoievsky's attempt to create a superman. He is the most real, the most vital, the most human, and, at the same time, the most lovable of all his characters. He is the essence of Myshkin and Stavrogin and Karamazov and Father Zosima, the residue that is left in the crucible when their struggles were reduced, their virtues and their vices distilled. He is Myshkin whose mind has not been destroyed by epilepsy, he is Stavrogin who has seen light before his soul was sold to the devil, he is Ivan Karamazov redeemed by prayer and good works, he is the apotheosis of Father Zosima. "He felt clearly and as it were tangibly that something firm and unshakable as the vault of heaven had entered into his soul. It was as though some idea had seized the sovereignty of his mind—and it was for all his life and for ever and for ever." In other words, Aloysha realises in a mild form and continuously that which Myshkin realises as the result of disease and spasmodically. Aloysha goes into a state of faith, of resignation, of adjustment with the Infinite, and Myshkin goes into dementia via ecstasy.

As a peace-maker, adjuster, comforter, and inspiration he has few superiors in profane literature. His speech at the Stone of Ilusha embodies the whole doctrine of brotherly love.

Dimitri's hatred of his father becomes intense when they are rivals for Grushenka's favours, so that it costs him no pang to become potentially a parricide on convincing himself that the father has been a successful rival. Psychologically he represents the type of unstable, weak-willed, uninhibited being who cannot learn self-control. Such individuals may pass unmarked so long as they live in orderly surroundings, but as soon as they wander from the straight path they get into trouble. Their irritability, manifested for the smallest cause, may give rise to attacks of boundless fury which are further increased by alcohol, and the gravest crimes are often committed in these conditions. The normal inhibitions are entirely absent; there is no reflection, no weighing of the costs. The thought which develops in the brain is at once translated into action. Their actions are irrational, arbitrary, dependent upon the moment, governed by accidental factors.

Despite overwhelming proof, Dimitri denies his guilt from the start. It is an open question if the motive of this denial is repentance, shame, love for Grushenka, or fear. The three experts of the trial each has his own opinion. The first two declare Dimitri to be abnormal. The third regards him as normal. The author himself has made it easy to judge of Dimitri's state of mind. Though on the boundary line of accountability, he is not in such a pathological condition as to exclude his free determination; however, he is not fully responsible for the crime, and extenuating circumstances have to be conceded by the judge.

Smerdyakov, the illegitimate child of the idiot girl whom Karamazov *pere* raped on a wager and who eventually murders his father (vicariously, as it were, his morality having been destroyed by Ivan), is carefully delineated by Dostoievsky. He is epileptic. Not only are the disease and its manifestations described, but there is a masterly presentation of the personality alteration which so often accompanies its progress. In childhood he is cruel, later solitary, suspicious, and misanthropical. He has no sense of gratitude and he looks at the world mistrustfully. When Fyodor Pavlovitch hears he has epilepsy he takes interest in him, sees to it that he has treatment, and sends him to Moscow to be trained as cook. During the three years of absence his appearance changes remarkably. Here it may be remarked that though Dostoievsky lived previous to our knowledge of the rôle that the ductless glands play in maintaining the appearance and conserving the nutritional equilibrium of the individual, he gives, in his delineation of Smerdyakov, an extraordinarily accurate description of the somatic and spiritual alteration that sometimes occurs when some of them cease functioning. It is his art also to do it in a few words, just as it is his art to forecast Smerdyakov's crime while discussing the nature and occurrence of epileptic-attack equivalents, which he called contemplations.

The way he disentangles the skeins from the confused mass of putridity, disease, and crime of which this novel is constituted, has been the marvel and inspiration of novelists the world over for the past fifty years. Dimitri wants to kill his father for many reasons, but the one that moves him to meditate it and plan it is: Grushenka, immoral and unmoral, will then be beyond the monster's reach; Grushenka whose sadism peeps out in her lust for Aloysha and who can't throw off her feeling of submission for the man who had violated her when she was seventeen. Dimitri loves Grushenka and Grushenka loves Dimitri "abnormals with abnormal love which they idealised." During an orgy which would have pleased Nero, Dimitri lays drunken Grushenka on the bed, and kisses her on the lips.

" 'Don't touch me,' she faltered in an imploring voice. 'Don't touch me till I am yours. . . . I have told you I am yours, but don't touch me . . . spare me. . . . With them here, with them close you mustn't. He's here. It's nasty here.' "

He sinks on his knees by the bedside. He goes to his father's house at a propitious time and suitably armed for murder; he hails him to the window by giving the signal that he has learned from Smerdyakov would apprise him of the approach of Grushenka; but before he can strike him Smerdyakov, carrying out a plan of his own, despatches him, and Dimitri flees. The latter half of the book is taken up with the trial of Dimitri and the preliminaries to it, which give Dostoievsky an opportunity to pay his respects to Jurisprudence and to medicine and to depict a Slav hypocrite, Rahkitin. Smerdyakov commits the crime to find favour in the eyes of his god Ivan. He knows that Ivan desired it, suggested it, and went away knowing it was going to be done—at least that is the impression the epileptic mind of Smerdyakov gets—and under that impression he acts when he despatches his father with the three-pound paper weight. The unprejudiced reader will feel the sympathies that have gradually been aroused for Smerdyakov because of his disease fade as he reads of the plan that the murderer made, and when he has hung himself after confessing to Ivan. In proportion as they recede for the valet, they will be rearoused for Ivan whose brain now gives away under the hereditary and acquired burden. This gives Dostoievsky the opportunity to depict the prodromata and early manifestations of acute mania as they have never, before or since, been depicted in lay literature.

Description of the visual hallucination which Ivan has in the early stages, that a "Russian gentleman of a particular kind is present," and the delusion that he is having an interview with him, might have been copied from the annals of an asylum, had they been recorded there by a master of the narrative art. It is one of the first, and the most successful attempts to depict dual personality, and to record the beliefs and convictions of each side of the personality. He listens to his *alter ego* sit in judgment upon him and his previous conduct, and is finally goaded by him to assault, as was Luther under similar though less dramatic circumstances. "Voices," as the delirious and insane call them, have never been more accurately rendered than in the final chapters of the Ivan section of the book.

An exhaustive psychosis displaying itself in intermittent delirium, and occurring in a profoundly psychopathic individual, is the label that a physician would give Ivan's disorder. Aloysha saw.in it that God, in whom Ivan disbelieved, and His truth were gaining mastery over his heart, which still refused to submit.

"The Idiot" was one of Dostoievsky's books which had a cold reception from the Russian reading public, but which has been, next to "The Brothers Karamazov" and "Crime and Punishment," the most popular in this country. The basic idea is the representation of a truly perfect and noble man, and it is not at all astonishing that Dostoievsky made him an epileptic. He had been impressed, he said, that all writers who had sought to represent Absolute Beauty were unequal to the task. It is so difficult, for the beautiful is the ideal, and ideals have long been wavering and waning in civilised Europe. There is only one figure of absolute beauty, Christ, and he patterns Prince Myshkin upon the Divine model. He brings him in contact with Nastasya Filipovna, who is the incarnation of the evil done in the world, and this evil is represented symbolically by Dostoievsky as the outrage of a child. The nine years of brooding which had followed the outrage inflicted upon Nastasya as a child by Prince Tosky had imprinted upon her face something which Myshkin recognises as the pain of the world, and from the thought of which he cannot deliver himself, and which he cannot mitigate for her. She marries him after agonies of rebellion, after having given him to her *alter ego* in virginal state, Aglaia Epanchin, and then takes him away to show her power and demonstrate her own weakness; but she deserts him on the church steps for her lover Rogozhin, who murders her that night. Myshkin, finding Rogozhin next morning, says more than "Forgive them, Father, they know not what they do." He lies beside him in the night and bathes his temples with his tears, but fortunately in the morning when the murderer is a raving lunatic a merciful Providence has enshrouded Myshkin in his disease.

As Dimitri Merejkowski, the most understanding critic and interpreter of Dostoievsky who has written of him, truthfully says, his works are not novels or epics, but tragedies. The narrative is secondary to the construction of the whole work, and the keystone of the narrative is the dialogue between the characters. The reader feels that he hears real persons talking and talking without artifice, just as they would talk in real life; and they express sentiments and convictions which one would expect from individuals of such inheritance, education, development, and environment, obsessed particularly with the injustices of this world and the uncertainties of the world to be, concerned day and night with the immortality of the soul, the existence of God, and the future of civilisation.

It has been said that he does not describe the appearance of his characters, for they depict themselves, their thoughts and feelings, their faces and bodies, by their peculiar forms of language and tones of voice. Although he does not dwell on portraiture, he has scarcely a rival in delineation, and his portraits have that quality which perhaps Leonardo of all who worked with the brush had the capacity to portray, and which Pater saw in the *Gioconda;* the revelation of the soul and its possibilities in the lineaments. The portrait of Mlle. Lebyadkin, the imbecile whom the proud Nikolay Stavrogin married, not from love or lust, but that he might exhaust the list of mortifications, those of the flesh, for himself, and those of pride for his family; that he might kill his instincts and become pure spirit, is as true to life as if Dostoievsky had spent his existence in an almshouse sketching the unfortunates segregated there. The art of portraiture cannot surpass this picture of Shatov, upon whose plastic soul Stavrogin impressed his immoralities in the shape of "the grand idea" and who said to Stavrogin in his agony, "Sha'n't I kiss your foot-prints when you've gone? I can't tear you out of my heart, Nikolay Stavrogin:"

"He was short, awkward, had a shock of flaxen hair, broad shoulders, thick lips, very thick overhanging white eyebrows, a wrinkled forehead, and a hostile, obstinately downcast, as it were shamefaced, expression in his eyes. His hair was always in a wild tangle and stood up in a shock which nothing could smooth. He was seven or eight and twenty."

It is not as a photographer of the body that Dostoievsky is a source of power and inspiration in the world today, and will remain so for countless days to come—for he has depicted the Russian people as has no one else save Tolstoi, and his pictures constitute historical documents—but as a photographer of the soul, a psychologist. Psychology is said to be a new science, and a generation ago there was much ado over a new development called "experimental psychology," which was hailed as the key that would unlock the casket wherein repose the secrets of the mind; the windlass that would lift layer by layer the veil that has, since man began, concealed the mysteries of thought, behaviour, and action. It has not fulfilled its promise. It would be beyond the truth to say that it has been sterile, but it is quite true to say that the contributions which it has made have been as naught compared with those made by abnormal psychology. Some, indeed, contend that the only real psychological contributions of value have come from a study of disease and deficiency, and their contentions are granted by the vast majority of those entitled to opinion.

Dostoievsky is the master portrayer of madness and of bizarre states of the soul and of the mind that are on the borderland of madness. Not only has he depicted the different types of mental alienation, but by an intuition peculiar to his genius, by a species of artistic divination, he has understood and portrayed their display, their causation, their onset—so often difficult to determine even for the expert—and finally the full development of the disease. Indeed, he forestalled the description of the alienists. "They call me a psychologist," says Dostoievsky; "it is not true. I am only a realist in the highest sense of the word, that is I depict all the soul's depth. Arid observations of every-day trivialities I have long ceased to regard as realism—it is quite the reverse."

It is the mission of one important branch of psychology to depict the soul's depth, the workings of the conscious mind, and as the interior of a house that one is forbidden to enter is best seen when the house has been shattered or is succumbing to the incidences of time and existence, so the contents of the soul are most discernible in the mind that has some of its impenetralia removed by disease. It was in this laboratory that Dostoievsky conducted his experiments, made his observations, and recorded the results from which he drew conclusions and inferences. "In my works I have never said so much as the twentieth part of what I wished to say, and perhaps could actually have said. I am firmly convinced that mankind knows much more than it has hitherto expressed either in science or in art. In what I have written there is much that came from the depth of my heart," he says in a letter to a friendly critic, to which may be added that what he has said is in keeping with the science of today, and is corroborated by workers in other fields of psychology and psychiatry.

"The Possessed," in which Dostoievsky reached the highwater mark of personality analysis, has always been a stumbling block to critics and interpreters. The recent publication by the Russian Government of a pamphlet containing "Stavrogin's Confession" sheds an illuminating light on the hero; and even second-hand knowledge of what has gone on in Russia, politically and socially, during the past six years facilitates an understanding of Pyotr Stepanovitch, Satan's impressario, and of Kirillov, nihilist.

The task that Dostoievsky set himself in "The Possessed" was not unlike that which the Marquis de Sade set himself in "Justine, or the Misfortunes of Virtue," and Sacher-Masoch in "Leibesgeschichten"; viz., to narrate the life of an unfortunate creature whose most important fundamental instinct was perverted and who could get the full flavour of pleasure only by inflicting cruelty, causing pain, or engendering humiliation.

"Every unusually disgraceful, utterly degrading, dastardly, and above all, ridiculous situation in which I ever happened to be in my life, always roused in me, side by side with extreme anger, an incredible delight."

Stavrogin was apparently favoured by fortune: he had charm, education, wealth, and health. In reality he was handicapped to an incalculable degree. After a brilliant brief career in the army and in St. Petersburg society, he withdrew from both and associated with the dregs of the population of that city, with slip-shod government clerks, discharged military men, beggars of the higher class, and drunkards of all sorts. He visited their filthy families, spent days and nights in dark slums and all sorts of low haunts. He threw suspicion of theft on the twelve-year-old daughter of a woman who rented him a room for assignations that he might see her thrashed, and a few days later he raped her. The next day he hated her so he decided to kill her and was preparing to do so when she hanged herself. This is not featured in the novel as it now stands. Until the publication of "Stavrogin's Confession" interpreters of Stavrogin's personality who maintained that he was a sadist were accused of having read something into his character that Dostoivesky did not intend him to have. After committing this "greatest sin in the world," he determined to cripple his life in the most disgusting way possible, that he might pain his mother, humiliate his family, and shock society. He would marry Marya, a hemiplegic idiot who tidied up his room. After the ceremony he went to stay with his mother, the granddame of their province. He went to distract himself, which included seducing and enslaving Darya, Shatov's sister, a ward of his mother, and a member of the family.

Suddenly, apropos of nothing, he was guilty of incredible outrages upon various persons and, what was most enigmatic, these outrages were utterly unheard of, quite inconceivable, entirely unprovoked and objectless. For instance, one day at the club, he tweaked the nose of an elderly man of high rank in the service. When the Governor of the club sought some explanation Stavrogin told him he would whisper it in his ear.

"When the dear, mild Ivan Ossipovitch hurriedly and trustfully inclined his ear Stavrogin bit it hard. The poor Governor would have died of terror but the monster had mercy on him, and let go his ear."

The doctor testified that he was temporarily unbalanced, and after a few weeks' rest and isolation he went abroad for four years and there Lizaveta Nikolaevna, Shatov's wife, and several others succumbed, and he also met his old tutor's son, Pyotr Stepanovitch, his deputy in the Internationale, who from that moment became his apologist, his tool, his agent, and finally the instrument of his destruction. The gratification of Stavrogin's perverted passion, the machinations of the Republicans and nihilists, and the revelations of Shatov's limitations and of Mr. Kirillov's nihilistic idealism are the threads of the story. Shatov was the son of a former valet of Stavrogin's mother who had been expelled from the University after some disturbance, a radical with a tender heart, who had held Stavrogin up as an ideal.

"He was one of those idealistic beings common in Russia who are suddenly struck by some overmastering idea which seems, as it were, to crush them at once and sometimes for ever. They are never equal to coping with it, but put passionate faith in it, and their whole life passes afterward, as it were, in the last agonies under the weight of the stone that has fallen upon them and half crushed them."

Shatov's overmastering idea was that Nikolay Vsyevolodovitch could do no wrong, and the stone that crushed him was Nikolay's misdeeds. Mr. Kirillov, the engineer, believed that he who conquers pain and terror will become a god.

"Then there will be a new life, a new man, everything will be new . . . then they will divide history into two parts: from the guerilla to the annihilation of God, and from the annihilation of God to the transformation of the earth and of man physically. Man will be God and will be transformed physically and all men will kill themselves."

"He who kills himself only to kill fear will become a god at once." Kirillov believed or feared that eternal life was now, not hereafter. There are moments when time suddenly stands still for men, and it was fear that it might become eternal that he could not tolerate. In Dostoievsky's books there is always one contemptible character, a sanctimonious hypocrite, a fawning holier-than-thou, a pious scandal monger, a venomous volunteer of first aid to the morally injured. In this book his name is Liputin, an elderly provincial official.

These are the chief figures of the drama.

When Shatov had been killed; when Kirillov's promise: namely, that he would commit suicide on request, had been exacted; when Stavrogin's imbecile wife and her brother Lebyadkin had been despatched; when Lisa, who was abducted by Stavrogin on the eve of her marriage and then abandoned, had been knocked on the head and killed by the mob because she was Stavrogin's woman who "had come to look at the wife he had murdered"; when Shatov's wife had come back to him and borne Stavrogin's child in his presence; when Stepan Trofimovitch had displayed his last infantile reaction and his son Peter, the Russian Mephistopheles, had made a quick and successful get-away, Stavrogin wrote to Darya and suggested that she go with him to the Canton of Uri, of which he was a citizen, and be his nurse. Darya, for whom humiliation spelled happiness, consented and Varvara Petrovna, hearing of the plan, succumbed to the sway of maternal love and arranged to go with them.

The day they had planned to begin their journey Stavrogin was not to be found, but search of the loft revealed his body hanging from a hook by means of a silken cord which had been carefully soaped before he slung it around his neck.

At the inquest the doctors absolutely and emphatically rejected all idea of insanity.

"The Possessed" has been the most enigmatic of the writer's books because critics could not agree as to the motives of Stavrogin's crimes and conduct. With the publication of "Stavrogin's Confession" the riddles were solved. In the book as originally planned (and modified at the request of the pub-

lisher of the periodical in which the novel originally appeared),
Stavrogin, instead of hanging himself, went to Our Lady
Spasso-Efimev Monastery and confessed himself to Bishop
Tikhon. Dostoievsky recruited his spiritual *menschenkenners*
from the ranks of those who, in youth, had played the game
of life hard, transgressed, and repented. Tikhon was one of
them, a strange composite of piety and worldliness chained to
his cell by chronic rheumatism and alcoholic tremours.

Stavrogin had been obsessed by a phrase from the Apoca-
lypse: "I know thy works; that thou art neither hot nor cold.
I would thou wert cold or hot. So then because thou art lukewarm, and neither cold nor hot, I will spew thee out of my
mouth." He would be lukewarm no longer. He handed
Tikhon three little sheets of ordinary small-sized writing paper
printed and stitched together. It was entitled "From Stavrogin" and was a confession of his sins. He couldn't dislodge
from his mind the vision of the little girl Matryosha. He
identified her with photographs of children that he saw in shop
windows. A spider on a geranium leaf caused the vision of her
as she killed herself to rise up before him, and this vision came
to him now every day and every night

"not that it comes itself, but that I bring it before myself and
cannot help bringing it although I can't live with it. I know
I can dismiss the thought of Matryosha even now whenever I
want to. I am as completely master of my will as ever. But
the whole point is that I never wanted to do it; I myself do
not want to, and never shall."

Tikhon suggested that he would be forgiven if his repentance was sincere, and told him he knew an old man, a hermit
and ascetic of such great Christian wisdom that he was beyond
ordinary understanding. He suggested that Stavrogin should
go to him, into retreat, as novice under his guidance, for five
years, or seven, for as many as were necessary. He abjured
him to make a vow to himself so that by this great sacrifice he

would acquire all that he longed for and didn't even expect, and assured him that he could not possibly realise now what he would obtain from such guidance and isolation and repentance.

Stavrogin hesitated and the Bishop suddenly realised that he had no intention of repenting. It dawned upon him that Stavrogin's plan was to flaunt his sin in the face of God as he had previously flaunted it in the face of society, and in a voice which penetrated the soul and with an expression of the most violent grief Tikhon exclaimed,

"Poor lost youth, you have never been so near another and a still greater crime as you are at this moment. Before the publication of the 'Confession,' a day, an hour perhaps before the great step, you will throw yourself on another crime, as a way out, and you will commit it solely in order to avoid the publication of these pages."

Stavrogin shuddered with anger and almost with fear and shouted "You cursed psychologist!", and left the cell without looking at Tikhon.

The annihilation of the sense of time in Dostoievsky's stories was first dwelt upon by Merejkowski, and it has been much discussed by all of his serious commentators. Events occur and things take place within a few hours in his books which would ordinarily take months and years. The reason for this timeless cycle of events may be sought in the experiences that the author had in the moments preceding his attacks of epilepsy in which he had thoughts and emotions which a lifetime would scarcely suffice to narrate.

Dostoievsky is the greatest of subjective writers because he goes deepest and is the most truthful. His books are narratives of sins and crimes and descriptions of attempts at expiation. He didn't invent sins, he took them from life; he presented those he had committed and seen committed. He invented only the expiation, and some of that, it must be admitted, he experienced. His sinners are never normal mentally. They are never insane legally, but all of them are insane medically.

Dostoievsky himself was far from "normal" mentally, aside from his epilepsy, though he made approximation to it as he grew older. His mind was a garden sown with the flower seeds of virtue and the thistle seeds of vice. All of them germinated. Some became full blown, others remained stunted and dwarfed.

"I have invented a new kind of enjoyment for myself," he wrote to his brother, "a most strange one—to make myself suffer. I take your letter, turn it over in my hand for several minutes, feel if it is full weight, and having looked on it sufficiently and admired the closed envelope, I put it in my pocket. You won't believe what a voluptuous state of soul, feeling and heart there is in that!"

That is the *anlage* of masochism. In the outline of "The Life of a Great Sinner," the novel whose completion would permit him to die in peace, for then he should have expressed himself completely, one sees the wealth of detail taken by the author from his boyhood and early manhood. The hero of the "Life" was unsociable and uncommunicative; a proud, passionate, and domineering nature. So was Dostoievsky. So here was to be apotheosis of individualism, consciousness of his superiority, of his determination, and of his uniqueness. Dostoievsky wrote of himself in 1867, "Everywhere and in everything I reach the furthest limits; I have passed beyond the boundaries of all life."

The most inattentive reader of his "Letters" will be reminded of Dostoievsky when they read that the hero of the "Life" "surprised everybody by unexpectedly rude pranks," "behaved like a monster," "offended an old woman," and that he was obsessed with the idea of amassing money; and the alternative stages of belief and disbelief of the hero are obviously recollections of his own trials. "I believe I shall express the whole of myself in it" he wrote of it to a friend, and no one

familiar with his books and his life can read the outline of it
and doubt that he would have succeeded. Wherever Dostoievsky looked he saw a question mark and before it was
written "Is there a God? Does God exist?" He was determined to find the answer. He had found Christ abundantly
and satisfactorily, but the God of Job he never knew, nor had
He ever overthrown him or compassed him with His net.

Dostoievsky was a rare example of dual personality. His
life was the expression of his ego personality (and what a life
of strife and misery and unhappiness it was!), revealed with
extraordinary lucidity in his "Letters" and "The Journal of
an Author"; and his legacy to mankind is the record of his
unconscious mind revealed in his novels. The latter is the life
he would have liked to live, and in it he depicts the changes in
man's moral nature that he would have liked to witness. His
contention was that man should be master of his fate, captain
of his soul. He must express his thought and conviction in
action and conduct, particularly in his relation to his fellow-
man. He must take life's measure and go to it no matter what
it entails or how painful, unpleasant, or disastrous the struggle,
or the end.

Many thoughtful minds believe that Dostoievsky has shown
us the only salvation in the great crisis of the European conscience. The people, it matters not of what nationality, still
possess the strength and equilibrium of internal power. The
conviction that man shall not live as a beast of burden still
survives in the Russian people and is shared with them by the
masses throughout the civilised world. Salvation from internal anarchy was his plea, and it is the plea that is today being
made by millions in other lands than his.

As a prophet he foresaw the supremacy of the Russian
people, the common people succoured to knowledge, faith, and
understanding by liberty, education, and health, and by con-
formation to its teaching the Renaissance of the Christian

faith, which shall be a faith that shall show man how to live and how to die, and which shall be manifest in conduct as well as by word of mouth; primacy of the Russian church; and the consummation of European culture by the effort and propaganda of Russia. "Russia is the one God-fearing nation and her ultimate destiny shall be to make known the Russian Christ for the salvation of lost humanity." No one can say at this day that his prophecies may not come true, and to the student of history there may seem to be more suggestive indication of it in the Russia of today than in that of half a century ago; for from a world in ferment unexpected distillations may flow. But to the person who needs proof Russia is silent now. Dostoievsky's doctrines have not dropped as the rain, nor has his speech been distilled as the dew, though he published the name of the Lord and ascribed greatness unto our God. Indeed, the fate that has overtaken Russia would seem to deny the possibility of the fulfillment of his prophecies either for his country or his people.

As a narrator of the events of life here, and of the thoughts of life here and hereafter, he has had few peers of any nation or language. That he did it in a disorderly way must be admitted; that the events of his tragedies had little time incidence is obvious to the most casual reader; that the reader has to bring to their perusal concentration and application is beyond debate; and that his characters are "degenerates," using that word in its biological sense, there is no doubt. But despite these defects, Dostoievsky succeeds in straining the essence of the Russian's soul through his unconscious to his conscious mind, and then expressing it; and his books are the imperishable soul-prints of his contemporaneous countrymen. Not only does he stand highest in literary achievement of all men of his time, but he is a figure of international significance in the world of literature. His life and struggle was Hauptmann's song,

"Always must the heart-strings vibrate in the breath of the world's sorrow, for the world's sorrow is the root of heaven's desire."

He foresaw with clairvoyancy the necessity of making religion livable, not professed with the lips and scorned in action, but a code or formulation that would combine Life, Love, and Light pragmatically; and although he was not able to formulate his thought or to express it clearly and forcibly, to synthetise and codify it, as it were, formulators of the new religion, of Christianity revivified or dematerialised, will consult frequently and diligently the writings of Feodor Dostoievsky.

# CHAPTER IV

## DOROTHY RICHARDSON AND HER CENSOR

THE novelists are behind the naturalists in the recording of minutiæ. Many of the latter have set down the life history of certain species of birds in exhaustive detail—every flip of the tail, every peck preceding the grand drama of courtship and marriage, every solicitude of paternity, every callousness of guardianship.

An analogous contribution to realism in the domain of fiction has been made by Dorothy M. Richardson, an interesting figure in English literature today. She has written six books about herself. When one considers that her life has been uneventful, one might say drab, commonplace, and restricted, this is an accomplishment deserving of note and comment.

Critics and connoisseurs of literary craftsmanship have given her a high rating, but they have not succeeded in introducing her to the reading public. She is probably the least known distinguished writer of fiction in England, but she has a certain public both in her own country, and in this in which all her novels have been republished.

Her influence on the output of English fiction since the publication of "Pointed Roofs," in 1913, is one of the outstanding features in the evolution of novel-writing during the present decade. Since Flaubert set the pace for a reaction against the conception of the realistic novel as the faithful transcription of life as perceived by the novelist; and his followers introduced into novel-writing a more subtle art than that of mere transcription of life, by making the hypothetical consciousness through which the story is presented a determining factor in its essence, this factor has been assuming a more and more important rôle. The autobiographical novel, tracing its lineage straight back to Rousseau, has become a prevailing fashion in fiction. It remained, however, for Miss Richardson to give the example—aside from James Joyce and Marcel Proust—of a novel in which the consciousness of the writer should assume the leading rôle in a drama that just missed being a monologue. Miss Richardson has made, not herself in the ordinary sense of the word, but her subjective consciousness, the heroine of her narrative; and the burden of it has been to present the development of this consciousness, or energy, directly to the reader in all its crudity and its dominancy. The result is a novel without plot, practically without story interest. It is a question what influence this "artistic subjectivism," as Mr. J. Middleton Murry has called it, will have upon the fiction of the future. Of its influence upon that of the present there can be no question.

Her technique is intensive, netting in words the continuous flow of consciousness and semi-consciousness. She is first and foremost a symbolist, an exponent of autistic thinking, a recorder of the product of what is called by the popular psychology her "unconscious mind," which has got by the "censor," a mythical sort of policeman who, in her case, often sleeps on his post, or is so dazed by the supply from her unconscious he cannot carry on.

This recently rechristened official, from the baptismal font of the Freudians, is responsible for much literature of questionable value. Latterly he has become something of a radical and has been permitting stuff to get by on many wires and postal avenues that seems to those whose "censors" have been doing duty in the name of Reason or *Amour Propre* to be, if not immoral, at least indecent. Miss Richardson's "censor" is a Socialist, but he is not a Red. He hasn't much time for appearances and diplomacy, and he has so many fish to fry that he cannot have all his time taken up with putting his best foot forward. Therefore Miriam Henderson doesn't believe in the religion of her forebears, she isn't strong for the National cause, and she doesn't hark to any party cry. She doesn't like her mother, and it is the tendency of the modern "censor" to emphasise that; but to "pater" her allegory and her ordered stream of thought are uniformly kind and indulgent. Her "censor" early in life warned her that he was no parent of shams and if she wanted to live a peaceful life she must be unconventional. So Miriam determined to be "different." She is unsociable. She cannot think of anyone who does not offend her. "I don't like men and I loathe women. I am a misanthrope. So is pater." He further assured her that "freedom" is the gateway and roadway to happiness, and to travel thereon, with a little money to satisfy the self-preservative urge, constituted the joy of life. Up to this point Miriam and the "censor" got on famously. It was when he announced that he was determined not to exhaust himself keeping down her untutored passions that she revealed a determination that staggered him. The "censor" capitulated. The result is that Miss Richardson's books are of all symbolic literature the least concerned with the sinfulness of the flesh, therefore furthest removed from comedy.

Miriam Henderson—who is Dorothy M. Richardson, the narrator of her own life—is the third of four daughters of a silly, inane, resigned little mother and an unsocial father of artistic temperament, the son of a tradesman whose ruling passion is to be considered a country gentleman. His attitude toward life and his efforts to sustain it have culminated in financial ruin, and Miriam finds herself at the age of eighteen, all reluctant and unprepared, confronted with the necessity of depending upon her own efforts for a living—unless she can achieve escape, as do two of her sisters, in marriage. She meets the situation bravely—cowardice is not one of her faults —and the six books contain a statement of her struggles against circumstance and a psychological analysis of her personality. As self is less able to accept compromises or to make adaptations in her case than in that of the average mortal, the conflict is fierce; but it is soul struggle, not action.

Miriam's first tilt with life, recorded in "Pointed Roofs," is as a governess in a small German boarding-school, from which she is politely dismissed, without assigned reason, at the close of the first term. Her second, in "Backwater," is as a teacher of drab youngsters in a North London school. After less than a year, ennui, restlessness, and discontent compel her to resign without definite outlook or prospects. She finds herself, in "Honeycomb," established as governess to two children in the country home of a prosperous Q.C. The situation suddenly becomes unendurable after a few months—for no stated reason—and she eagerly seeks escape in her mother's illness. In "The Tunnel" she at last finds a "job" to her taste when she becomes assistant in the office of several London dentists, and denizen of a hall bedroom in a dismal Bloomsbury rooming-house. In "Interim" she loses her opportunity of marrying a wholesome Canadian by flirting with a Spanish Jew. And in "Deadlock" she puts forth her first tentative efforts to write and becomes engaged to a man with whom she believes herself to be in love, but of whom she does not intellectually approve.

Her next novel is likely to be called "Impasse," for meanwhile, in real life, Miss Richardson has married and a new element has been introduced into her life which she will not be able to keep from tincturing and tinting her "unconscious," but which she will not be able to get past her "censor." It would not surprise us either should she switch from this series and cast her next book in the form of an episode or short story. Revelations of impulses, thoughts, determinations have been considered "good form" in literature when they were one's own, but when they were another's, submitted to the narrator's judgement or reason, especially a wife's or a husband's, it has been considered bad taste either to narrate or to publish them. Moreover the alleged facts are always questioned.

In the six books, whose titles are symbolic and which were originally meant to be grouped under the one head of "Pilgrimage"— her adventure of life—the author has presented what might be described as a cinema of her mind, not particularly what the New Psychology calls, with all the assurance of infallibility, the "unconscious mind." She has the faculty of taking a canvas and jotting down everything she sees in a landscape and then finishing it in the studio in such a way as to convince the person who has seen similar landscapes or who has an eye for scenic beauty that her work is nearly perfect. She does it by a skillful blending of the mind products of purposeful and autistic thinking.

The autonomic mechanism of man displays the closest approximation to perpetual motion that exists. It never rests. As yet we do not know how far thought is conditioned by the autonomic nervous system, but we know that the mind is never idle any more than the heart or the lungs. Constantly a stream of thoughts flows from it or through it. These thoughts vary in quality and quantity, and their variations have formed endless and bitter discussions of psychologists. Whenever the waking mind is not entirely occupied with directed thoughts, it is filled with a succession of more or less vivid or vague thoughts, often popularly referred to as "impressions," which seem to arise spontaneously and are usually not directed toward any recognised end or purpose. A significant feature of them is the prominence of agreeable impressions concerning oneself, people or things—or thoughts of these as one would wish them to be, rather than as they are known to be. It is these autistic, or wishful thoughts, which, constantly bubbling up to the surface of consciousness like the water of a spring, give colour to personality. They reveal it more luminously than anything else—unless one goes still deeper and lays bare the thoughts at the hidden source of the spring, thus penetrating the unconscious itself, as the Freudians claim to do through the symbolism of dreams.

Whether Miriam Henderson, proceeding in this fashion, revealed more of her real self than did Marie Bashkirtseff, or Anatole France in "Le Petit Pierre," "La Vie en Fleur" and the other charming books with which he has been ornamenting his old age, is an open question. However, Dorothy M. Richardson has established a reputation as one of the few Simon-pure realists of modern English literature.

Another faculty which is developed to an exceptional degree in Miriam is what psychologists call the association of cognitions and memories. The "Wearin' of the Green" on a hand organ while she is big with thoughts of what her trip to a foreign land may bring her makes her think of

"rambles in the hot school garden singing 'Gather roses while ye may,' hot afternoons in the shady north room, the sound of turning pages, the hum of the garden beyond the sun-blinds, meeting in the sixth form study . . . Lilla with her black hair and the specks of bright amber in the brown of her eyes, talking about free-will."

Then she stirs the fire and back her thoughts whisk to her immediate concerns.

Music more than anything else calls into dominancy these associated recollections. Listening to the playing of one of the schoolgirls at the German school she suddenly realises:

"That wonderful light was coming again—she had forgotten her sewing—when presently she saw, slowly circling, fading and clearing, first its edge, and then, for a moment the whole thing, dripping, dripping as it circled, a weed-grown mill-wheel. . . . She recognised it instantly. She had seen it somewhere as a child—in Devonshire—and never thought of it since— and there it was. She heard the soft swish and drip of the water and the low humming of the wheel. How beautiful . . . it was fading. . . . She held it—it returned—clearer this time and she could feel the cool breeze it made, and sniff the fresh earthly smell of it, the scent of the moss and the weeds shining and dripping on its huge rim. Her heart filled. She felt a little tremour in her throat. All at once she knew that if she went on listening to that humming wheel and feeling the freshness of the air, she would cry. She pulled herself together, and for a while saw only a vague radiance in the room and the dim forms grouped about. She could not remember which was which. All seemed good and dear to her. The trumpet notes had come back, and in a few minutes the music ceased. . . . Someone was closing the great doors from inside the schoolroom."

It would be difficult to find in literature a better illustration of revival of unconscious or "forgotten" memory than this. An extraordinary thing about it is that these and similar revivals are preceded by an aura or warning in the shape of a light, similar to the warnings that Dostoievsky had before having an epileptic attack during which he experienced ecstasy so intense and overpowering that had it lasted more than a few seconds the human mechanism would have broken beneath the display. Miriam's ecstasy is of a milder sort, and the result is like that which the occupant of a chamber with drawn blinds and sealed windows might experience should some magic power stealthily and in a mysterious way flood it gradually with sunshine and replace the stale atmosphere with fresh air.

Many can testify from personal experience the power that music has to influence purposeful thinking. It would not astonish me to hear that Einstein had solved some of the intricate problems of "relativity" under the direct influence of the music of Beethoven, Wagner, or Liszt. It is the rod with which most temperamental persons smite the rock of reality that romance may gush out and refresh those who thirst for it. Miriam often wields the rod in her early days to the reader's intense delight.

While giving Miss Richardson her full measure of praise as recorder of her unconscious mental activity in poetic and romantic strain, we must not overlook her unusual capacity to delineate the realities of life, as they are anticipated and encountered.

The description of her preparation for going away in the first chapter of "Pointed Roofs" is perfect realism: the thoughts of a young girl in whom a conflict between self-depreciation and self-appreciation is taking place. This is marvellously portrayed in the narration of her thoughts and apprehensions of her ability to teach English in the German school to which she is journeying. It is a fool's errand to be going there with nothing to give. She doubts whether she can repeat the alphabet, let alone parse and analyse.

This mastery of realism is displayed throughout the series. The inwardly rebellious governess in the country house of prosperous people is made vivid in her setting when she says:

"There was to be another week-end. Again there would be the sense of being a visitor amongst other visitors; visitor was not the word; there was a French word which described the thing, 'convive,' 'les convives' . . . people sitting easily about a table with flushed faces . . . someone standing drunkenly up with eyes blazing with friendliness and a raised wineglass . . . women and wine, the rose of Heliogabalus; but he was a Greek and dreadful in some way, convives were Latin, Roman; fountains, water flowing over marble, white-robed strong-faced people reclining on marble couches, feasting . . . taking each fair mask for what it shows itself; that was what this kind of wealthy English people did, perhaps what all wealthy people did . . . the maimed, the halt, the blind, *compel* them to come in . . . but that was after the others had refused. The thing that made you feel jolliest and strongest was to forget the maimed, to *be* a fair mask, to keep everything else out and be a little circle of people knowing that everything was kept out. Suppose a skeleton walked in? Offer it a glass of wine. People have no right to be skeletons, or if they are to make a fuss about it. These people would be all the brighter if they happened to have neuralgia; some pain or emotion made you able to do things. Taking each fair mask was a fine grown-up game. Perhaps it could be kept up to the end?

Perhaps that was the meaning of the man playing cards on his
death-bed."

The author has the gift of narration, too, of making a picture with a few sweeps of the brush. In "Pointed Roofs"
Miriam gives a synopsis of her parents and their limitations
in a few words, which is nearly perfect. She does it by narration of her thoughts in retrospection, which is another striking
feature of her technique.

"She thought sleepily of her Wesleyan grandparents, gravely
reading the 'Wesleyan Methodist Recorder,' the shop at Bab-
ington, her father's discontent, his solitary fishing and reading,
his discovery of music . . . science . . . classical music in
the first Novello editions . . . Faraday . . . speaking to
Faraday after lectures. Marriage . . . the new house . . .
the red brick wall at the end of the garden where young peach-
trees were planted . . . running up and downstairs and singing . . . both of them singing in the rooms and the garden
. . . she sometimes with her hair down and then when visitors
were expected pinned in coils under a little cap and wearing a
small hoop . . . the garden and lawns and shrubbery and the
long kitchen-garden and the summer-house under the oaks beyond and the pretty old gabled 'town' on the river and the
woods all along the river valley and the hills shining up out of
the mist. The snow man they both made in the winter—the
birth of Sarah and then Eve . . . his studies and book-buying
—and after five years her own disappointing birth as the third
girl, and the coming of Harriet just a year later . . . her
mother's illness, money troubles—their two years at the sea to
retrieve . . . the disappearance of the sunlit red-walled garden always in full summer sunshine with the sound of bees in it
or dark from windows . . . the narrowings of the house-life
down to the Marine Villa—with the sea creeping in—wading
out through the green shallows, out and out till you were more
than waist deep—shrimping and prawning hour after hour for
weeks together . . . poking in the rock pools, watching the
sun and the colours in the strange afternoons . . . then the
sudden large house at Barnes with the 'drive' winding to the
door. . . . He used to come home from the City and the

Constitutional Club and sometimes instead of reading 'The Times' or the 'Globe' or the 'Proceedings of the British Association' or Herbert Spencer, play Pope Joan or Jacoby with them all, or Table Billiards and laugh and be 'silly' and take his turn at being 'bumped' by Timmy going the round of the long dining-room table, tail in the air; he had taken Sarah and Eve to see 'Don Giovanni' and 'Winter's Tale' and the new piece, 'Lohengrin.' No one at the tennis-club had seen that. He had good taste. No one else had been to Madame Schumann's Farewell . . . sitting at the piano with her curtains of hair and her dreamy smile . . . and the Philharmonic Concerts. No one else knew about the lectures at the Royal Institution, beginning at nine on Fridays. . . . No one else's father went with a party of scientific men 'for the advancement of science' to Norway or America, seeing the Falls and the Yosemite Valley. No one else took his children as far as Dawlish for the holidays, travelling all day, from eight until seven . . . no esplanade, the old stone jetty and coves and cowrie shells . . ."

Nature was in a satirical mood when she equipped Miriam for her conflict. Early the casual reader recognises her as the kind of girl who is socially difficult and who seems predestined to do "fool things." The psychologist looks deeper and sees a tragic jest. Plain in appearance, angular in manner, innocent of subtlety, suppleness, or graciousness of body or soul, with a fine sensitiveness fed by an abnormal self-appreciation, which she succeeds in covering only at the cost of inducing in it a hot-house growth, Miriam Henderson enters upon the task of an unskilled wage-earner with a mind turned inward and possessed by that modern and fashionable demon politely known as a "floating libido." Dogged, if not actually damned, by her special devil, Miriam is driven in frenzied and blinded unrest from one experience to another, in vain efforts to appease its insistent demands, placing the blame for her failure to achieve either success or happiness everywhere except where it belongs.

Tortured by romantic sentimentalism unrelieved by a glimmer of imagination or humour; over-sexed but lacking the magnetism without which her sex was as bread without yeast; with a desire for adulation so morbid that it surrounded itself with defences of hatred and envy, Miriam's demon drove or lured her through tangled mazes of the soul-game, and checkmated every effort to find herself through her experiences.

In "Pointed Roofs," even through the wall of self, the reader catches the charm with which the German school held Miriam, in the music floating through the big *saal*, the snatches of schoolgirl slang and whimsical wisdom, and Fraulein Pfaff with her superstitions, her rages, her religiosity, and her sensuality. But this is the background of the picture, just as the background of the home which she had so clingingly left had been the three light-hearted sisters with their white plump hands and feminine graces, the tennis, the long, easy dreamy days; and the foreground had been Miriam cherishing a feeling of "difference" toward the feminine sisters, feeding her smarting self-love by her fancied resemblance to her father who hated men and loathed women, and dreaming of the "white twinkling figure coming quickly along the pathway between the rows of hollyhocks every Sunday afternoon."

The "high spot" in her experience at the German school is revealed in the answer to the question: Why could not Miriam get on with "tall Fraulein Pfaff smiling her horse smile"? Miriam leaves the school cloaked in injured innocence. But the cloak is no mask for the native wit of the schoolgirls. They know—and Miriam knows—that the answer is the old Swiss teacher of French upon whom the Fraulein herself has designs. Even before he is revealed reading poetry to the class with a simper while Miriam makes eyes at him, or in a purported chance encounter alone in the *saal*, the girls have twitted Miriam in a way that would have warned a more sensible girl that she was venturing upon dangerous ground. But Miriam's demon had made her insensible to such hints, just as it had robbed her of the common sense which would have made her understand, even without warnings, that she could not work for a woman and "go vamping" on her preserves.

If Miriam's flirtation with the Swiss professor had been in a spirit of frolicsomeness it would have presented at least one hopeful symptom. But Miriam is incapable of frolicing—abnormally so. The absence of the play impulse in her is striking, as is the lack of spontaneous admirations or enthusiams for people or things. Her impressions are always in terms of sensuous attraction or repulsion—never influenced by appeal to intellect, æsthetic taste, admiration, or ambition. Other girls exist for her, not as kindred spirits, but as potential rivals—even her sisters—and she is keen to size them up solely by qualities which she senses may make them attractive to the other sex. The exceptions to this are certain German girls whose over-sentimental make-up furnishes easy material for Miriam's starved libido.

The next picture is at her country home where a dance has been staged, in Miriam's own consciousness, especially as a temporary farewell appearance of the "white twinkling figure," now materialised into Ted. Ted appears on programme time bringing with him a strange young man with a German name and manner of speech, with whom she promptly goes off spooning in a dark conservatory, where she is discovered by Ted. She hopes the scene will stir Ted to emulation. But it does not. When she returns to the light Ted has gone home. And that seems to be the last of him. The strange young man is keen to announce his departure the coming day for foreign parts. So Miriam is left to set off for her next school without further adventures in love-making, and the reader is left to wonder whether she is not one of the girls who are incurably given to taking their Teds more seriously than they intend to be taken.

In "Backwater" Miriam is a teacher of little girls in a Bambury Park school kept by three quaint refined little old English women—a palatable contrast to the coarseness of Fraulein Pfaff—for nine months. She is successful as a teacher, but finds her situation unendurable and resigns. The emotional shallowness of the girls and their lower middle-class mothers with aspirations to "get on" are dreary, but hardly sufficiently dismal to provoke the black despair and unreasoning rage which cause her to cry out in her moments of revolt, "But why must I be one of those to give everything up?" There is no masculine element connected with the school life, as there had been with that of the German school. She contrasts herself with her sisters who have made adaptations to life, two having become engaged and the third having settled happily into a position as governess. But Miriam can not settle, nor adapt. Her demon will not permit.

A girl of nineteen, brought up in middle-class culture, without previous experiences except as teacher in two girls' schools, becomes governess, as "Honeycomb" relates, in the country home of a Q. C., upon the introduction of friends of a future brother-in-law. From the day of her arrival her wishful thinking revolves around the man of the family. She loathes teaching the children and fails to hide from them her boredom. By lampooning the eccentricities and stupidities of Mrs. Corrie she betrays her hatred of women, her besetting "inferiority complex," which, in this instance, is partly justified by the adult infantilism of the lady and her absorbing attachment to a woman of questionable morality. Without anything to which to tie it on the other side, Miriam constructs—as a spider might a web out of her own unconscious self—a bridge of affinity between herself and the Q. C., placing such significance as her demon prompts upon his insignificant words or looks, until he snubs her at dinner when she attempts to take too leading a part in the conversation. Immediately she hates it all, with the collapse of her bridge, and is ready to throw up her "job" and all it implies.

Romance would seem remote from a hall bedroom in a sordid London rooming-house and the duties of first aid to a firm of dentists. But this is where Miriam finds it, for a time at least. The central figure is one of the dentists in whom her autistic thoughts discover a lonely sensitive man eager for the sympathetic understanding which Miriam is ready to offer. The boredom of teaching gives place to ecstasy in the discharge of the details, often repellent, which go to fill up the "strange rich difficult day." Her drab existence becomes a charmed life until Miriam's libido, which has been running away with her like a wild horse, shies right across the road at the first young girl she sights within the orbit of the dentist. Judging from the reaction of the latter, the explosion of jealousy and hatred that took place in Miriam's mind must have found outward expression, for he retreats behind a barrier of an "official tone," which infuriates Miriam into demanding an explanation and brings in reply to her demand a letter from him beginning: "Dear Miss Henderson—You are very persistent"; and concluding "foolish gossip which might end by making your position untenable." For the first time Miriam admits her folly, saying,

"I have nothing now but my pained self again, having violently rushed at things and torn them to bits. It's all my fault from the very beginning . . . I make people hate me by *knowing* them and dashing my head against the wall of their behaviour . . . I did not know what I had. Friendship is fine fine porcelain. I have sent a crack right through it . . . Mrs. Bailey (her landlady) . . . numbers of people I never think of would like to have me always there. . . . At least I have broken up his confounded complacency."

When Miriam's dingy lodging-house becomes a boarding-house new food comes to her creative urge in the form of daily association with masculine boarders. Her resolution in the early pages of "Interim" to take "no more interest in men," collapses like a house of cards upon the first onslaught. A close companionship develops between her and a Spanish Jew of more than unconventional ideas and habits. But her special devil is soon busy again, and Miriam discovers romance in the presence in the house of a young Canadian who is studying in London. When he comes into the dining-room where Miriam is sitting with other boarders after dinner, and sits down with his books to study:

"He did not see that she was astonished at his coming nor her still deeper astonishment in the discovery of her unconscious certainty that he would come. A haunting familiar sense of unreality possessed her. Once more she was part of a novel; it was right, true like a book for Dr. Heber to come in in defiance of every one, bringing his studies into the public room in order to sit down quietly opposite this fair young English girl. He saw her apparently gravely studious and felt he could 'pursue his own studies' all the better for her presence. . . . Perhaps if he remained steadily like that in her life she could grow into some semblance of his steady reverent observation. He did not miss any movement or change of expression. . . . It *was* glorious to have a real, simple homage coming from a man who was no simpleton, coming simple, strong and kindly from Canada to put you in a shrine. . . ."

And yet all he does is to look at her! She goes for a walk and

"the hushed happiness that had begun in the dining-room half an hour ago seized her again suddenly, sending her forward almost on tiptoe. It was securely there; the vista it opened growing in beauty as she walked; bearing within her in secret unfathomable abundance the gift of ideal old-English rose and white gracious adorable womanhood given her by Dr. Heber."

When he goes to church she interprets it as a symptom of falling in love, but if it is, the further progress of the disease is along lines which would baffle even those who have specialised in the study of the malady in fiction and poetry through ages. He goes back to Canada, along with his companion students, without saying a word to his fellow-boarder and leaves to the landlady the difficult task of warning Miriam that her association with the Spanish Jew has furnished a subject of gossip in the house, and that another boarder has confided

to her that Dr. Heber had "made up his mind to speak," but
that he had been scared by Miriam's flirtation with the little
Jew.

Miriam never questions the correctness of the landlady's
diagnosis, nor the authenticity of her information. Still less
does she doubt her own interpretation of the wholesome direct-
minded Canadian's silent looks in her direction.

Finally a man comes into her life who literally proposes
marriage. He is a young Russian Jew student, small of stature
and suggestive of an uncanny oldness. Under his influence she
begins translating stories from the German and seems to find
some of the beneficial possibilities of "sublimation" in the
task. The test is not a true one, however, because this little
stream into which the current of her libido is temporarily
turned is too closely associated with the main channel—
Shatov—and when she becomes engaged to him the translation
seems to be forgotten.

"Deadlock" is the conflict between instinct and taste, involved in marrying a man with whom she is in love but who
arouses a revolt of her inherited traditions and intellectual
and æsthetic biases; or between her ego instinct and her herd
instinct. There the reader takes leave of her at the end of the
sixth volume.

A far more serious deadlock than that presented by her
engagement is the deadlock imposed upon Miriam by nature in
creating her a woman and endowing her with qualities which
keep her in a state of revolt against her Creator and against
what to her is the indignity of being a woman. This is epito-
mised splendidly in "The Tunnel," when she is fretting her
mind through the wearying summer days to keep pace with
the illness that is creeping upon her. Entries in the dentists'
index under the word "Woman" start the train of thought:

"inferior; mentally, morally, intellectually and physically . . .
her development arrested in the interest of her special func-

tions . . . reverting later towards the male type . . . old women with deep voices and hair on their faces . . . leaving off where boys of eighteen began. . . . Woman is undeveloped man . . . if one could die of the loathsome visions. . . . Sacred functions . . . highest possibilities . . . sacred for what? The hand that rocks the cradle rules the world? The future of the race? What world? What race? Men. . . . Nothing but men; forever. . . . It will go on as long as women are stupid enough to go on bringing men into the world . . . even if civilised women stop the colonials and primitive races would go on. It was a nightmare. They despise women and they want to go on living—to reproduce—themselves. None of their achievements, no 'civilisation,' no art, no science can redeem that. There is no possible pardon for men. The only answer to them is suicide; all women ought to agree to commit suicide. . . . All the achievements of men were poisoned at the root. The beauty of nature was tricky femininity. The animal world was cruelty. Jests and amusements were tragic distractions from tragedy. . . . The woman in black works. It's only in the evenings she can roam about seeing nothing. But the people she works for know nothing about her. She knows. She is sweeter than he. She is sweet. I like her. But he is more me."

Earlier, but less consciously, she expresses it when, watching the men guests at the Corrie's,

"Miriam's stricken eyes sought their foreheads for relief. Smooth brows and neatly brushed hair above; but the smooth motionless brows were ramparts of hate; pure murderous hate. That's men, she said, with a sudden flash of certainty, that's men as they are, when they are opposed, when they are real. All the rest is pretence. Her thoughts flashed forward to a final clear issue of opposition, with a husband. Just a cold blank hating forehead and neatly brushed hair above it. If a man doesn't understand or doesn't agree he's just a blank bony conceited thinking, absolutely condemning forehead, a face below, going on eating—and going off somewhere. Men are all hard angry bones; always thinking something, only one thing at a time and unless that is agreed to, they murder. My husband shan't kill me . . . I'll shatter his conceited brow—

*make* him see . . . two sides to every question . . . a million sides . . . no questions, only sides . . . always changing. Men argue, think they prove things; their foreheads recover— cool and calm. Damn them all—all men."

Few writers could have sketched Miriam Henderson without condemning her and without inviting the condemnation of the reader. Miss Richardson has done it. She has given us Miriam as she knows herself, without explanation, plea, or sentence, and left us to judge for ourselves. She does not label her. And this is probably the reason Miss Richardson's work has found so small an audience. People demand labels. They want to be "told." And she does not "tell" them. She invites them to think, and original thinking is an unpopular process.

If ten people were to read these books and write their impressions of them, the results would be as different as were the thoughts of the ten people. Because each result would add what the author has left out: a judgment, or an estimate of Miriam. And this judgment would be rendered upon the evidence, but according to the mind of the judge.

The question which everyone must decide for himself is: when such revelations of the conscious and the unconscious are spread before him in words and sentences, does the result constitute gibberish or genius; is it slush or sanity; is it the sort of thing one would try to experience; or should one struggle and pray to be spared? It may be the highroad to dementia—this concentrating of all one's thoughts upon oneself, and oneself upon a single instinct. And Miriam might well have been headed for it when she failed to differentiate between ideas based upon objective evidence and ideas created solely out of her instinctive craving, which is an approach toward the belief of the insane person in his own delusions.

We identify ourselves, motives, and conduct with the characters of fiction who cut a good figure; we identify with the ones who do not, those we dislike, disdain, or condemn. Has anyone identified himself with Miriam Henderson and added to his or her stature?

The strongest impression made upon an admirer of Miss Richardson's craftsmanship is a wish that it might be applied to the study of a different, a more normal, type of personality. But the wish that such a study might be given us is burdened with a strong doubt whether its fulfillment would be humanly possible. Could anyone but an extreme type of egocentric person make such a study of himself? Could anyone whose libido was normally divided in various channels follow its course so graphically? And would not such division destroy the unity essential to even so much of the novel form as Miss Richardson preserves?

Here is a deadlock for the reader: Miss Richardson's art and Miriam as she is; or a Miriam with whom one could identify oneself as a heroine of fiction.

The novel, according to Miss Richardson, may be compared to a picture-puzzle in a box. Properly handled, the pieces may be made to constitute an entity, a harmonious whole, a thing of beauty, a portrait or a pergola, a windmill or a waterfall. The purpose of the novel is to reveal the novelist, her intellectual possessions, emotional reactions, her ideals, aspirations, and fulfilments, and to describe the roads and short-cuts over which she has travelled while accomplishing them. People and things encountered on the way do not count for much, especially people. They are made up largely of women, whom she dislikes, and men, whom she despises. It should be no part of its purpose to picture situations, to describe places, to narrate occurrences other than as media of author-revelation. Undoubtedly it is one of the most delightful things in the world —this talking about oneself. I have known many persons who pay others, physicians for instance, to listen. But unless the narration is ladened with adventure, or interlarded with humour, or spiced with raciness, it is often boring; and reluctantly it must be admitted that when we have ceased to admire

Miss Richardson's show of art, when we no longer thrill at her mastery of method, when we are tired of rising to the fly of what Miss Sinclair calls her "punctilious perfection" of literary form, she becomes tiresome. Egocentrics should have a sense of humour. Samuel Butler thus endowed might have been assured of immortality. Lacking that, they should have extensive contact with the world. That is what enlivens the psychological jungle of Marcel Proust. If Henri Amiel had had a tithe of Jean Jacques Rousseau's worldly and amatory experiences his writings might have had great influence and a large sale.

Miss Dorothy M. Richardson has revealed herself a finished technician. She may be compared to a person who is ambitious to play the Chopin Studies. She practices scales steadily for a year and then gives a year to the Studies themselves. But when she essays to play for the public she fails because, although she has mastered the mechanical difficulties, she has not grasped the meaning. She reveals life without drama and without comedy, and that such life does not exist everybody knows.

She may have had compensation for her effort from two sources: her imitators and her benefactors. The former are too numerous to mention, but Mr. J. D. Beresford and Miss May Sinclair would undoubtedly admit their indebtedness.

It is vicarious compensation, also, to be praised by one's peers and superiors. If Dorothy M. Richardson hasn't yet had it, in the writer's judgment she may look forward to it with confidence.

# CHAPTER V

MARCEL PROUST may justly be hailed as the greatest psychological novelist of his time. He was to normal psychology what Dostoievsky was to abnormal psychology: an unsurpassed observer, interpreter, and recorder of men's thoughts and conduct.

If would be hazardous to attempt to estimate the place he will eventually have in literature until the remaining volumes of "A la Recherche du Temps Perdu," and "Le Temps Retrouvé" are published. But the volumes of the former that have appeared: "Du Côté de Chez Swann," "Á l'Ombre des Jeunes Filles en Fleurs," "Le Côté de Guermantes," and "Sodome et Gomorrhe" justify the statement that with the death of their author in November, 1922, France lost a writer whose fame will rank with that of Balzac. It is not likely that he will ever have a popularity comparable to Balzac or even to Bourget, Barbusse, or several other contemporaries, for M. Proust is an author for writers. He will never be read by the large class of novel readers who create the market demand for novels of action and plot; nor will he appeal to that hardly less numerous class—chiefly women—who find the emotional novel palatable food. However, those who, like the writer, cannot punish themselves by struggling through a detective story and by whom the most skillfully contrived plot can be endured only if the harassment which it causes is counterbalanced by the charm of its literary style or its interpretation of the personality of the author reacting to conditions more or less common to all mankind, may find in M. Proust a novelist whom they can ill afford to ignore. And no writer of fact or fiction today would be just to himself were he to proceed with his art without making the acquaintance of this master artificer and psychologist. Proust will be remembered as a pioneer who explored the jungle of the unconscious memory, and a marvellous interpreter of the laws governing associated memories. I doubt not his name will be as inseparably connected with the novel of the future as that of de Maupassant or Poe has been with the short story of the last few decades, even while his wares will still find scant sale, save to writers, dilettantes, professional students of letters, of form, and of psychology.

The measure of success that was vouchsafed him came late in life. He was fifty when the Goncourt Prize was awarded "A l'Ombre des Jeunes Filles en Fleurs" in 1919. Until that time his writings were known to readers of "La Nouvelle Revue Française," to friends, and to a limited circle whose members have an urge for the unusual, and a flair for the picturesque in literature. Then readers began to nibble at "Du Côté de Chez Swann," and the more they nibbled, that is the oftener they read it, or attempted to read it—for it is difficult even for a cultured Frenchman—the more keenly aware did they become that they had encountered a new force, a new sensibility in literature, and, like appetite that comes with eating, the greater was their desire to develop an intimacy with him. "Le Côté de Guermantes" showed that he walked and talked, dined and wined, registered the thoughts and interpreted the dreams of the aristocracy with the same security, understanding, perspicacity, and clairvoyance that he had brought to bear on the bourgeoisie in "Du Côté de Chez Swann." In "Sodome et Gomorrhe" he did the impossible. He talked with frankness and with a tone of authority of an enigmatic, inexplicable aberration of nature, inversion of the genesic instinct, which antedates possibly by millions of years the differentiation of man from anthropoid stock; which has always been with us, now the patent of good form, the badge of intellectual superiority, the hallmark of æsthetic refinement, as in the days of Hellenic supremacy; now the stigma of sin, the scarlet letter of infamy, the key of the bottomless pit, as today; and which unquestionably will always continue to be with us. He divested it of pruriency; he rescued it from pornography; he delivered it from pathology; and at the same time he made the penologist pause and "normal" man thoughtful.

Whether this freakishness of nature is as common as M. Proust says, whether it bulks so large in the conduct of daily life as he intimates, is a matter for the individual to estimate. No statistics are available, but experienced psychiatrists and discerning pedagogues know that a considerable proportion of mankind is so constituted. To deny it is equivalent to acknowledging that one is immune to evidence; to consider it a vice is to flaunt an allegation of falsehood in the face of biology. One can imagine the shock the world would have today if everyone told the truth, the whole truth, and nothing but the truth about his genesic instinct. If, then, it was decided to segregate and deprive of liberty the inverted, what a strange medley it would be of general and soldier, of prince and pauper, of priest and parishioner, of genius and moron, of ambassador and attaché, of poet, artist, and savant. It will mark an epoch in modern civilisation when this strange variation from the normal shall be subject to study by such investigators as Mendel, de Vries, Tschermak, and the host of biologists who are slowly solving the mysteries of heredity. Meanwhile the preparation for such work is the formation of public opinion, and probably there is no better way to accomplish it than that adopted by M. Proust.

So far the only one of M. Proust's books that has appeared in English is "Du Côté de Chez Swann," (Swann's Way), by C. K. Scott Moncrieff. The translation itself is a work of art,

MARCEL PROUST IN 1890

and the reading public is under profound obligation to this master stylist.

The narrator is M. Proust himself, but the reader who would understand Proust must keep in mind that he has distributed his own personality between two characters, the narrator of the story, and Swann. Those who see Proust only in the first, or only in Swann, see but half of him.

In the overture he recalls the memories of a precocious, sentimental, sickly childhood spent in his aunt's house in Combray, with an indulgent mother, a sensible matter-of-fact father, an archaic paternal grandmother, and two silly sentimental grandaunts. He succeeds in introducing in the most incidental way M. Swann, the son of a stockbroker, "a converted Jew and his parents and grandparents before him," who has successfully unlocked the door of smart and savant society; his former mistress Odette de Crecy whom he has now married, to the disgust of his neighbours; his daughter with whom the narrator is to fall in love; M. Vinteuil whose sonata contains the solvent of Swann's amatory resistance, and his daughter, a Gomorrite; M. de Villeparisis; and M. de Charlus, who we shall see in "Sodome et Gomorrhe" is not like other men.

The setting is in Brittany.

"Combray at a distance, from a twenty-mile radius, as we used to see it from the railway when we arrived there every year in Holy Week, was no more than a church epitomising the town, representing it, speaking of it and for it to the horizon, and as one drew near, gathering close about its long, dark cloak, sheltering from the wind, on the open plain, as a shepherd gathers his sheep, the woolly grey backs of its flocking houses, which a fragment of its mediæval ramparts enclosed, here and there, in an outline as scrupulously circular as that of a little town in a primitive painting."

He who invokes his memories is a boy of ten or thereabouts, lying in bed and awaiting dinner to end and M. Swann to depart that his mother may kiss him goodnight. Memory of it was like a luminous panel, sharply defined against a vague and shading background.

"The little parlour, the dining-room, the alluring shadows of the path along which would come M. Swann, the unconscious author of my sufferings, the hall through which I would journey to the first step of that staircase, so hard to climb, which constituted, all by itself, the tapering 'elevation' of an irregular pyramid; and, at the summit, my bedroom, with the little passage through whose glazed door Mamma would enter; in a word, seen always at the same evening hour, isolated from all its possible surroundings, detached and solitary against its shadowy background, the bare minimum of scenery necessary (like the setting one sees printed at the head of an old play, for its performance in the provinces); to the drama of my undressing, as though all Combray had consisted of but two floors joined by a slender staircase, and as though there had been no time there but seven o'clock at night."

The power not only of reproducing scenes and events, but also of revivifying states of consciousness long past through invoking associated memories, is utilised with an effect rarely parallelled in literature. It is invoked through any of the special senses, but chiefly through taste and hearing. The little cake soaked in tea which, taken many years after the trivial events of his childhood at Combray had been all but forgotten, unlocks, as if by magic, the chamber stored with memories.

"No sooner had the warm liquid, and the crumbs with it, touched my palate than a shudder ran through my whole body, and I stopped, intent upon the extraordinary changes that were taking place. An exquisite pleasure had invaded my senses, but individual, detached, with no suggestion of its origin. And at once the vicissitudes of life had become indifferent to me, its disasters innocuous, its brevity illusory— this new sensation having had on me the effect which love has of filling me with a precious essence; or rather this essence was not in me, it was myself. I had ceased now to feel mediocre, accidental, mortal."

He then tries to analyse the state, and

"that nothing may interrupt it in its course I shut out every obstacle, every extraneous idea, I stop my ears and inhibit all attention to the sounds which come from the next room. . . . Undoubtedly what is thus palpitating in the depths of my being must be the image, the visual memory which, being linked to that taste, has tried to follow it into my conscious mind. . . . Will it ultimately reach the clear surface of my consciousness, this memory, this old, dead moment which the magnetism of an identical moment has travelled so far to importune, to disturb, to raise up out of the very depths of my being?"

It does reach the surface of consciousness, for

"once I had recognised the taste of the crumb of madeleine soaked in her decoction of lime-flowers which my aunt used to give me (although I did not yet know and must long postpone the discovery of why this memory made me so happy) immediately the old grey house upon the street, where her room was, rose up like the scenery of a theatre to attach itself to the little pavilion, opening on to the garden. . . . And just as the Japanese amuse themselves by filling a porcelain bowl with water and steeping in it little crumbs of paper which until then are without character or form, but, the moment they become wet, stretch themselves and bend, take on colour and distinctive shape, become flowers or houses or people, permanent and recognisable, so in that moment all the flowers in our garden and in M. Swann's park, and the water-lilies on the Vivonne and the good folk of the village and their little dwellings and the parish church and the whole of Combray and of its surroundings, taking their proper shape and growing solid, sprang into being, town and gardens alike, from my cup of tea."

M. Proust's description of the first effect upon him of the little "madeleine" dipped in tea, when, "weary after a dull day, with the prospect of a depressing morrow, I raised to my lips a spoonful of the tea in which I had soaked a morsel of the cake" is almost a paraphrase of the words of Locke in his "Essay Concerning Human Understanding."

Music, more than anything else, has the power of invoking Swann's associated memories. A little phrase of old Vinteuil's Sonata runs like a fine thread all through the tangle of Swann's love for Odette de Crocy, although the memory of the phrase goes back prior to his meeting Odette—to the night of the party at which he had heard it, after going home from which

"he was like a man into whose life a woman, whom he has seen for a moment passing by, has brought a new form of beauty, which strengthens and enlarges his own power of perception, without his knowing even whether he is ever to see her again whom he loves already, although he knows nothing of her, not even her name."

Swann had tried in vain to identify the fugitive phrase which had awakened in him a passion for music that seemed to be bringing into his life the possibility of a sort of rejuvenation.

"Like a confirmed invalid whom all of a sudden, a change of air and surroundings, or a new course of treatment, or, as sometimes happens, an organic change in himself, spontaneous and unaccountable, seems to have so far removed from his malady that he begins to envisage the possibility, hitherto beyond all hope, of starting to lead—and better late than never— a wholly different life, Swann found in himself, in the memory of the phrase that he had heard, in certain other sonatas which he had made people play over to him, to see whether he might not, perhaps, discover his phrase among them, the presence of one of those invisible realities in which he had ceased to believe, but to which, as though the music had had upon the moral barrenness from which he was suffering a sort of recreative influence, he was conscious once again of a desire, almost, indeed, of the power to consecrate his life."

"It is a labour in vain to attempt to recapture our own past; all the efforts of our intellect must prove futile. The past is hidden somewhere outside the realm, beyond the reach of intellect, in some material object (in the sensation which that material object will give us) which we do not suspect. And as for that object, it depends on chance whether we come upon it or not before we ourselves must die."

Associative memory depends upon the fact that though the grouping of the stimuli is novel, the elementary components are individually similar to previous stimuli, and Proust avails himself of this established fact. These elementary stimuli leave retention traces in the central nervous system. When the same stimuli recur in a new grouping the pathways and centres that bear such traces are brought into connection and are combined in new ways. This modifies the form of the response. As the separate retention traces were due to conditions resembling the present, the new response will tend to be adaptive. This associative memory is known in psychology as mnemonic combination.

Although no attempt is made to describe the development of the personality of the sensitive, sentimental, impressionable, precocious child who narrates the story, one gets an extraordinarily vivid picture of him. He has the hallmarks and habituations of neuropathy, and amongst them phantasying and substitution.

"In those days, when I read to myself, I used often, while I turned the pages, to dream of something quite different. And to the gaps which this habit made in my knowledge of the story more were added by the fact that when it was Mamma who was reading to me aloud she left all the love-scenes out. And so all the odd changes which take place in the relations between the miller's wife and the boy, changes which only the birth and growth of love can explain, seemed to me plunged and steeped in a mystery, the key to which (as I could readily believe) lay in that strange and pleasant-sounding name of *Champi*, which draped the boy who bore it, I knew not why, in its own bright colour, purpurate and charming."

That his neuropathic constitution was a direct inheritance is obvious. He got it through his Aunt Leonie

"who since her husband's death, had gradually declined to leave, first Combray, then her house in Combray, then her bedroom, and finally her bed; and who now never 'came down,' but lay perpetually in an indefinite condition of grief, physical exhaustion, illness, obsessions, and religious observances. . . . My aunt's life now was practically confined to two adjoining rooms, in one of which she would rest in the afternoon while they aired the other."

Despite these apparent restrictions of life's activities she knows more of the happenings of the village than the town crier, and in a way she conditions the conduct of her neighbours whose first question is "What effect will it have on Aunt Leonie?" Her contact with people is limited to Françoise, a perfect servant, to Eulalie, a limping, energetic, deaf spinster, and to the reverend Curé.

"My aunt had by degrees erased every other visitor's name from her list, because they all committed the fatal error, in her eyes, of falling into one or other of the two categories of people she most detested. One group, the worse of the two, and the one of which she rid herself first, consisted of those who advised her not to take so much care of herself, and preached (even if only negatively and with no outward signs beyond an occasional disapproving silence or doubting smile) the subversive doctrine that a sharp walk in the sun and a good red beefsteak would do her more good (her, who had had two dreadful sips of Vichy water on her stomach for fourteen hours) than all her medicine bottles and her bed. The other category was composed of people who appeared to believe that she was more seriously ill than she thought, in fact that she was as seriously ill as she said. And so none of those whom she had allowed upstairs to her room, after considerable hesitation and at Françoise's urgent request, and who in the course of their visit had shown how unworthy they were of the honour which had been done them by venturing a timid: 'Don't you think that if you were just to stir out a little on

A PAGE OF CORRECTED PROOF SHOW-
ING MARCEL PROUST'S METHOD
OF REVISION

really fine days . . . ?' or who, on the other hand, when she said to them: 'I am very low, very low; nearing the end, dear friends!' had replied: 'Ah, yes, when one has no strength left! Still, you may last a while yet'; each party alike might be certain that her doors would never open to them again."

With all his literary art, and mastery of the mysterious powers that suggestion has to heighten awareness and deepen information, M. Proust does not succeed in enlightening us as to how the boy at Combray comes to possess so much information of people and such knowledge of the world. Part of it is intuitive, but understanding of Vinteuil's daughter, who "after a certain year we never saw alone, but always accompanied by a friend, a girl older than herself, with an evil reputation in the neighbourhood, who in the end installed herself permanently at Montjouvain," thus leading M. Vinteuil broken-hearted to the grave because of the shame and scandal of her sadism, is beyond possibility even for a boy of his precocity and prehensibility.

"For a man of M. Vinteuil's sensibility it must have been far more painful than for a hardened man of the world to have to resign himself to one of those situations which are wrongly supposed to occur in Bohemian circles only; for they are produced whenever there needs to establish itself in the security necessary to its development a vice which Nature herself has planted in the soul of a child, perhaps by no more than blending the virtues of its father and mother, as she might blend the colours of their eyes. And yet however much M. Vinteuil may have known of his daughter's conduct it did not follow that his adoration of her grew any less. The facts of life do not penetrate to the sphere in which our beliefs are cherished; as it was not they that engendered those beliefs, so they are powerless to destroy them; they can aim at them continual blows of contradiction and disproof without weakening them; and an avalanche of miseries and maladies coming, one after another, without interruption into the bosom of a family, will not make it lose faith in either the clemency of its God or the capacity of its physician."

Thus does he introduce most casually a subject which bulks large in "Sodome et Gomorrhe," and which M. Proust understands like a composite priest, physician, and biologist.

Most of the grist of the boy's mill comes over the road that skirts Swann's park, but some comes the Guermantes Way. In "Le Côté de Guermantes," which followed "A l'Ombre des Jeunes Filles en Fleurs," he makes us as intimately acquainted with the Duchesse de Guermantes, Mme. de Villeparisis, and other notables of the *société élegante,* as he does in "Swann's Way" with the Verdurins and their "little nucleus" which furnishes a background to Odette, and furnishes M. Proust with canvas upon which to paint the portrait of an Æsculapian bounder, Dr. Cottard, who, it has been said, is still of the quick. M. Proust was the son and the brother of a physician and had abundant opportunity not only to get firsthand information but to have his natural insight quickened. In the same way one discovers his Jewish strain (his mother was a Jewess) in his mystic trends and in his characters such as Bloch and Swann. "Whenever I formed a strong attachment to any one of my friends and brought him home with me that friend was invariably a Jew." Moreover his lack of a sense of humour is an Hebraic trait. With the exception of the reaction provoked in his grandfather by the advent of one of these friends, "Swann's Way," and indeed all M. Proust's writings, are humourless.

The genesis of Swann's love and the dissolution of Odette's take up one volume. If it is not a perfect description of the divine passion in a mature man surfeited by conquest and satiated by indulgence, it is an approximation to it.

He was introduced one day at the theatre to Odette de Crocy by an old friend of his, who had spoken of her to him as a ravishing creature with whom he might very possibly come to an understanding. She made no appeal to Swann; indeed she not only left him indifferent, aroused in him no desire, but gave him a sort of physical repulsion. But

Odette knew the *ars amandi* as did Circe or Sappho, and ere long she had entangled him in the meshes of Eros' net. When the net was drawn to her craft and the haul examined, it didn't interest her, though she kept it, for it contributed to her material welfare. Then M. Proust did a psychological stunt which reveals an important aspect of his mastery of the science. Swann identified Odette with Zipporah, Jethro's daughter, whose picture is to be seen in one of the Sixtine frescoes by Botticelli. Her similarity to it enhanced her beauty and rendered her more precious in his sight. Moreover it enabled him to introduce the image of Odette into a world of dreams and fancies where she assumed a new and nobler form. And whereas the mere sight of her in the flesh, by perpetually reviving his misgivings as to the quality of her face, her figure, the whole of her beauty, used to cool the ardour of his love, those misgivings were swept away and that love confirmed now that he could re-erect his estimate of her on the sure foundations of his æsthetic principles. Instead of placing a photograph of Odette on his study table, he placed one of Jethro's daughter, and on it he lavished his admiration and concentrated his intensity in all the abandon of substitution.

The author utilises the potency of suspense to bring Swann's ardour to the boiling point. One evening when Odette had avoided him he searched the restaurants of the Boulevards in a state of increasing panic.

"Among all the methods by which love is brought into being, among all the agents which disseminate that blessed bane, there are few so efficacious as the great gust of agitation which, now and then, sweeps over the human spirit. For then the creature in whose company we are seeking amusement at the moment, her lot is cast, her fate and ours decided, that is the creature whom we shall henceforward love. It is not necessary that she should have pleased us up till then, any more, or even as much as others. All that is necessary is that our taste for her should become exclusive."

He proceeded to cultivate his love in an emotional medium and to inoculate himself with the culture which rendered him immune to love of another. The culture medium was furnished by Vinteuil, the old composer, who had died of a broken heart. "He would make Odette play him the phrase from the sonata again ten, twenty times on end, insisting that, while she played, she must never cease to kiss him."

"Watching Swann's face while he listened to the phrase, one would have said that he was inhaling an anæsthetic which allowed him to breathe more deeply.

The effect that it had was deep repose, mysterious refreshment. He felt himself transformed into a "creature foreign to humanity, blinded, deprived of his logical faculty, almost a fantastic unicorn, a chimera-like creature conscious of the world through his two ears alone."

Swann's discovery of the spiritual and bodily inconstancies of his mistress, the perfidies and betrayals of the Verdurins, his jealousy, planned resentments, and resurrection are related in a way that convinces us that Proust saw life steadily and saw it whole.

To appease his anguish, to thwart his obsession, to supplant his preoccupation he decided to frequent again the aristocratic circles he had forsaken. The description of the reception at Mme. de Saint Euverte's, showing the details of fashionable life, is of itself a noteworthy piece of writing. Not only is it replete with accurate knowledge of such society, but it gives M. Proust the opportunity to display understanding of motives and frailties and to record impressions of contact with the world abroad. Speaking of one of the guests he says:

"She belonged to that one of the two divisions of the human race in which the untiring curiosity which the other half feels about people whom it does not know is replaced by an unfailing interest in the people whom it does."

The peculiar tendency which Swann always had to look for analogies between living people and the portraits in galleries reasserted itself here in a more positive and more general form. One of the footmen was not unlike the headsman in certain Renaissance pictures which represent executions, tortures, and the like. Another reminded him of the decorative warriors one sees in the most tumultuous of Mantegna's paintings. "He seemed as determined to remain as unconcerned as if he had been present at the massacre of the innocents or the martyrdom of St. James." As he entered the salon one reminded him of Giotto's models, another of Albert Dürer's, another of that Greek sculpture which the Mantuan painter never ceased to study, while a servant with a pallid countenance and a small pig-tail clubbed at the back of his head seemed like one of Goya's sacristans.

It was this soirée that conditioned irrevocably Swann's future life, and the little phrase from Vinteuil's Sonata did it for him. To have heard it "in this place to which Odette would never come, in which no one, nothing was aware of her existence, from which she was entirely absent" made him suffer insupportably. While listening to it

"suddenly it was as though she had entered, and this apparition tore him with such anguish that his hand rose impulsively to his heart. . . . All his memories of the days when Odette had been in love with him, which he had succeeded, up till that evening, in keeping invisible in the depths of his being, deceived by this sudden reflection of a season of love, whose sun, they supposed, had dawned again, had awakened from their slumber, had taken wing and risen to sing maddeningly in his ears, without pity for his present desolation, the forgotten strains of happiness."

It raised the flood-gate of the dam in which he had stored the memories of Odette when she loved him and before he loved her. Not only did it liberate the memories of her, but the memories that were associated with them: all the net-work of mental habits, of seasonable impressions, of sensory reactions, through which it extended over a series of groups its uniform meshes, by which his body now found itself inextricably held.

"When, after that first evening at the Verdurins', he had had the little phrase played over to him again, and had sought to disentangle from his confused impressions how it was that, like a perfume or a caress, it swept over and enveloped him, he had observed that it was to the closeness of the intervals between the five notes which composed it and to the constant repetition of two of them that was due that impression of a frigid, a contracted sweetness; but in reality he knew that he was basing this conclusion not upon the phrase itself, but merely upon certain equivalents, substituted (for his mind's convenience) for the mysterious entity of which he had become aware, before ever he knew the Verdurins, at that earlier party, when for the first time he had heard the sonata played. . . .

"In his little phrase, albeit it presented to the mind's eye a clouded surface, there was contained, one felt, a matter so consistent, so explicit, to which the phrase gave so new, so original a force, that those who had once heard it preserved the memory of it in the treasure-chamber of their minds. Swann would repair to it as to a conception of love and happiness. . . .

"Even when he was not thinking of the little phrase, it existed, latent, in his mind, in the same way as certain other conceptions without material equivalent, such as our notions of light, of sound, of perspective, of bodily desire, the rich possessions wherewith our inner temple is diversified and adorned. Perhaps we shall lose them, perhaps they will be obliterated, if we return to nothing in the dust. But so long as we are alive, we can no more bring ourselves to a state in which we shall not have known them than we can with regard to any material object, than we can, for example, doubt the luminosity of a lamp that has just been lighted, in view of the changed aspect of everything in the room, from which has vanished even the memory of the darkness. . . .

"So Swann was not mistaken in believing that the phrase of the sonata did, really, exist. Human as it was from this point of view, it belonged, none the less, to an order of supernatural creatures whom we have never seen, but whom, in spite of that, we recognise and acclaim with rapture when some explorer of the unseen contrives to coax one forth, to bring it down from that divine world to which he has access to shine for a brief moment in the firmament of ours."

From that evening Swann understood that the feeling which Odette had once had for him would never revive. He had made his bed, and he resolved to share it in holy matrimony with Odette, though this discomforted his friends and made him a species of Pariah.

Mme. Swann in Combray was a solitary, but not in Paris. There she queened it, as many lovely ladies had done before her. The account of that, and of the narrator's love for Gilberte, Swann's daughter, who, when he had encountered her casually at Combray, had made a stirring and deep impression on him; and the advent of Albertine, a potential Gomorrite, make up the contents of the succeeding instalment, entitled "A l'Ombre des Jeunes Filles en Fleurs." Gilberte, Swann's daughter, and the narrator now approaching puberty, came to play together in the Champs Elysées, frolicking like children, innocently, though another feeling began soon to bud in him, a feeling which he did not yet understand. In this volume the narrator relates the experiences he had when a youth, and therefore there is more precision in the description of the persons with whom he came in contact. The volume also throws much light indirectly on Proust's personality. From a certain incident which he tells regarding the way he was brought up, one sees that his father was a rigourous aristocrat, stiff in his demeanour, and very particular in the choice of his connections. He, the narrator, was brought up in a way the Germans would call "schablonenmässig": everything was discussed at a family council, as though he were an inanimate plaything. His naïvete, the result of such training, is very characteristic.

For some time he had been longing to see "Phèdre" played

by the famous Mme. La Berma (evidently Sarah Bernhardt, for at that time she was the only one who played "Phèdre"). After long deliberation because of his illness, it was decided he should go chaperoned by his grandmother, to see his ideal actress. The scene opened with two men who rushed on in the throes of heated argument. He did not know that this was part of the play and that the men were actors; he thought they were some ruffians who had forced their way into the theatre and who would surely be ejected by the officials. He wondered, though, that the spectators not only did not protest, but listened to them with the greatest attention. Only when the theatre re-echoed with applause did he understand that the two men were actors. Afterwards, when two ladies came upon the stage, both of portly bearing, he could not decide which one was La Berma; a little later he learned that neither of them was the great actress. To reconcile such unsophistication with the account of the peeping Tom episode when he laid bare Mlle. Vinteuil's deforming habituation is very difficult.

Swann, now ill, and repentant, was consumed with ambition to introduce his wife, Odette, into high society, in which he succeeded to a great extent. Though he did not like M. Buntemps because of his reactionary opinions, he, "the director of the minister's office," was an important personage and his wife, Mme. Buntemps, was a steady visitor in Odette's salon. But once in a while he was malicious enough to exasperate Mme. Buntemps. He told her once he would invite the Cottards and the Duchesse de Vendome to dinner. Mme. Buntemps protested, saying it was not seemly that the Cottards should be at the same table with the Duchesse. In reality she was jealous of the Cottards who were going to share the honour with her. The Prince d'Agrigente was invited, because it was altogether "private"! Odette is described as a woman of low intelligence, without education, speaking faulty French, but shrewd, dominating her husband. One of her guests was Mme. Cottard, the wife of Dr. Cottard, the medical bounder who had now become Professor, a woman who did not belong to her present circle. But she had to invite a person who could tell her former friends of her high connections, so as to raise their envy.

The Marquis de Norpais, a former ambassador, is admirably drawn. He was naturally considered by the narrator's father as the cream of society. Just think of it! a man with two titles: Monsieur l'Ambassadeur, and Son Excellence Monsieur le Marquis! It is true that he was an ambassador under a republican government. But because of this he was interesting, for despite his antecedents he was entrusted with several extraordinary missions by very radical ministers. When a monarchist would not accept that honour, the republican government having had no fear that he might betray it, M. de Norpais himself willingly accepted the charge. Being in his blood a diplomat, he could not help exercising the functions of a diplomat, though in his heart he detested the republican spirit of government.

The narrator's mother did not admire his intelligence, but for the father every word of M. l'Ambassadeur de Norpais was an oracle. He had always wished that his son should become a diplomat, while the son wished to take up literature so as not to be separated from Gilberte. M. de Norpais, who did not much like the new style diplomats, told the narrator's father that a writer could gain as much consideration and more independence than a diplomat. His father changed his mind.

It is quite impossible, within the space of an essay, to give even an outline of the remaining volumes that have already appeared of this amazing and epochal novel.

Without doubt M. Proust had a definite idea in mind, a determination to make a contribution: to prove that the dominant force in mental life is association, the chief resource of mentality reminiscence. Thus the primitive instincts of mankind and their efforts to obtain convention's approbation furnish the material with which he has built. It is extraordinary how large association bulks: individuals remind him of famous paintings, not merely the general characters of the people whom he encounters in his daily life, but rather what seem least susceptible of generalisation, the individual features of men and women whom he knows. For instance, a bust of the Doge Loredan by Antonio Rizzo, is suggested by the prominent cheekbones, the slanting eyebrows, in short a speaking likeness to his own coachman Rami; the colouring of a Ghirlandajo, by the nose of M. de Palancy; a portrait by Tintoretto, by the invasion of the plumpness of the cheek by an outcrop of whisker, the broken nose, the penetrating stare, the swollen eyelids of Dr. du Bolbon.

If, on descending the stairs after one of the Doncières evenings, suddenly on arriving in the street, the misty night and the lights shining through suggest a time when he arrived at Combray, at once there is thrown on the screen of his consciousness a picture of incidents there and experiences elsewhere that are as vivid and as distinct as if he were looking at them on a moving-picture screen. Then suddenly there appears a legend "the useless years which slipped by before my invisible vocation declared itself, that invisible vocation of which this work is the history." Like the monk who seeks God in solitude, like Nietzsche who sought Him in reason, M. Proust has sought to reveal his soul, his personality, the sum total of all his various forms of consciousness by getting memory to disgorge her contents, the key to the chamber being association.

"We try to discover in things, endeared to us on that account, the spiritual glamour which we ourselves have cast upon them; we are disillusioned, and learn that they are in themselves barren and devoid of the charm which they owed, in our minds, to the association of certain ideas; sometimes we mobilise all our spiritual forces in a glittering array so as to influence and subjugate other human beings who, as we very well know, are situated outside ourselves, where we can never reach them."

There are so many features of M. Proust's work that excite admiration that it is possible to enumerate only a few. Despite a studied style of confusion and interminable sentences, suspended, hyphenated, alembicated, and syncopated, that must forever make him the despair of anyone whose knowledge of French is not both fundamental and colloquial, he makes telling, life-like pen pictures of things and persons. Such is one of Françoise, the maid at Combray,

"who looked as smart at five o'clock in the morning in her kitchen, under a cap whose stiff and dazzling frills seemed to be made of porcelain, as when dressed for church-going; who did everything in the right way, who toiled like a horse, whether she was well or ill, but without noise, without the appearance of doing anything; the only one of my aunt's maids who when Mamma asked for hot water or black coffee would bring them actually boiling; she was one of those servants who in a household seem least satisfactory, at first, to a stranger, doubtless because they take no pains to make a conquest of him and show him no special attention, knowing very well that they have no real need of him, that he will cease to be invited to the house sooner than they will be dismissed from it; who, on the other hand, cling with most fidelity to those masters and mistresses who have tested and proved their real capacity, and do not look for that superficial responsiveness, that slavish affability, which may impress a stranger favourably, but often conceals an utter barrenness of spirit in which no amount of training can produce the least trace of individuality.

"The daughter of Françoise, on the contrary, spoke, thinking herself a woman of today and freed from all customs, the Parisian argot and did not miss one of the jokes belonging to it. Françoise having told her that I had come from a Princess: 'Ah, doubtless a Princess of the cocoanut.' Seeing that I was expecting a visitor, she pretended to think that I was called Charles. I answered 'No,' naïvely, which permitted her to exclaim 'Ah, I thought so! And I was saying to myself Charles waits (charlatan).' It wasn't very good taste, but I was less indifferent when as a consolation for the tardiness of Albertine, she said, 'I think you can wait for her in perpetuity. She will not come any more.' Ah, our gigolettes of today!

"Thus her conversation differed from that of her mother but what is more curious the manner of speaking of her mother was not the same as that of her grandmother, a native of Bailleau-le-Pin which was near the country of Françoise. However the patois were slightly different, like the two country places. The country of the mother of Françoise was made up of hills descending into a ravine full of willows. And, very far from there, on the contrary, there was in France a little region where one spoke almost exactly the same patois as at Meseglise. I made the discovery at the same time that I was bored by it. In fact, I once found Françoise talking fluently with a chambermaid of the house who came from the country and spoke its patois. They understood each other mostly. I did not understand them at all. They knew this but did not stop on this account, excused, so they thought, by the joy of being compatriots, although born so far apart, for continuing to speak before me this foreign language as if they did not wish to be understood. This picturesque study of linguistic geography and comradeship was followed each week in the kitchen without my taking any pleasure in it."

Time, M. Proust was convinced, was made for slaves. It takes longer to read his account of a soirée at the Prince de Guermantes' than it would to attend it. It requires half a volume to narrate it. The account is masterly, and the reader is filled with the feelings that actual experience might produce. Those who have had contact with aristocracy, and whose lucidity of mind has not been impaired by it, also find such an account interesting. Here one meets aristocrats of every complexion, heirs of the oldest and proudest names in Gotha's Almanach, and those whose pedigree is not so ancient, upon whom the former look condescendingly. As in a Zoo, one sees a great variety of the aristocrat genus, and if one has believed that the nobility is formed of people different and better than the common herd the delusion is dissipated. Here is a light that fairly dazzles those who are susceptible to the appeal of clothes, wealth, and jewels. If one's yearnings are for things more substantial in human nature he will not be satisfied as a guest of the Prince de Guermantes. Diogenes there would have used his lantern in vain.

One becomes intimately acquainted with the *haut monde*, their colossal pride, and overweening conceit, concealed from the eyes of those below them in the hierachy by thin veils of conventional and shallow amiability which they make more and more transparent as the people they deal with are further removed from the blue zone of the *nobilior spectrum*. One discovers also another characteristic: the capacity for putting up with such pride and conceit from above, and for making the best of it for the sake of securing the lustre which comes with the good will of those higher up, and contact with them.

In the society of the Guermantes one becomes acquainted with such specimens of human meanness and hatefulness, such hypocrisy, such paucity of the sentiments that ennoble life, that he finds himself wondering why better flowers do not grow in the enchanted gardens. Those which seemed so beautiful at a distance turn out to be not only without fragrance, but with a bad odour. The *grand monde*, in truth, seems to be nothing but a small world of gossiping and shallow talk, a world aware of no other nobility than that of inherited titles, and scorning the idea that real nobility is a refinement of the soul, produced by education, to which rich and poor, high and low, may all aspire. The feeling of a man not recognised as an aristocrat who, for some special reason, gains admission to this circle, is made vivid in the experience of a talented physician who has saved the life of the Prince de Guermantes and who owes his invitation to the reception to the Prince's gratitude. The experience of a Bavarian musician is also interesting. It shows how great can be the insolence of aristocracy swollen with vanity. At the soirée we meet nobles who never possessed ideals which acted as

armour against pollution, nobles with imaginations easily in-
flamed by the attractions of women servants, whose lust for a
chambermaid is sufficient to dim all consciousness of their
pedigrees. And we meet others who are even lower, noblemen
and ladies who keep up the traditions of Sodom and Gomorrah
in modern society.

It may be beside the question to inquire the intention of
the author in painting this picture of high society and then
dwelling on aspects of it that can only cause disgust. His
words at times seem to reveal a sarcastic intention. His
descriptions are so full of minute details and so rich in incidents
of extreme naturalness that it is impossible to believe that
even a lively imagination could fabricate them. One easily
sees that they are fragments of real life. This keeps the
interest alive, despite the involved style. His periods are so
twisted and turgid with associated thoughts, so bristling with
parenthetical clauses that often profound effort is required
to interpret them. There is none of the plain, clear, sane,
sunny style of a Daudet, or of Paul Bourget. This causes a
sensation of discomfort at times, especially when the author
indulges in introspection that reveals a morbid imagination
and pathological sensitiveness; as, for instance, in the distinction between abiding sorrows and fugitive sorrows; on
how our beloved departed ones live in us, act on us, transform
us even more than the living ones; and how those who are
dead grow to be more real to us who love them than when
they were alive.

We feel an unhealthiness under it all. We have to stop
and analyse, to unravel the main idea from the tangled skein
in which it is hidden. But it is a work that brings its own
reward. It brings real jewels of *finesse de pensée et d'observation,* such as those on the reminiscence of departed sensations
and feelings; on the different selves which we have been in the
past and which coexist in our present individuality; on the
eclipses to which the latter is subject when one of its com-

ponents suddenly steps from the dark recesses into the vivid light of consciousness; on the elements of beauty apparent in different individuals who are partial incarnations of one great beauty without; on reminiscence of Plato; on the anxiety of expectation while awaiting a person; on the effect which consciousness of his own sinfulness has on the sinner; on the interchange of moral qualities and idiosyncrasies of persons bound by mutual sympathy; on the permanence of our passions—in mathematical jargon, a function of the time during which they have acted on our spirit. It also discloses treasures of delicate feeling, such as are awakened in a person by the image of a beloved one that flashes vivid in his memory.

But to discover such treasures one has often to wade through a series of long and indigestible sentences of thirty or forty lines.

I recall reading in an English magazine, a number of years ago, an article entitled "A Law in Literary Expression." Stated in its plainest terms, the law is this: that the length of the phrase—not the sentence, but its shortest fraction, the phrase—must be measured by the breath pause. M. Proust breaks this law oftener than any citizen of this country breaks the prohibition law, no matter how imperious may be his thirst.

Finally the frank and scientific way in which he has discussed a subject that has always been tabooed in secular literature calls for remark. Of the posterity of Sodom he says it forms a colony spread all over the world, and that one can count it as one can count the dust of the earth. He studies all the types and varieties of sodomists. Their manners and ways, their sentiments, their aberrations of the senses, their shame are passed in review. It is a sort of scientific, poetical treatise. The actions in which the sodomistic instinct finds its outlet are often compared to the seemingly conscious actions by which flowers attract the insects that are the instruments of their fecundation. Botany and sexuality are mixed together. Sometimes the scientific spirit, gaining the upper hand, leads him to look upon these phenomena of genesic inversion as manifestations of a natural law, and therefore marvellous, like all the workings of nature. He is nearly carried away, and finds excuses for what is considered a vice, and seems to be on the verge almost of expressing his admiration.

Some of his observations on sodomistic psychology are highly interesting, although expressed in long periods.

I append a few pages of literal translation from the opening chapter of "Sodome et Gomorrhe"; first, that the reader may have a sample of M. Proust's style; second, that he may gain an insight of the grasp the writer has of one of nature's most unsolvable riddles; and finally, that he may have the description of an individual who plays an important part in the novel.

"At the beginning of this scene, before my unsealed eyes, a revolution had taken place in M. de Charlus, as complete, as immediate as if he had been touched by a magic wand. Until then, not understanding, I had not seen. The vice (so-called for convenience), the vice of each individual, accompanies him after the manner of those genii who are invisible to those who ignore their presence. Goodness, deceit, a good name, social relations do not allow themselves to be discovered, they exist hidden. Ulysses himself did not at first recognise Athene. But gods are immediately perceptible to gods, the like to the like, so M. de Charlus was to Julien. Until now, in the presence of M. de Charlus, I was like an absent-minded man in company with a pregnant woman, whose heavy figure he had not remarked and of whom, in spite of her smiling reiteration 'Yes, I am a bit tired just now,' he persists in asking indiscreetly, 'What is the matter with you then?' But, let some one say to him, 'She is pregnant,' he immediately is conscious of her abdomen and hereafter sees nothing but that. Enlightenment opens the eyes; an error dissipated gives an added sense.

"Those persons who do not like to believe themselves examples of this law in others—towards the Messieurs de Charlus of their acquaintance whom they did not suspect even until there appears on the smooth surface of a character, apparently in every respect like others, traced in an ink until then invisible, a word dear to the ancient Greeks, have only to recall, in order to satisfy themselves, how at first the surrounding world appeared naked, devoid of those ornamentations which it offers to the more sophisticated, and also, of the many times in their lives that they had been on the point of making a break. For instance, nothing upon the characterless face of some man could make them suppose that he was the brother, the fiancé or the lover of some woman of whom they are on the point of making an uncomplimentary remark, as, for example, to compare her to a camel. At that moment, fortunately, however, some word whispered to him by a neighbour freezes the fatal term on his lips. Then immediately appears, like a *Mene, Mene, Tekel, Upharsin,* these words, 'This is the fiancé, or the brother, or the lover of the woman, therefore it would be impossible to call her a camel before him,' and, this new notion alone causes the retreat or advance of the fraction of those notions, heretofore completed, that he had had concerning the rest of the family.

"The real reason that M. de Charlus was different from other men was because another being had been engrafted upon him, like the horse upon the centaur, that his being was incorporated with that of the Baron. I had not hitherto perceived. The abstract had not become materialised, the being, finally understood had lost its power of remaining invisible, and the transmutation of M. de Charlus into a new person was so complete that not only the contrasts of his face, of his voice, but retrospectively the heights and depths of his relations with me, everything, in fact, which had until then appeared incoherent, became intelligible, disclosed itself, like a phrase which, without meaning so long as the letters composing it are scattered becomes, if the characters be placed in their proper order, a thought impossible to forget.

"Moreover I now understood why, a short time ago, when I saw M. de Charlus coming out from Mme. de Villeparisis' I thought he looked like a woman. It was because he was one! He belonged to that race of beings whose ideal is virile because their temperament is feminine, and who are, in appearance only, like other men. The silhouette cast in the facet of their eyes, through which they see everything in the universe, is not that of a nymph but of a beautiful young man. One of a race upon whom rests a curse, who is forced to live

in an atmosphere of falsehood and perjury because he knows
that his desire, that which gives to all creatures the greatest
satisfaction in life, must be unavowed, being considered pun-
ishable and shameful, who must even deny God himself, since
when even as a Christian he appears as an accused at the bar
of the tribunal he must before Christ and in his name defend
himself as if from a calumny from that which is his very life;
son without a mother, forced to lie to her all her life, even to
the moment when he is closing her eyes, friend without friendships, in spite of all those who are attracted by his charm, fully
recognised, and whose hearts would lead them to be kind—
for can those relations, which bloom only by favour of a lie,
be called friendship, when the first burst of confidence he might
be tempted to express, would cause him to be rejected with
disgust?  Should he, by chance, have to do with an impartial
mind, that is to say a sympathetic one, even then diverted
from him by a psychology of convention, would permit to flow
from the confessed vice even the affection which is the most
foreign to him—as certain judges extenuate and excuse more
easily assassination amongst inverts and treason amongst Jews
from reasons drawn from original sin and fatality of race.

"Finally, lovers (at least according to the first theory advanced which one will see modified by the continuation and
which would have angered them above everything had not this
contradiction been wiped out from before their eyes by the
same illusion that made them see and live) to whom the possibility of this love (the hope of which gives them the force to
bear so many risks, so much solitude) is nearly closed since
they are naturally attracted to a man who does not resemble
in any way a woman, a man who is not an invert and who
therefore cannot love them; consequently their desire would
remain forever unappeased if money did not deliver to them
real men or if the imagination did not cause them to take for
real men the inverts to whom they are prostituted.  Whose
only honour is precarious; whose only liberty provisory,
up to the discovery of the crime; whose only situation is
unstable like the poet, who, fêted at night in all the salons,
applauded in all the theatres of London is chased from his
lodgings in the morning and can find no place to lay his head.
Turning the treadmill like Sampson and saying like him, 'The
two sexes will die each on his own side.' Excluded even (ex-

cept during the days of great misfortune when the greatest number rallies around the victim like the Jews around Dreyfus—from the sympathy—sometimes of society) excluded even from their kind who see with disgust, reflected as in a mirror which no longer flatters, all those blemishes which they have not been willing to see in themselves and which make them understand that that which they call their love (and to which, playing upon the word, they have annexed everything that poetry, painting, music, chivalry, asceticism can add to love) comes not from an ideal of beauty which they have chosen, but from an incurable malady. Like the Jews again (save a few who only care to consort with their own race and have always on the lips ritualistic words and consecrated pleasantries); they fly from each other, seeking those who are most unlike them, who will have nothing to do with them, pardoning their rebuffs, intoxicating themselves with their condescensions; but also reassembled with their kind by the very ostracism which strikes them, the opprobrium into which they have fallen, and finally taking on (as a result of a persecution similar to that of Israel) the physical and moral characteristics of a race, sometimes beautiful, often frightful, finding (in spite of all the mockeries that those more homogeneous, better assimilated to the other race, in appearance less of an invert heap upon him who is apparently more of one) finding even a kind of expansion in frequenting with their kind, even an aid from their existence so that while denying that they belong to that race (whose very name is the greatest of injuries) those who have succeeded in hiding the truth, that they also are of that despised race, unmask those others, less to injure them, not detesting them, than to excuse themselves, as a physician seeks the appendicitis inversion in history, they find pleasure in recalling that Socrates was one of them and that the same thing was said of Jesus by the Israelites, without remembering that then when homo-sexuality was normal there was no abnormality, as there were no anti-Christians before Christ, also that opprobrium alone makes it crime, since it has been only allowed to exist as crime because it is refractory to all predication, all example, to all punishment by virtue of special innate disposition which repulses men more (although it may accompany high moral qualities) than certain vices which contradict high moral qualities, such as theft, cruelty, bad faith, better understood, therefore more easily excused by men in general.

"Forming a free-masonry, much more extended, more efficacious and less suspected than that of the lodges, because it rests upon an identity of tastes, of needs, of habits, of dangers, of apprenticeships, of knowledge, of traffic and of language. Whose members avoid one another and yet immediately recognise each other by natural or conventional signs, involuntary or studied, which disclose to the mendicant one of his kind in the lord whose carriage door he opens, to the father in the fiancé of his daughter, to him who had wished to be cured, to confess, in the physician, the priest or the lawyer whom he had gone to consult; all obliged to protect their secret, but, at the same time, sharing the secret of the others, which was not suspected by the others and which makes the most improbable romances of adventure seem true to them, for, in their romantic life, anachronically, the ambassador is the friend of the criminal, the prince who, with a certain freedom of manner, (which an aristocratic education gives and which would be impossible with a little trembling bourgeois) leaves the house of the duchess to seek the Apache. Rejected part of the human collectivity but all the same an important part, suspected where it does not exist, vaunting itself, insolently with impunity where it is not divined; counting its adherents everywhere, amongst the people, in the army, in the temple, in the prison, upon the throne; finally living, at least a great number of them, in a caressing and dangerous intimacy with men of the other race, provoking them, enticing them to speak of this vice as if it were not theirs, a game which is made easy by the blindness or the falseness of the others, a game which may be prolonged for years—until the day of Scandal, when these conquerors are devoured. Until this time obliged to hide their true life, to turn away their regards from where they would wish to fix them, to fix them upon that from which they would naturally turn away—to change the meaning of many adjectives in their vocabulary, a social constraint merely, slight compared to that interior constraint which their vice, or that which is improperly called so, imposes upon them, less with regard to others than to themselves and in a manner which makes it seem not to be a vice—to themselves. But certain ones, more practical, more hurried, who have not time to bargain and to renounce the simplification of life and the gain of time that might result from cooperation, have made two societies, of which the second is exclusively composed of beings like themselves."

M. Proust's work is the first definite reply in the affirmative to the question whether fiction can subsist without the seductive power due to a certain illusory essence of thought. Whether in this respect he will have many, if any, successful followers is to be seen. But his own volumes stand as an astonishing example of an organic and living fiction obtained solely by the effort to portray truth.

Because of the unique qualities of his novels and the fact that they are developed on a definite psychological plan, more than the usual interest in a favourite writer is attached to the personality of M. Proust. During his lifetime inaccessible both because of aristocratic taste and of partial invalidism, his figure is likely to become more familiar to the reading world— even to those who never read his books—than the figures of great authors who walked with the crowd and kept the common touch.

Neither Proust the man nor Proust the author can be considered apart from his invalidism. It shows all through his writings, although what the malady was which rendered him, if not a *de facto* invalid, certainly a potential invalid, is not known. Some of his friends accused asthma, others a disease of the heart, while still others attributed it to "nerves." In reality his conduct and his writings were consistent with neuropathy and his heredity. And if the hero of "A la Recherche du Temps Perdu" is to be identified with himself, as is popularly supposed, he was from early childhood delicate, sensitive, precocious, and asthmatic, that is profoundly neuropathic.

He was fastidious in his tastes; he liked the best styles, the most elegant ladies, aristocratic salons, and fashionable gatherings. He was noted for the generosity of his tips. His life reminds one of the hero of Huysman's famous novel. In his early days, M. Proust was a great swell, and there is no doubt that many of his descriptions of incidents and persons are elaborations of notes that he made after attending a reception given by the Duchesse de Rohan, or other notables of the Faubourg St. Germain, in whose houses he was an habitué.

His social activity may have been deliberate preparation for his work, as his fifteen-year apprenticeship to Ruskin was preparation. Or it may have been a pose, much the same as his mannerisms, habits, customs, and possibly some features of his invalidism, were a pose. Surely he enjoyed the reputation of being "different."

He ruminated on Rousseau and studied Saint-Simon. When he arrived at the stage where he could scoff at one and spurn the other, he learned Henry James by heart. Then he wrote; he had prepared himself. The deficit which art and endeavour failed to wipe out was compensated by his maternal inheritance.

One may infer whither he is going by reading Proust once, but to accompany him he must be read a second time. Those who would get instruction and enlightenment must read him as Ruskin, his master, said all worth while books must be read: "You must get into the habit of looking intensely at words and assuring yourself of their meaning, syllable by syllable."

The discerning reader must look intensely at M. Proust's words. If he looks long enough they seem to take on the appearance of *Mene, Tekel, Phares.*

# CHAPTER VI

TWO LITERARY LADIES OF LONDON: KATHERINE MANSFIELD
AND REBECCA WEST

**M**ANY persons are so constituted that they accept any positive statement as fact unless they know it to be false. Few more positive statements are made in print than "So and So is England's or America's or France's leading or most popular writer of fiction or verse." Publicity agents have found apparently that such claim sells books and needs no substantiation. The reading public rarely protests. It denies in a more effective way, but before the denial gets disseminated many credulous seekers of diversion and culture are misled.

There are several young women writing fiction in England today of whom it can be said truthfully that they ornament the profession of letters. Women have long justified their reputation for being intuitive by their fictional writing. It is likely that they may proceed to establish an equal reputation for accurate observation, logical inference, and temperate narrative. Had not the waves of death recently encompassed Katherine Mansfield in her early maturity she would have remained at the top of the list, the place where now, varying with individual taste and judgment, stand the names of Dorothy Richardson, Rebecca West, Stella Benson, Virginia Woolf, Sheila Kaye-Smith, Mary Webb, Rose Macaulay, to mention no others. For the first time in history women prose writers preponderate, and it is a good augury for a country which has been so quickly and successfully purged of anti-feminism.

Katherine Mansfield's output has been small, but quality has made up for quantity. Her reputation is founded on two volumes of short stories. To say that they reveal capacity to create life, to recognise the temperament, intellectuality, and morality of the ordinary human beings that one encounters, and to display their behaviour; as well as a power to analyse personality and to depict individuality that equals de Maupassant, is to make a truthful statement, and a temperate one. Indeed, she seemed to her contemporaries to be possessed of some unsanctified and secret wisdom.

Her history is brief. She was Kathleen Beauchamp, third daughter of a man of affairs, recently knighted, and was born in Wellington, New Zealand. She was 23 years old when she married, just before the war, J. Middleton Murry, the British critic and novelist. Her first book "In a German Pension," published when she was 21, gave no promise of great talent. Her first mature work was a series of book reviews in *The Nation and Athenæum,* about 1919. She was quickly recognised to be a subtle and brilliant critic. In 1920 the publication of "Bliss and Other Stories" revealed her metal and temper. Development and maturity marked her second and last collection, "The Garden-Party and Other Stories," which followed in 1922. Hardly had the promise of her early work been recognised before it was overshadowed by progressive pulmonary disease, and after long months of illness, during which she was obliged to spend most of her time away from England, she died in France on January 9, 1923.

Katherine Mansfield had a technique which may be compared to that of a great stage manager. When the play is put on, the scenes and the characters, the atmosphere and the environment, the sentiment and the significance are satisfying, intelligent and convincing. The world seen through her eyes, and the conduct of its most highly organised product, is the world that may be seen by anyone who has normal, keen vision. The conduct of the people who encumber it is that which an observer without inherited bias or acquired bigotry knows intuitively, and has learned from experience, is the conduct that

KATHERINE MANSFIELD

reflects our present development, our attitudes, our interests, our desires, and most of all our dispositions.

She prepared the stage and then her characters came on. She didn't bore with narrative of their birth, weary with incidents of their development, or disgust with details of their vegetative existence. They reacted to their immediate desires and environment in the way that people act in real life. She had a comprehensive understanding of human motives, and she realised how firmly engrained in man is the organic lust to live and to experience pleasure.

To find the balance in fiction midway between the "joy stuff" which for the last decade has been threatening to reduce American literature to a spineless pulp, and morbid realism which, in both England and this country, has been reflecting the influence of so-called psychoanalysis, is an accomplishment deserving of the thanks of all admirers of sanity in art. Miss Mansfield has succeeded in doing this, with the result that a large measure of the charm of her art lies in its sanity, its extraordinary freedom from obsessions, from delusions, and from excessive egocentricity. To borrow a term from music, she may be said to have possessed an unerring sense of pitch.

The easiest way of estimating any unknown element is to compare it to something already known, and Katherine Mansfield has been called the Chekhov of English fiction. Such a comparison may be useful as an approach to her work. In truth, however, while her position in English fiction may be compared with that of the illustrious Russian, she is in no sense an imitator, a disciple of him or of any one else. Her art is her own.

It can best be estimated from study of her last published story. If Katherine Mansfield, feeling herself already drawn into the shadow of approaching death, had tried to leave the world one final sample of her art which would epitomise her message and her method, "The Fly," published in *The Nation and Athenæum* of March 18, 1922, is a lasting triumph of her success. In a story of twenty-five hundred words she has said more than most authors say in a one-hundred-thousand word novel, or, indeed, in many novels. Not only is every word pregnant with meaning, but for those who can read between the lines there is an indictment of the life she is picturing too poignant for any but strong souls who can look upon the wine of life when it is red; who can even drain the cup to the bitter dregs in their sincere desire to learn its truth, without suffering the draft to send its poison into their souls. It is not that Katherine Mansfield was poisoned with the bitterness of life, or weakened with the taint of pessimism. On the contrary, she was as immune to bitterness, to poison, to weakness, as a disembodied spirit would be to disease. She was like pure white glass, reflecting fearlessly the part of life that was held before her, but never colouring it with her own personality. Her reflection was impartial.

In "The Fly" the *dramatis personæ* are old Mr. Woodifield, the boss, and the fly. Old Mr. Woodifield is not described, but the reader sees him, small of body and of soul, shrivelled, shaky, wheezy, as he lingers in the big, blatantly new office chair on one of the Tuesdays when, since the "stroke" and retirement from his clerkship, he has escaped from the solicitude of the wife and the girls back into his old life in the city— "we cling to our last pleasures as the tree clings to its last leaves"—and revelled in the sense of being a guest in the boss's office. The boss is more graphic because he remains nameless. "Stout, rosy, five years older than Mr. Woodifield and still going strong, still at the helm" is what we are told he is, but this is what we see: A brutal, thick man, purring at the admiration of the old clerk for his prosperity revealed in the newly "done-up" office; self-satisfied, selfish, and supercilious, offering a glass of whiskey as a panacea for the old man's tottering pitifulness, and then listening, insolently tolerant, to the rambling outpourings of the old soul, harmless, disciplined to long poverty of purse, of life, of thought, about the "Girls" visit to the soldier's grave in Belgium and the price they paid for a pot of jam. Then the picture changes. The shuffling footsteps of the old man have died out, the door is closed for half-an-hour, the photograph of a "grave-looking boy in uniform standing in one of those spectral photographers' parks with photographers' storm-clouds behind him," looks out at the boss who has "arranged to weep." But the flood-gates which have opened at the tap of the one sentiment of which the boss was capable are now suffering from the rust of six years. Tears refuse to come.

A fly drops into the pot of ink, and the boss, absent-mindedly noticing its struggles for freedom, picks it out with a pen and shakes it on to the blotting paper, where the little animal makes a heroic effort to clean off the ink and get ready for life again. But the boss has an idea. In spite of himself, his admiration is aroused by the fly's struggle, his pluck—"that was the way to tackle things, that was the right spirit. Never say die; it was only a question of . . . But the fly has again finished its laborious task and the boss has just time to refill his pen, to shake fair and square on the newly cleaned body yet another dark drop. What about it this time?" And yet another. "He plunged his pen back into the ink, leaned his thick wrist on the blotting paper, and as the fly tried its wings, down came a great heavy blot. What would it make of that? . . . Then the boss decided that this time should be the last, as he dipped the pen deep in the inkpot. It was. The last blot fell on the soaked blotting-paper and the bedraggled fly lay in it and did not stir." And as he rings for some new blotting-paper, a feeling of unaccountable wretchedness seizes him and he falls to wondering what it was he had been thinking about before the fly had attracted his attention. "For the life of him, he could not remember." And that is the end of the story.

Katherine Mansfield's art resembles that of the great Russian physician-novelist in that she preaches no sermon, points no moral, expounds no philosophy. Although there is no available exposition of her theories, her work is evidence that her conception of art was to depict the problematic as it was presented to her, and leave the interpretation to the reader's own philosophy. She made Raoul Duquette say, in "Je ne parle pas Française," one of the most psychologically remarkable of her stories: "People are like portmanteaux, packed with certain things, started going, thrown about, tossed away, dumped down, lost and found, half emptied suddenly or squeezed fatter than ever until finally the Ultimate Porter swings them on to the Ultimate Train, and away they rattle." That may have been her own belief.

While it may be true in a certain sense that the artist sees only himself in his art, there is an essential difference between seeing himself reflected in life and in seeing life as in himself. Katherine Mansfield habitually did the latter. And it is this fact that enabled her to use as models, or accessories, or background any of the chance travellers she may have encountered with almost equal success. If she ever reflected herself in her art, it was a normal and objective self, a self which was interested in the drama being enacted about her, not merely the drama of her own soul; and in the fine points of this drama as well as in its leading actors and more obvious aspects.

Her world from which she has gathered the material for her two books of stories has been richly variegated, and her readers are given the full benefit of a versatile experience. She was *La Gioconda* of English fiction writers. "Je ne parle pas Française" shows that she knew the soul maladies and, like Walter Pater's conception of Leonardo's masterpiece, she knew some of the secrets of the grave: though she had not "been a diver in deep seas," nor "trafficked for strange webs with Eastern merchants." She did not *finish* an individual. She narrated an episode which revealed his or her character; she didn't lead up to some epochal event like marriage, a dramatic reconciliation, a studied folly, or a crime. She depicted an episode, and left you to put such interpretation upon it, or to continue it, as your experience, imagination, or desire might suggest. She was a picture maker, not pigment by pigment, cell by cell, but with great sweeps of the brush.

She usually depicted sentimental *men,* whose long suits were fidelity and constancy, or men whose fundamental urges were not harmonised to convention. Her women were, in the main, fickle, designing, inconstant, shallow, truckling, vain. "Marriage à la Mode," is a specimen. William keeps his romantic and sentimental view of life after prosperity and progeny come. Isabel doesn't. She is all for progress and evolution—new house, new environment, new friends, new valuation of life's possessions. He goes home for week-ends chockful of love and sentimentality. She meets him at the station with her new friends—sybarites and hedonists in search of sensation. He soon finds he isn't in the game at all as Isabel now plays it. So he decides to abbreviate his visit. On the way back to town he concocts a long letter full of protestations of unselfish love, and willingness to stand aside if his presence is a drag on her happiness. She reads it aloud to her guests who receive it with sneers and jeers. Isabel has a moment of self-respect, and withdraws to her room and experiences the vulgarity and loathesomeness of her conduct. She will write to William at once and dispel his fears and reassure him, but while she is holding her character up to her eyes disparagingly she hears her guests calling her and decides "I'll go with them and write to William later—some other time. Not now. But I shall *certainly* write." Procrastination, not hesitation, condition her downfall.

In "Je ne parle pas Française" she handled a subject—the implantation of the genesic instinct—in such a way that the reader may get little or much from it, depending upon his knowledge and experience. But in the lines and between the lines there is exposition of practically all that is known of the strange deviations of the libido. Raoul Duquette and

Dick, his English friend, who cannot kill his mother, cannot give her the final blow of letting her know that he has fallen in love with Mouse, are as truly drawn to life as Paul Verlaine and Arthur Rimbaud, or as Encolpius and Giton of the Satyricon.

It is a far cry from the depths glimpsed—but with such terrible sureness—in this story, to the budding soul of a young girl from the country as pictured in Leila in "Her First Ball"; or to the very spirit of healthy youth, both frivolous, superficial youth, and sensitive idealising youth, which exudes from the pages of "The Garden-Party."

She depicted transformation of mental states, the result of suggestion or impulse, much as a prestidigitator handles his Aaron's rod. This is particularly well seen in Leila. The reader shares her joyous mental state, full of vistas of hope and love and joy. Then a fat man who has been going to parties for thirty years dances with her and pictures her future follies, strifes, struggles, and selfishness at forty. At once she realises her doll is stuffed with sawdust, and cries and wants to go home, but a young man comes along, dances with her again, and behold the filling isn't sawdust, but radium!

Katherine Mansfield's art may be studied in such a story as "At the Bay." The *dramatis personæ* are: Beryl, a temperamental young lady looking for romance, seeking fulfilment of destiny, thwarted by a Narcissus inhibition; Linda, her sister, without temperament, to whom fulfilment is repellant; Mrs. Harry Kember, unmoral and immoral, a vampire with a past and keen for a future; Harry Kember, her husband of whom many things are said, but none adequate to describe him; Stanley Burnell, a conventional good man—mollycoddle; Jonathan Trout, a poet compelled by fate to be a drone; Alice, a servant in transformation from chrysalis to butterfly; Mrs. Stubbs, a vegetative hedonist; and several delightful children and a devoted "Granma."

They spend a holiday at the seashore and Beryl looks for romance. Here is the picture:

"Very early morning. The sun was not yet risen, and the whole of Crescent Bay was hidden under a white sea-mist. The big bush-covered hills at the back were smothered. You could not see where they ended and the paddocks and bungalows began. The sandy road was gone and the paddocks and bungalows the other side of it; there were no white dunes covered with reddish grass beyond them; there was nothing to mark which was beach and where was the sea. A heavy dew had fallen. The grass was blue. Big drops hung on the bushes and just did not fall; the silvery, fluffy toi-toi was limp on its long stalks, and all the marigolds and the pinks in the bungalow gardens were bowed to the earth with wetness. Drenched were the cold fuchsias, round pearls of dew lay on the flat nasturtium leaves. It looked as though the sea had beaten up softly in the darkness, as though one immense wave had come tippling, rippling—how far? Perhaps if you had waked up in the middle of the night you might have seen a big fish flicking in at the window and gone again. . . ."

You feel the wetness of it. Then come the first signs of waking up in the place: the shepherd with his dog and flock making for the Downs, the cat waiting on the gatepost for the milk-girl—harbingers of the day's activities.

Then the picture is animated.

"A few minutes later the back door of one of the bungalows opened, and a figure in a broad-striped bathing suit flung down the paddock, cleared the stile, rushed through the tussock grass into the hollow, staggered up the sandy hillock, and raced for dear life over the big porous stones, over the cold, wet pebbles, on to the hard sand that gleamed like oil. Splish-splosh! Splish-splosh! The water bubbled round his legs as Stanley Burnell waded out exulting. First man in as usual! He'd beaten them all again. And he swooped down to souse his head and neck."

This is a complete revelation of his character—smug, righteous, selfish, the centre of a world in which every tomorrow shall be like today, and today is without romance. He feels cheated when Jonathan Trout tries to talk to him.

"But curse the fellow! He'd ruined Stanley's bathe. What an unpractical idiot the man was! Stanley struck out to sea again, and then as quickly swam in again, and away he rushed up the beach."

There is something pathetic in his determination to make a task of everything, even the entailments of matrimony.

"You couldn't help feeling he'd be caught out one day, and then what an almighty cropper he'd come! At that moment an immense wave lifted Jonathan, rode past him, and broke along the beach with a joyful sound. What a beauty! And now there was another. That was the way to live—carelessly, recklessly, spending oneself. He got on to his feet and began to wade towards the shore, pressing his toes into the firm, wrinkled sand. To take things easy, not to fight against the ebb and flow of life, but to give way to it—that was what was needed. It was this tension that was all wrong. To live— to live!"

The whole world of his home moves round Stanley. When he returns for breakfast he has every member of the family working for him. When Beryl does not help him at once, its mechanism must be dislocated. But Linda he can't draw into the net. "Linda's vagueness on these occasions could not be real, Stanley decided."

The bathing hour on the beach for the women and children is as vivid as if taken by a camera.

"The firm, compact little girls were not half so brave as the tender, delicate-looking little boys. Pip and Rags, shivering, crouching down, slapping the water, never hesitated. But Isabel, who could swim twelve strokes, and Kezia, who could nearly swim eight, only followed on the strict understanding they were not to be splashed. As for Lottie, she didn't follow at all. She liked to be left to go in her own way, please. And that way was to sit down at the edge of the water, her legs straight, her knees pressed together, and to make vague motions with her arms as if she expected to be wafted out to sea. But when a bigger wave than usual, an old whiskery one, came lolloping along in her direction, she scrambled to her feet with a face of horror and flew up the beach again."

Mrs. Harry Kember and Beryl give an exhibition of the vampire and the novice, while Linda dreams the morning away in revery and retrospect. Beryl's dream of romance when she is alone in the garden after everybody else in the household has gone to bed receives a rude jolt from Harry Kember.

The story is illustrative of Miss Mansfield's art in leaving her characters without killing or marrying them or bringing great adventure into their lives. It leaves one with a keen interest in what is next for Beryl, although she is not the most attractive of the figures in the story, but there is no indication that we shall meet her again. "Granma" and the children are the features of this story, and appear as real as life. The author's faculty in making the reader interested in characters who do not play heroic or leading rôles is distinctive. Even the sheep-dog's encounter with the cat on the gate-post is delightful, also the glimpse of Mrs. Stubbs' cottage with its array of bathing suits and shoes and the lady's reception of Alice are art: "With her broad smile and the long bacon knife in her hand, she looked like a friendly brigand."

"Prelude," the introductory story of "Bliss and Other Stories," is a further revelation of Beryl, with side lights on her sister Linda and Linda's husband, Stanley, and her quite wonderful mother. The Narcissus in Beryl has bloomed. Forced to accept bed and board from her brother-in-law, she bewails her fate while chanting the praises of her physical charms and mental possessions. Linda, by this time, has given herself all the air of confirmed invalidism. Linda gets her emotional appeasement from what might have been; Beryl, from what is going to be—both foundationed in introspection. When Linda first met Stanley out in Australia she scorned him, but previous to or after their marriage she fell in love with him. But her antipathy to childbearing and her fear of it are so profound that they colour all her thoughts and emotions. This is best seen when she relates her dream about birds.

"Prelude" is not a story of Linda, but of Beryl and her hypocrisy. It should be dovetailed into "At the Bay." The overtures and the temptation which were made to her by Mr. and Mrs. Harry Kember have not borne fruit. She is in love with herself and it may be that that is what the author meant to convey. The description of herself and her comment on her own appearance: "Yes, my dear, there is no doubt about it, you really are a lovely little thing" is very illuminating. She persuades herself that she is a potential Nina Declos and that if opportunity had not been denied her she could rival Messalina. Hypocrisy is bearing in on her and it is not quite evident, at the close of "Prelude," where it is going to lead her.

The burden of the story is to intensify interest in Beryl, and her influences and surroundings, and to heighten the suspense of the reader. On finishing "At the Bay" one has a picture of the romantic girl; at the close of "Prelude" one feels that something is going to happen to her before the author finishes with her. The reader gets no clue, however, to what it might be, except that it would be the working out of her temperament—admiration for self and longing for romance through which to express this self. Her longing at first seemed to be for expression of self biologically and intellectually; now it seems to be to find a setting in which to frame becomingly this adorable self—an essential difference in character and the difference that is the axis upon which the story might be expected to turn. If people are their temperaments, it is such subtle differences of temperament which determine destiny, or what they shall work out for themselves from given circumstances.

Beryl is more cold-blooded, more calculating than she at first appeared to be, and never again will she be in danger of capitulating to a Kember. What she wants is to shine, and she is going to use her valued attractions designedly as currency to accomplish this. Beryl and Linda are studies in selfishness and introspection. The latter is phlegmatic and lazy, mentally and emotionally as well as physically.

"Granma" and the children are still the most attractive figures in the family. How such a woman as "Granma" could have had daughters like Beryl and Linda is truer to life than to fiction. Had we known their father they might not have been so enigmatic.

Katherine Mansfield had a genius for catching the exact meaning of the little touches in life, the little ironies and comedies as well as the single little wild flower in a rank growth of weeds. She was delightfully objective. She had a quality rare in women writers, especially, of not putting all her treasures in one basket, of not concentrating upon one character and that character more or less the expression of herself; and of being interested in the whole drama as it passed. She could enter into the soul of a charwoman or a cat and take a snap-shot of it which made the reader love the charwoman or the cat, as well as she could paint a picture that gives the very atmosphere of children at play or of dawn at the seashore or night in a quiet house—even better than she could make an X-ray study of the soul of a selfish woman or a stupid self-righteous man.

The "high light" of "The Garden-Party" is the contrast between a typical happy prosperous family and an equally unhappy poor one; a garden-party for the young girls of the first family, the accidental death of the man and the wage-earner of the second. One lives on the hill in the sunlight; the other in the damp forbidding hollow below. They are near neighbours in point of space; strangers in all other respects. One makes an art of the graces and pleasures of life; the other is familiar with the gloom typified by poverty and death. Both accept their existences unquestioningly, in worlds as different psychologically as they are physically.

The author does not preach; there is no straining for effect. Laura, one of three sisters, is more sensitive than the other members of the family. She alone feels contrasts. She is revelling in the preparations for the garden-party when she hears from the workmen of the man's sudden death, and her joy is clouded. But her mother and sisters make light of it, and the party proceeds—a picture of average wholesome young joyousness. Then the mother sends Laura, with a basket of cakes, to the man's family. The dramatic contrast is in Laura's impressions when she goes, in her party clothes, with the frivolous-looking basket, down into the hollow at dusk. That is all. There is no antagonism, no questioning of fate, no sociology—just a picture. Only the ability not to use an extra word, the taste and the humour which kept out any mawkishness saved the story from being "sob stuff."

When Katherine Mansfield read virtues into her female characters she usually made them humble, lowly, or plain, such as Ma Parker, Miss Brill, and Beryl's mother. She could introduce Ma Parker who cleaned the flat of the literary gentleman every Tuesday, and in eleven pages, without a single approach to sentimentality, make you in love with the old scrubwoman, with her hard life and heroic unselfish soul, when you left her standing in the cold street wondering whether there was any place in the world where she could have a cry at last. The motive of this story is much the same as that of "The Garden-Party," the sharp contrast between two extreme types of life which circumstances bring close together.

In "The Daughters of the Late Colonel" the author walked with a sure step on thin ice from the first sentence to the last, never taking a false step or undignified slide. Humour alone preserved the balance where the ice was not too thin, and kept her from slipping over the invisible line of safety in the direction of bathos on the one side, or of the coarsely comic on the other. To make two old ladies who had spent their lives "looking after father, and at the same time keeping out of father's way" and who at father's death find themselves among those whom life had passed by, interesting and intriguing, is a severe test for a writer. Not only are they dead emotionally, but their habit of thought has become too set to be readjusted to their new freedom. Miss Mansfield made them as funny as they naturally would have been, without "making fun" of them. Their funniness is lovable. For instance:

"At the cemetery while the coffin was lowered, to think that she and Constantia had done this thing without asking his permission. What would father say when he found out? For he was bound to find out sooner or later. He always did. 'Buried. You two girls had me buried.' She could hear his stick thumping."

Or when the organ-grinding and the spot of sunshine on their mother's picture start in both silent reminiscence as to whether life might have been different if she had lived.

"Might they have married? But there had been nobody for them to marry. There had been father's Anglo-Indian friends before he quarrelled with them. But after that she and Constantia never met a single man except clergymen. How did one meet men? Or even if they'd met them, how could one have got to know men well enough to be more than strangers? One read of people having adventures, being followed, and so on. But nobody had ever followed Constantia and her."

"Miss Brill" is a sketch with a whimsical pathos. A little old maiden lady who dresses up every Sunday and goes to the *Jardin Publiques* in Paris and sits on a bench, getting her romance out of watching people and feeling that she is a part of the passing life, goes one Sunday as usual. The feature in the sketch is the little fur piece around her neck.

"Miss Brill put up her hand and touched her fur. Dear little thing! It was nice to feel it again. She had taken it out of its box that afternoon, shaken out the mothpowder, given it a good brush, and rubbed the life back into the dim little eyes."

It is to her like a pet animal or even a child. At first she finds the park less interesting than usual, but finally, as she senses romance in a pair of park lovers who sit down on her bench, she hears the boy say, "that stupid old thing at the end there. Why does she come here at all—who wants her? Why doesn't she keep her silly old mug at home?" And the girl, giggling, replies, "It's her fu-fur which is so funny. . . . It's exactly like a fried whiting." Suddenly the romance and the joy have all gone out of the old lady, and when she lays away her little fur piece in its box sadly and puts on the lid she thinks she hears something crying.

Ability to depict the hidden speck of beauty under an uncompromising exterior not only inspired some of Katherine Mansfield's finest touches, but is especially refreshing after acquaintance with many writers who seem bent solely upon discovering some inmost rottenness and turning upon it the X-rays. There are many old ladies in this book, and the loving skill with which she has reproduced for the reader the charm she was able to see in them is indicative not only of her art, but also of her essential wholesomeness.

"The Man Without a Temperament" is an objective study of an unpopular man. One knows him from the few outward glimpses given of him as well as if the author had made an intensive psychological study of him. That is, one knows him as one knows other people, not as he knows himself. The sketch is pregnant with irony and pathos. Without a temperament—unfeeling—is the world's verdict of him. In reality, he has more feeling than his critics. What he lacks is not feeling, but expression. He is like a person with a pocketful of "paper" who has to walk because he hasn't change to pay his carfare, or to go hungry because he can't pay for a meal.

People who know him trust him, even if they do not fancy him or feel quite at ease with him; but with strangers he has no chance. A life study of such a character would make him ·interesting. A photograph shows him as one of the people who "never take good pictures."

In "Bliss and Other Stories," the author went into deeper water than in the other collection. She was less concerned with the little ironies and with the fine points of her characters, and more with great passions.

"Bliss," the story, shows the same method as do many of her other stories, but reversed. It is as if her reel were being run before the reader backwards. Instead of hunting out the one flower in a patch of weeds, she painted a young married woman's Garden of Eden and then hunted down the snake. From the first note of Bertha Young's unexplainable bliss one knows that the snake motive is coming, but does not know how or where. The feeling of it runs through Bertha's psychical sense of secret understanding—the "something in common" between herself and Pearl Fulton, who, by a subtle uncanniness, is made to suggest a glorified "vamp." The leading motive of the story is the psychic sympathy between the women, who are antitheses. Commonly such a sense of understanding would take the form of antipathy. That it is attraction—harking back in all likelihood to something in Bertha remote and unrecognised—constitutes the distinctiveness of the motive. The art is revealed in a clear-cut picture—nothing more. Katherine Mansfield knew so marvellously where to stop. She had a good eye, a deft hand, an understanding mind, a sense of humour, and she loved her fellow-beings.

Until "The Judge" was published Miss Rebecca West, in the opinion of many amateur and professional critics, was the most promising young woman to enter the field of literature in the reign of King George. Her advent to the literary world was impressive, and in a little book on Henry James in the "Writers of the Day" series she revealed a capacity of interpretation and facility of expression which made her elders envious and her contemporaries jealous. It was obvious to the casual reader of this book, and of her journalistic contributions, that not only had she the artistic temperament, but that she was familiar with its display in others, and that she had read widely, discriminatingly, and understandingly. Moreover, she was a thoroughly emancipated young woman and bore no marks of the cage that had restrained her sex. Her cleverness, her erudition, her resourcefulness were admitted. It was rated to be an asset, also, that she did not hesitate to call a spade a spade or to use the birch unsparingly when she felt it was for the benefit of the reading public, misled and deluded as it so often is by false prophets, erring evangelists, and self-seeking promoters. In other words, though she had sentiment and sympathy, she knew how to use them judiciously. In "Notes on Novels" she constantly reminds herself that there is a draught that we must drink or not be fully human. One must know the truth. When one is adult one must raise to one's lips the wine of truth, heedless that it is not sweet like milk but draws the mouth with its strength, and celebrate communion with reality, or else walk forever queer and small like a dwarf. Miss West does not intend that her countrymen shall display these deformities.

Her first novel, "The Return of the Soldier," a fictional exposition of the Freudian wish, was acclaimed by critics as the first fulfilment of the promise she had given. The teachings of the Austrian mystic were not much known then in England, the country that now seems to have swallowed them, bait, line, and sinker, not only in the fields of fiction but in pedagogy and in medicine; so Miss West's little book was more widely read and discussed than it might be today when Miss May Sinclair, Mr. J. D. Beresford, Mr. D. H. Lawrence, and many other popular novelists have made his theories look like facts to the uninitiated.

The story is of Christopher, the ideal type of young Englishman who knows how to fight and to love.

"He possessed in a great measure the loveliness of young men, which is like the loveliness of the spring, foal or the sapling, but in him it was vexed with a serious and moving beauty by the inhabiting soul. To see him was to desire intimacy with him so that one might intervene between this body which was formed for happiness and the soul which cherished so deep a faith in tragedy."

It is narrated by his cousin who has loved him platonically since youth. Chris had a romantic and ardent love affair with an inn-keeper's daughter in his youth, but he married Kitty, a beautiful little conventional non-temperamental young woman with a charming and cultivated soprano voice, of the class of women who

"are obscurely aware it is their civilising mission to flash the jewel of their beauty before all men so that they shall desire and work to get the wealth to buy it, and thus be seduced by a present appetite to a tilling of the earth that serves the future."

He goes to the war, gets concussion of the brain which causes amnesia, or forgetfulness of certain epochal events in his life, particularly his marriage to Kitty. "Who the devil is Kitty?" he replies when he is told she might have something to say on hearing of his plan to marry Margaret Allingham. Though some of the events of his life from twenty-one, when he fell in love with Margaret, to thirty-six, when he got injured, can be revived in his memory by Jenny, a resourceful understanding person, the sort of cousin every man should have, no argumentation can reconcile him to Kitty, and "he said that his body and soul were consumed with desire for Margaret and that he would never rest until he once more held her in his arms."

After exhausting every means that love and science can

suggest to jog his memory or wipe out the amnesia, it is decided to bring him and Margaret together. No one who had known her as the "Venus of Monkey Island," a composite of charity and love, would recognise her now, seamed and scarred and ravaged by squalid circumstance, including dreary matrimony to a man with a weak chest that needed constant attention. Moreover, "all her life long Margaret had partaken of the inalienable dignity of a requited love, and lived with men who wore carpet slippers in the house." Such experience had left deforming scars. However, Chris sees her with the eyes of youth, and her presence resurrects juvenile emotions. Under their influence Margaret undergoes transformation.

"She had a little smile in her eyes as though she were listening to a familiar air played far away, her awkwardness seemed indecision as to whether she would walk or dance to that distant music, her shabbiness was no more repulsive than the untidiness of a child who had been so eager to get to the party that it has not let its nurse fasten its frock."

However, their interviews do not get them anywhere from Kitty's standpoint, and she decides to send for Dr. Gilbert Anderson.

"Heaven knows she had no reason for faith in any doctor, for during the past week so many of them sleek as seals with their neatly brushed hair and their frockcoats, had stood around Chris and looked at him with the consequential deliberation of a plumber."

But Dr. Anderson was different.

"He was a little man with winking blue eyes, a flushed and crumpled forehead, a little grey moustache that gave him the profile of an amiable cat and a lively taste in spotted ties, and he lacked that appetiteless look which is affected by distinguished practitioners."

Dr. Anderson explains to the family that Christopher's amnesia is the manifestation of a suppressed wish and that his

REBECCA WEST
Photograph by *Yevonde, London.*

unconscious self is refusing to let him resume his relations with his normal life. He forgot his life with his wife because he was discontented, and there was no justification for it for "Kitty was the falsest thing on earth, in tune with every kind of falsity." The doctor proposes psychoanalysis, but Margaret says she knows a memory so strong that it will recall everything else, in spite of his discontent, the memory of the boy, his only child who had died five years before. Dr. Anderson urges her to take Christopher something the boy had worn, some toy they used to play with. So she takes a jersey and ball and meets Chris in the garden where there is only a column of birds swimming across the lake of green light that lays before the sunset, and as Chris gazes at Margaret mothering them in her arms the scales fall from his eyes and he makes obeisance to convention and bids his creative libido *au revoir*.

Jenny is witness of the transformation and when Kitty asks "How does he look?" she answers, though her tongue cleaves to the roof of her mouth, "Every inch a soldier."

When Miss West next essayed fiction in "The Judge" it was the diagnosis of the creative urge that was her theme. It is one of Freud's contentions that the male child, before it hears the voice of conscience and the admonition of convention, has carnal yearnings for the mother, the female child for the father. With the advent of sense, with the development of individuality, with the recognition of obligation to others, and particularly with the acquisition of the sense of morality, these are replaced with what are called normal desires. In some instances the transformation does not take place. The original trend remains, and it is spoken of as an infantile fixation. Its juvenile and adult display is called sin ethically and crime socially.

The wages of sin still is death, according to Miss West's portrayal, but it is not called sin. It is merely behaviourism interpreted in the light of the New Psychology.

"Every mother is a judge who sentences the children for the sins of the father" is her thesis. As a work of art "The Judge" has elicited much praise. As a human document, a mirror held up to actual life, a statement of the accepted facts of heredity and of behaviour, and of the dominancy and display of passion, lust, jealousy, anger, revenge, I doubt that it merits unqualified approbation.

Marion Yaverland, daughter of a Kentish father and a French mother, had yielded without compunction to the wooing of the local squire and had borne a child, Richard, around whose development, personality, and loving the story is built.

"Vitality itself had been kneaded into his flesh by his parents' passion. He had been begotten when beauty, like a strong goddess, pressed together the bodies of his father and mother, hence beauty would disclose more of her works to him than to other sons of men with whose begetting she was not concerned."

But the goddess did not give him straight genesic endowment, so he was not able to keep filial love and carnal love in their proper channels. And from this flowed all the tragedy. His mother realised his infirmity, though she didn't look upon it as an infirmity, from the earliest days; and, unfortunately, she did not attempt to eradicate it—if it is ever eradicable.

Squire Harry behaved badly to Marion, save financially, and public opinion backed up by a stoning in the streets (a real Old Testament touch) by a moron and his more youthful companions, made her accept an offer of marriage from the squire's butler, a loathsome creature called Peacey. In proposing marriage and promising immunity to its obligations he said:

"Marion, I hope you understand what I'm asking you to do. I'm asking you to marry me. But not to be my wife. I never would bother you for that. I'm getting on in life, you see, so that I can make the promise with some chance of keeping it."

But Peacey deceived no one save Marion. Miss West's description of the one visit of violence which he made to his wife, and which was followed in due time by Roger, whom Richard hated from birth, is a bit of realism that in verisimilitude has rarely been excelled. Roger was a pasty, snivelling, rhachitic child who developed into a high-grade imbecile of the hobo type, and finally managed to filter through the Salvation Army owing to some filter paper furnished by his mother that bore the legend "For the Gov$^t$ and Comp$^a$ of the Bank of England."

From earliest childhood Richard and his mother both realised that their intimacy was unnatural and unpromising for happiness. When he was two years old

"He used to point his fingers at her great lustrous eyes as he did at flowers, and he would roll his face against the smooth skin of her neck and shoulders; and when he was naked after his bath he liked her to let down her hair so that it hung round him like a dark, scented tent."

Poor little monster, how unfortunate that he could not then have been given a hormone that would extrovert his budding perversion!

"She always changed her dress for tea, and arranged her hair loosely like a woman in a picture, and went out into the garden to gather burning leaves and put them in vases about the room, and when it fell dark she set lighted candles on the table because they were kinder than the lamp to her pain-flawed handsomeness and because they kept corners of dusk in which these leaves glowed like fire with the kind of beauty that she and Richard liked. She would arrange all this long before Richard came in, and sit waiting in a browse of happiness, thinking that really she had lost nothing by being cut off from the love of man for this was very much better than anything she could have had from Harry."

Somewhat like the way the daughter of Senator Metellus Celere, called by some Claudia and by others Lesbia, arranged the visits of Catullus.

.

When Richard was sixteen he forced life's hand and leapt straight from boyhood into manhood by leaving school where he had shown great promise in science, and becoming a sailor so that he should be admirable to his mother. His wanderings took him to South America where he had great success in affairs of the heart and of the purse. It is with disposition of the latter that the book opens in the office of a lubricitous old Scotch solicitor where sits a young red-haired temperamental suffragette whimpering for the moon.

Ellen Melville is a lovable Celt of seventeen, and her creator displays a comprehensive insight into her mind and emotions. She is what Rebecca West once was and wished to be. It is sad that the pathway of her life leads so early to the *Via Dura* and that Richard Yaverland had not tarried in Vienna or Zurich to be psychoanalysed.

Richard falls in love with her at first sight. He woos her ardently, though simply, and she responds like a "nice" girl, like a girl who feels that for the endowment of that most wondrous thing in the world, the cerebral cortex, it is vouchsafed her to exercise restraints and make inhibitions which insects and animals cannot. In the highest sense she is rational and instinctive.

Ellen goes south to visit her future mother-in-law and a few days later Richard joins them. Roger meanwhile has "found Jesus," and Poppy, a Salvation Army lassie, one stage removed from "Sin." While knocking at Marion's door to gain entry that they may announce their intention to marry, their gaze floats upward and they see Ellen being kissed by the man to whom she will be married in three months. Roger, who is instinctive but not rational, puts a wrong interpretation upon it, and from that mal-interpretation the final tragedy flows. A few days later Marion realises there is no happiness for Richard and Ellen so long as she lives. She walks out into the marshes. Roger accuses Richard of driving his mother to it "because she saw that there was something wrong between you two." He elaborates the accusation, and Richard drives a bread-knife into Roger's heart.

Richard knows his doom is sealed. So he invites Ellen to share a cattlemen's hut with him on the farther side of the creek where his mother had drowned herself, until the people come to take him—and to share it comprehensively.

"Her love had not been able to reach Richard across the dark waters of his mother's love and how like a doom that love had lain on him. Since life was like this she would not do what Richard asked."

But she does.

The mode in which "The Judge" is cast is noteworthy because of its novelty and of the success attending it. Here is no sequential narrative, no time-table of events in the order in which they happened. The contact of Richard and Ellen is set forth in a straightforward way, but the main thesis of the book, the Laocoon grip of mother-love on Richard is conveyed indirectly, surreptitiously, atmospherically rather than verbally. Ellen, though she is quite normal, senses it at once when she meets Marion, and the writer approximates perfection of her art most closely in narrations of the first interviews of these two women, who are as unlike as the Colonel's lady and Judy O'Grady.

While this mode may not prove an obstacle to an easy grasp of the novel upon first reading by writers or critics, it is doubtful whether the casual reader for diversion will comprehend its significance without special effort and perhaps several attempts at mastering the intricacies in the development of the story. The plan which the author has adopted of beginning, in direct narrative form, with the mature life of Richard and his love for Ellen, and then revealing through retrospect and suggestion the events of his early life and that of his mother, is a tax upon the technique of any novelist. The form has been used with notable success by Miss Elizabeth Robins in

"Camilla." But Miss West has not entirely mastered its difficulties, and her failure to do so seriously mars the story.

Miss West's reputation for brilliancy has not suffered by "The Judge," but if one were to sentence her after reading it, he would be compelled to say she is no novelist. If it is an index of her imaginative capacity, of her conception of life, of her insight into conduct, of her knowledge of behaviour, we must content ourselves with her contributions as critic and guide.

The subject of her two novels is behaviourism of sexual motivation. It is an index of the change that has taken place in Great Britain within the past ten years, a change that should be acclaimed by everyone desirous of the complete emancipation of women.

Rebecca West has leaned her ear in many a secret place where rivulets dance their wayward round, and beauty born of murmuring sound has passed into her soul, to paraphrase the words of one who, were he in the flesh, would likely not meet Miss West's entire approbation.

# CHAPTER VII

## TWO LESSER LITERARY LADIES OF LONDON: STELLA BENSON AND VIRGINIA WOOLF

M ISS STELLA BENSON and Mrs. Virginia Woolf are young women who have come to the fore very rapidly. The former, who lived in this country for two years after the war, published in 1915, when she was barely out of her teens, a novel called "I Pose" which revealed an unusual personality with an uncommon outlook on life, and an enviable capacity to describe what she saw, felt, and fabricated. Until the appearance of her last novel it might be said that she created types which symbolised her ideas and attitudes and gave expression to them through conveniently devised situations, rather than attempting to paint models from life and placing them in a realistic environment.

"I Pose" is a story of allegorical cast lightened with flashes of whimsical sprightliness. A pensive Gardener who likes to pose as "original," a Suffragette who disguises romance under a mask of militancy, a practical girl, Courtesy, and a number of others take an ocean voyage and have many adventures, at the end of which the Suffragette and the Gardener find themselves in love, just as any other young people who had been dancing and playing tennis, instead of posing as individuals with convictions.

For the setting of her two succeeding books, "This is the End," and "Living Alone," Miss Benson created a world of her own, and in a foreword to the latter book she says:

"This is not a real book. It does not deal with real people, nor should it be read by real people. But there are in the world so many real books already written for the benefit of real people, and there are still so many to be written, that I cannot believe that a little alien book such as this, written for the magically-inclined minority, can be considered too assertive a trespasser."

Her world is not the traditional fairyland of the nursery, nor are the supernatural endowments of some of the characters the classic equipment of witches and fairies, although her *dramatis personæ* include both who function under the law of Magic. Rather is her dramatic machinery in these books a vehicle in the form of a sort of delicate symbolism for getting over a very sane attitude toward certain social foibles and trends of today. Incidentally it gives her opportunity of expressing this attitude in frequent witticisms and epigrammatic sayings for which she has a gift. In "Living Alone" social service and organised charity are the targets for her irony. She says,

"Perception goes out of committees. The more committees you belong to, the less of ordinary life you will understand. When your daily round becomes nothing more than a round of committees you might as well be dead . . . organizing work consists of sitting in 'busses bound for remote quarters of London, and ringing the bells of people who are almost always found to be away for a fortnight."

So after Sarah Brown, whose work consists of

"sitting every morning in a small office, collecting evidence from charitable spies about the Naughty Poor, and, after wrapping the evidence in mysterious ciphers, writing it down very beautifully upon little cards, so that the next spy might have the benefit of all his forerunners' experience,"

eats the magic sandwiches which the witch has given her for her lunch, the scales fall from her eyes. "I am sentimental," she says to herself.

STELLA BENSON

"It is sentimental to feel personal affection for a Case, or to give a child of the Naughty Poor a penny without full enquiry, or to say 'a-goo' to a grey pensive baby eating dirt on the pavement . . . or in fact to confuse in any way the ideas of charity and love."

She resigns her "job" and her place on the committees and goes to live in the House of Living Alone.

In other words, Miss Benson gives the artist in her what is called "rope." She doesn't ask herself, "Will people think I am mad, or infantile?" She doesn't care what "people think." And that is an encouraging sign. Women writers will come to their estates more quickly and securely the more whole-heartedly they abandon themselves to portraying instincts as they experience them, behaviour as they observe it, motives and conduct as they sense and encounter them, accomplishments and aspirations as they idealise them, the ideals being founded, like the chances of race horses, on past performances.

In her last novel, "The Poor Man," Miss Benson's art shows tremendous development. This story is characterisation in the finest sense. Edward, the poor man, as a psychological study, is living, vivid, almost tragically real in the reactions which betray his inherent defects—a poor devil who never gets a chance. Miss Benson preaches no sermon, points no moral, makes no plea. She gives us a slice of life—and gives it relentlessly, but justly. It is the Old Testament justice which visits the iniquity of the father upon the third and fourth generations, and leaves the reader with the congenial task of finishing the sentence by supplying the mercy without which this old world could hardly totter under the weight of this Commandment. The story, however, makes no reference either to eugenics or to religion. The application is for the reader to supply—if he is so inclined. The author is not concerned with "science," but with art. She does not bore us with a history of Edward's heredity or of his early life. She introduces him to us sitting in Rhoda Romero's room in San

Francisco—an unwelcome guest—without throwing light upon his previous existence, except that he had been "shell-shocked" and had experienced three air raids in London.

From his introduction we know Edward as we know an acquaintance, not as we know ourselves. His tragedy is his feeble mentality and still feebler temperament, and the heart of the tragedy is the contrast between his intentions and his acts. Edward always means well. He is not vicious; not lazy. But he is stupid. He wants to be decent; wants to be liked; even wants to work. He is weak, sickly, drinks too much, and there is nothing he knows how to do well. It is as a victim, rather than as an aggressive wrong-doer, that we see him secretly currying favour with school-boys he is supposed to be teaching, and ignoring their insults, selling what belongs to others, and at last robbing a boy of thirteen who has been left alone by his father in a hotel in Pekin, whence Edward has gone in headlong and blind pursuit of Emily, with whom he has become infatuated without even knowing her name. But such is the art of his delineator that one finds oneself almost pitying him when his infatuation climaxes in the declaration from Emily: "Can't you leave me alone? I can't bear you. I couldn't bear to touch you—you poor sickly thing." It is on this note that the drama ends.

If one were obliged to confine himself to backing one entry in the Fiction Sweepstakes now being run in England (entries limited to women above ten and under forty), he would do well to consider carefully the Stella Benson entry. Many would back Sheila Kaye-Smith, but the expert and seasoned bettor would be likely to find so many characteristics of the plough-horse that he would not waste his money.

Had Rose Macaulay not succumbed to smartness and become enslaved by epigram, her chances would have been excellent. As it is, she attempts to carry too much weight. The committee, the literary critics, have done what they could to lighten it, but "Mystery at Geneva" is her answer.

E. M. Delafield, Clemence Dane, and even G. B. Stern would be selected by many, no doubt. But judged from their record, not on form, they cannot be picked as winners.

The entry that is most likely to get place, if it doesn't win, is the youngest daughter of the late Sir Leslie Stephen, Mrs. Virginia Woolf.

"Mark on the Wall," her most important story, deals with the flood of thought, conscious and unconscious, when so-called abstraction is facilitated by intent gazing. The hypnotist anæsthetises the consciousness by having the subject gaze at some bright object, she by gazing at a snail. The illusion facilitates thought of the place and of the lives that have been lived there. The richness of the thought stream thus induced gives full play for her facility of expression and capacity for pen pictures.

There is in Mrs. Woolf a note of mysticism, of spirituality which reveals itself in a conscious or unconscious prayer for the elusive truth. This note of itself sets her apart from the realistic woman writers of today. Although often vividly realistic in her form, there is in her work an essence which escapes the bounds of realism. This is most strongly acknowledged in "Monday or Tuesday," a volume of short stories and sketches. The book takes its name from a little sketch of three hundred and fifty words, for which the only accurate label is "prose poem." It is a direct illustration of the author's meaning when she makes her hero say, in "The Voyage Out":

"You ought to write music. . . . Music goes straight for things. It says all there is to say at once. In writing it seems to me there's so much scratching on the match-box."

For prose writing "Monday or Tuesday" is a triumph in the elimination of "scratching on the match-box." One recognises in it the longing, more or less vaguely felt by all people, but inexpressible by most of them who are not poets, musicians, or artists in form or colour, for some supreme good which she calls truth. The New Psychology would attribute it to the unconscious and call it an ugly name. But Mrs. Woolf does not name it; she merely gives voice to the aspiration welling up from somewhere in people's deeper selves and hovering hauntingly, just out of range but near enough to colour the quality of their thoughts, even when they are occupied with the most trivial and commonplace business of life. They can never elude it, any more than they can long elude the "Hound of Heaven," but unlike the latter it is not a relentless pursuer, but a lovely, tantalising wraith—always present but never attainable or definable.

In "An Unwritten Novel," in the same collection, Mrs. Woolf again reveals a power of discernment, as well as the irony which is a part of her large human sympathy, in the conclusion of the story, which opens with:

"Such an expression of unhappiness was enough by itself to make one's eyes slide over the paper's edge to the poor woman's face—insignificant without that look, almost a symbol of human destiny with it."

During a railway journey the writer makes up a novel to fit the face of the old woman opposite her—a story of an old maid whom life had cheated, thwarted, and denied all expression of sex, and left her embittered, resentful, envious, and starved.

"They would say she kept her sorrow, suppressed her secret—her sex, they'd say—the scientific people. But what flummery to saddle her with sex!"

When she reaches her destination the old woman is met by her son—and the "story" remains unwritten.

In "A Society," Mrs. Woolf shies a few brick-bats—and well-aimed ones—at modern feminism. Her gesture is, however, more one of the irresistible impulse of the humourist to enjoy herself than any intention to do serious violence.

The members of the Society, who are a number of young girls bent upon self-education and believing that the object of life is to produce good people and good books, find themselves as a result of their investigations forced to acknowledge that if they hadn't learned to read they might still have been bearing children in ignorance, and that was the happiest life after all. By their learning they have sacrificed both their happiness and their ability to produce good people, and they are confronted, moreover, with the awful thought that if men continue to acquire knowledge they will lose their ability to produce good books.

"Unless we provide them with some innocent occupation we shall get neither good people nor good books; we shall perish beneath the fruits of their unbridled activity; and not a human being will survive to know that there once was Shakespeare."

The Society disbands with the conclusion that when a little girl has learned how to read "there's only one thing you can teach her to believe in—and that is in herself."

"Kew Gardens" is as vivid a picture as if it had been painted in colour, of the public gardens on a hot summer day, with their procession of varied humanity, old, young, and in the flush of life, each flashing for a moment with all of its own intense personality, like a figure in a cinema, before the reader, and then passing into the shadow as vague as the breath of the flowers, the buzzing of the dragon-fly, or the memories which for a moment the garden had invoked.

The two novels, "The Voyage Out," published in 1915, and "Night and Day," in 1919, are love stories in which, through the efforts of the lovers to find and express themselves, the author reveals her own ideas of life. Her machinery is largely that of dialogue between the lovers, and her chief actors are normal young men and women, wholesome in their outlook, as well as frank in their expression of their problems, which revolve largely around matrimony. The result is that while the novels are introspective in a way, as well as daring in their analysis of the author's psychology, they are free from the morbidness of many of the introspective books of today. "The Voyage Out" is the expression of healthy, normal youth reverently but straightforwardly seeking in marriage the deeper values that underlie its superficialities and justify the quality of its idealism.

In no more striking and creditable way have the women of Britain demonstrated the legitimacy of "Rights" than by their fiction of the past few years.

# CHAPTER VIII

## THE PSYCHOLOGY OF THE DIARIST: W. N. P. BARBELLION

> "The life of the soul is different. There is nothing
> more changing, more varied, more restless . . . to de-
> scribe the incidents of one hour would require eternity."—
> *Journal of Eugénie de Guérin.*

B RUCE FREDERICK CUMMINGS, an English entomologist and assistant at the Natural History Museum,
South Kensington, developed in early life an infectious disease
of the central nervous system called disseminated sclerosis,
which riddles the brain and spinal cord with little islets of
tissue resembling scars, and died of it October 22, 1919, in the
thirtieth year of his age. Six months before his death he published a book entitled "The Journal of a Disappointed Man,"
under the pen name of W. N. P. Barbellion. It is not destined
to live as long as Pepys' "Diary" or Amiel's "Journal," but it
may outlive "The Journal of Marie Bashkirtseff"—the three
great diaries of the past century. "The Journal of a Disappointed Man," in conjunction with another called "A Last
Diary," published after his death, may be looked upon as the
revelation of a conscious mind, as complete as the conscious
mind can make it. These books afford us opportunity to study
the psychology of one variety of self-revelation, just as the
books of James Joyce and Dorothy Richardson permit study
of the sub-conscious mind, and more specifically undirected or
wishful thinking, technically called autistic.

While absolute classification of people is always inaccurate
and misleading, still for the convenience of this study, in order
to bring into high relief the features which distinguish
Barbellion's diaries from the other three great self-revelations

of the conscious mind, the authors mentioned may be said to typify four distinct classes of diarists. The immortal Pepys may be dismissed with the words: pedant, philosopher, humourist. Amiel may be considered the mystic poet, with emphasis upon the spiritual side of his nature; Marie Bashkirtseff, the emotional artist whose talent was interpretive rather than creative; and Barbellion, the man of science, direct, forceful, effective on his objective side, but subjectively morbid and egocentric, unable to estimate correctly his own limitations or to direct his emotions into channels which would have made for happy living or sane thinking.

Cummings began to keep a diary when he was thirteen years old, and after seventeen years he had accumulated twenty post-quarto volumes of manuscript. Two years before his death he made an entry "Am busy rewriting, editing and bowdlerising my Journal for publication against the time when I shall have gone the way of all flesh. Reading it through again, I see what a remarkable book I have written." In it and in another small volume published posthumously, called "The Joy of Life," he said,

"You will find much of Bruce Frederick Cummings as he appears to his Maker. It is a study in the nude, with no appeal to pemmicanised intellects, but there is meaty stuff in it, raw, red or underdone."

The noteworthy features of his life may be stated briefly. He was the youngest child of a journalist known in the little town of Barnstable, in Devon, as a shrewd and facile man, and of a timid, pious mother of the lower middle class. A puny child, backward in development mentally and physically, solitary, sensitive, shy, secretive, and self-conscious, he displayed an uncommon interest in nature, birds, fishes, insects, and all wild creatures. When he was fourteen he determined to become a naturalist, but his father's illness obliged him to contribute to the family maintenance. At sixteen he wrote,

"Signed my death warrant, i.e. my articles apprenticing me to journalism for five years. By Jove, I shall work frantically during these years so as to be ready at the end of them to take up a natural history appointment."

And work he did, for in little more than a year he was offered a small appointment at the Plymouth Marine Laboratory, which he had to refuse because of his father's complete incapacity. But after another year of newspaper work and intensive study at night and at odd moments, he won an appointment in competitive examination to the staff of the Natural History Museum at South Kensington. There he remained six years, until July, 1917, when he was compelled to resign owing to the progress of his disease. In September, 1915, he married, after he had been declared unfit for military duty and after the secret of his obscure and baffling disease, and its outcome, had been revealed to some of his family and to his fiancée.

Two months after he married, despite his infirm state, he offered his services to his King and Country, having previously obtained from his own physician a letter addressed to the Medical Officer Examining Recruits. The recruiting officer promptly rejected him, so the letter was not presented. On his way home Barbellion opened it and read his death sentence. "On the whole, I am amazed at the calm way in which I take this news." At first he thought he would read up his disease in some System of Medicine, but the next day he wrote,

"I have decided never to find out what it is. I shall find out in good time by the course of events. A few years ago the news would have scared me. But not so now. It only interests me. I have been happy, merry, quite high spirited today."

But this was soon followed by depression and despair, as the progress of the disease was attested by the occurrence of rapidly increasing incapacity to get about, to use his arm, and to see. At that time he was ignorant of the fact that his wife had been informed of the nature and outcome of his disease previous to their marriage, and he was very much concerned lest she should find out. Within a year he discovered that she had known from the beginning and he was "overwhelmed with feelings of shame and self-contempt and sorrow for her."

The last months of his life were made as comfortable as possible by funds subscribed by a few literary men who had become interested in him from the publication of some chapters of the book in the London *Mercury,* and by the royalties from the publishers of the "Journal" in book form.

Barbellion's appearance, as described by his brother A. J., in the Preface to "The Last Diary," was striking. He was more than six feet tall, thin as a rake, and looked like a typical consumptive. His head was large and crowned with thick brown hair which fell carelessly about his brow; his face pale and sharply pointed; eyes deepset, lustrous and wide apart; nose slightly irregular; mouth large and firm; and chin like a rock. "Few people, except my barber, know how amourous I am. He has to shave my sinuous lips." He had an indescribable vividness of expression, great play of features, and a musical voice. His hands were strong and sensitive and he had a characteristic habit of beating the air with them in emphasising an argument. He moved and walked languidly, like a tired man, and stooped slightly, which gave him an attitude of studiousness.

Barbellion's fame depends entirely upon "The Journal of a Disappointed Man." "Enjoying Life and Other Literary Remains" is commonplace and might have been done by any one of countless writers whose years transcend their reputations. "The Last Diary," on the other hand, has a note of superficiality which is prejudicial to permanence. It suggests that it was done for effect and displays studious effort to be wise and philosophical. Although the book contains many beautiful specimens of sentiment and shows that Barbellion had enhanced his literary skill and added to his capacity for expression and sequential statement, it also shows that the processes of dissolution, physical and mental, were going on apace.

So much for the outward facts of his life. The value of the record lies entirely in the sincerity and completeness of the "portrait in the nude" which the author has painted of himself and which furnishes the basis for a psychological study of the original.

Three characteristics make the shape and colour of this portrait. Whether seen in one comprehensive glance as a composite picture, or subjected to a searching analysis of its separate parts, these three facts must be reckoned with in any estimate of his life or of his personality as a whole; or of the smallest act, thought, or emotion which entered into it. The features or leading motives which shaped the human study that Barbellion has given us in his diaries are what he calls ambition to achieve fame, a passion for the study of zoology, and a struggle against disease.

Every life which raises its possessor above the level of the clod may be called a battleground. The battle, in Barbellion's case a hard-fought one, was between ambition which inspired and actuated him and disease which seriously handicapped him during most of his life and finally caused his death—not, however, until after the victory had been won, since the odds were between fame and sickness, not between life and death. Judged, therefore, solely by the strength of the forces involved in the conflict and not at all by the value of the stakes, Barbellion's struggle and early death may claim a little of the glory suggested in the lines "Oft near the sunset are great battles won."

That the second motive mentioned, the love of zoology, entered into the conflict only as an ally, and not even an essential one, of the desire to become famous, has a special psychological interest. Unquestionable and persistent as was this passion for the science, it did not seem to form the basis for his ambition nor even to be inextricably bound up with it, as is usually the case with persons possessed of one strongly marked talent or taste combined with a dominant ambition. When nature has favoured an individual with a gift in the way of desire and ability to do one thing particularly well he usually concentrates on it. In fact the desire to achieve success through the talent, and the impulse for self-expression along the line of the talent, are so closely related that it is impossible to disentangle them and to say where the impulse for self-expression ends and the ambition to succeed begins. Barbellion's diaries, however, present no such difficulty. Conscious from early childhood of a great attraction to zoology for the sheer love of the science, his early life-plan naturally took the form of a career as a zoologist. Thwarted by circumstances, he still held to the plan with an admirable persistence and a measure of success which, considering his handicaps in the way of illness and lack of opportunities for study and training, would have been satisfactory to a less ambitious man. Such success would not, however, have given him the fame which it was the ruling motive of his life to achieve. Whether or not it was the recognition of this that determined the direction of his ambition it is impossible to say. The fact that stands out with great clearness, after reading his diaries, is that the consuming passion of his life was the desire for fame for its own sake, to be known of men, and to stand out from the mass of humanity as a man of distinction, a successful man. This seemed to be the full measure of Barbellion's ambition, and in this he succeeded, since the diaries have made him famous as the author of a record which shows him to the world as the winner of a losing game with life, though not as a scientist or as a writer of distinction.

A closer analysis of the particular qualities of Barbellion's ambition is the first step in an estimate of his personality.

The urge to keep a journal may come from within or from

without the individual. Barbellion does not tell us which it was with him. In late childhood he began making frequent records of his doings, which were those of a lonely romantic child interested in natural history. During the first three years there is no record of thought, but beginning with his sixteenth year it makes its appearance, and there is ample evidence that he was not only mature beyond his years, but ambitious as well. He says of himself,

"I was ambitious before I was breeched. I can remember wondering as a child if I were a young Macaulay or Ruskin and secretly deciding that I was. My infant mind even was bitter with those who insisted on regarding me as a normal child and not as a prodigy. Since then I have struggled with this canker for many a day, and as success fails to arrive it becomes more gnawing."

That the "canker" was eating its way into his soul as life progressed and success seemed no nearer from day to day is evidenced by the statements:

"I owe neither a knee nor a bare grammercy to any man. All that I did I did by my own initiative, save one exception. R. taught me to love music."
"I am daily facing the fact that my ambitions have over-taxed my abilities and health. For years my whole existence has rested on a false estimate of my own value, and my life has been revolving around a foolish self-deception. And I know myself as I am at last and I am not at all enamoured."

As the "Journal" progresses it becomes evident that the author's hopes for the realisation of his ambition rested entirely on its publication, and it is in the expressions concerning his hopes and fears in connection with the book that the struggle of the soul in its death grip with advancing disease and threatening failure is most poignantly expressed. Three years before he died he said,

"It is the torture of Tantalus to be so uncertain. I should be relieved to know even the worst. I would almost gladly burn my MSS. in the pleasure of having my curiosity satisfied. I go from the nadir of disappointment to the zenith of hope and back several times a week, and all the time I am additionally harassed by the perfect consciousness that it is all petty and pusillanimous to desire to be known and appreciated, that my ambition is a morbid diathesis of the mind. I am not such a fool either as not to see that there is but little satisfaction in posthumous fame, and I am not such a fool as not to realise that all fame is fleeting, and that the whole world itself is passing away."

A few months later, after a reference to his infant daughter, he said,

"If only I could rest assured that after I am dead these Journals will be as tenderly cared for—as tenderly as this blessed infant! It would be cruel if even after I have paid the last penalty, my efforts and sufferings should continue to remain unknown or disregarded. What would I give to know the effect I shall produce when published! I am tortured by two doubts—whether these MSS. (the labour and hope of many years) will survive accidental loss and whether they really are of value. I have no faith in either."

Again he wrote:

"My Journal keeps open house to every kind of happening in my soul. Provided it is a veritable autochthon—I don't care how much of a taterdemalion or how ugly or repulsive—I take him in and—I fear sponge him down with excuses to make him more creditable in other's eyes. You may say why trouble whether you do or whether you don't tell us all the beastly little subterranean atrocities that go on in your mind. Any eminently 'right-minded' *Times* or *Spectator* reader will ask: 'Who in Faith's name is interested in your retrospective muck-rakings—in fact, who the Devil are you?' To myself, a person of vast importance and vast interest, I reply—as are other men if I could but understand them as well. And in the firm belief that whatever is inexorably true however unpleasant and discreditable (in fact true things can never lack a certain dignity), I would have you know Mr. *Times*- and Mr.

*Spectator-* reader that actual crimes have many a time been enacted in the secrecy of my own heart and the only difference between· me and an habitual criminal is that the habitual criminal has the courage and the nerve and I have not. . . ."

It is more than probable that the hope of getting the "Journal" published was suggested by acquaintance with "The Journal of Marie Bashkirtseff" when Barbellion was twenty-four years old. On encountering a quotation from her in a book on Strindberg at that time, he noted,

"It would be difficult in all the world's history to discover any two persons with temperaments so alike. She is the very spit of me. We are identical. Oh, Marie Bashkirtseff, how we should have hated one another! She feels as I feel. We are of the same self-absorption, the same vanity and corroding ambition. She is impressionable, volatile, passionate—ill, so am I. Her Journal is my Journal. She has written down all my thoughts and forestalled me. Is there anything in the transmigration of souls? She died in 1886. I was born in 1889."

Barbellion's own estimate of what he calls his ambition is well summed up in the following words:

"My life appears to have been a titanic struggle between consuming ambition and adverse fortune. Behold a penniless youth thirsting for knowledge introduced into the world out of sheer devilment, with a towering ambition, but cursed with ill health and a two-fold nature, pleasure loving as well as labour loving."

It would be interesting to find out in what way he was pleasure loving. As far as I can see from reading the "Journal," the only pleasure that he sought was the occasional pleasure of contemplating nature, which was really a part of his work, and from hearing music.

"You can search all history and fiction for an ambition more powerful than mine and not find it. No, not Napoleon, nor Wilhelm II, nor Keats. No, I am not proud of it, not at all. The wonder is that I remain sane, the possessed of such a demon."

In the same way it is difficult to find evidence of this colossal ambition, save his statement of it. In reality he was ambitious for one thing: call it favour, applause, publicity, notoriety, or what not. He wanted to do something in literature which would focus the vision of the world upon him, and to accomplish this he devoted an incredible energy and labour to the production of a diary which was the record of aggressive, directed, logical thinking. He may have had capacity for creative literature, or he may have developed such capacity, but he did not display it. His career can be compared with no other because of the immeasurable handicap of his illness. But if it were not for this illness, it would be interesting to compare him with Huysmans, who, working as a clerk in a Governmental office in Paris, produced a series of books which gave him a commanding and perhaps a permanent place in French literature.

Unquestionably some resemblance exists between the passion for fame, or whatever it may be called, that Barbellion and Marie Bashkirtseff had in common, although in the case of the latter its relation to a definite talent was more evident. But that in either of the two cases it partook in any great measure of the nature of what is generally understood as ambition—the ambition, for instance, of Napoleon, Wilhelm II, or Keats to whom Barbellion compares himself—is not proved by either of their self-revelations. There is a quality well known to psychologists that may be described as the passion to attract attention, which is a distinguishing attribute of the neurotic temperament. It sometimes acts as an urge to the expression of a talent in case the possessor of the temperament is also the possessor of a talent—which is by no means infrequent and which was undoubtedly true in the case of Marie Bashkirtseff. It, however, exists in innumerable other cases where the neurotic has been gifted by nature with no special talent or ability for expression of any kind. The mere reiteration, therefore, of a passion to focus the attention of the world upon himself, while it would invite questions as to his balance or the lack of it, affords no proof of mental qualities upon which the hope of achieving such distinction might reasonably be placed.

The next question which arises in relation to Barbellion's ambition or desire for distinction is: What were his intellectual possessions? And the first step in answering this question is the examination of his interests. By a man's admirations, as by his friends, you may know him. He identified himself, in a measure, with Keats; he had great admiration for Sir Thomas Browne; James Joyce was a writer after his own heart; and he admired Dostoievsky and Francis Thompson.

Barbellion's objective intellect stands out rather clearly in his record, particularly as the evidence is written more forcibly between the lines than in his statements. Deduction, induction, and analysis are rather high. In fact, he possessed wisdom, ingenuity, caution, and perception; that is, the elements of objective thought. He showed no great ability to estimate the nature and bearing of his surroundings or to devise ways of dealing with them so as to turn them to his advantage, but had it not been for illness he might have done so. As to the actual results of his intellectual efforts, naturalists say he made some important contributions to their science; and, although these were trifling, they were in the right direction. His working life really ended at twenty-five, an age at which the working life of most men of science has scarcely begun.

It is almost entirely upon his subjective thought, that is upon his estimate of himself, that the value of his record rests. Everyone in his progress through life and his intercourse with his fellows measures himself more or less deliberately against, and estimates his own capacity relatively to, theirs, not only with respect to wisdom, cleverness, or caution, but with respect to special accomplishments. Besides this relative estimate, he learns to form an absolute estimate of his intellectual powers. He knows what he can understand at once, what he has to study hard before he can understand, and what is wholly beyond his comprehension. Some people habitually underestimate their ability; others, the majority, overestimate it. It is very difficult to say, from the literary remains of Barbellion, whether he was of the latter class or not. He had literary taste, a prodigious appetite, and he displayed considerable capacity for assimilation. It is quite possible that, as the result of these, he might have revealed constructive imagination; but his life was very brief, it was riddled with illness, and he matured slowly.

Barbellion's estimate of himself may be fairly judged by the epitome of his whole life which he made in an entry of August 1, 1917, in connection with his retirement from the staff of the British Museum:

"I was the ablest junior on the staff and one of the ablest zoologists in the place, but my ability was always muffled by the inferior work given me to do. My last memoir was the best of its kind in treatment, method and technique—not the most important—that ever was issued from the institution. It was trivial because the work given me was always trivial, the idea being that as I had enjoyed no academic career I was unsuited to fill other posts then vacant—two requiring laboratory training—which were afterwards filled by men of less powers than my own. There was also poor equipment for work and I had to struggle for success against great odds. In time I should have revolutionised the study of Systematic Zoology, and the anonymous paper I wrote in conjunction with R. in the *American Naturalist* was a rare *jeu d'esprit,* and my most important scientific work. In the literary world I fared no better. I first published an article at fifteen, over my father's name. My next story was unexpectedly printed in the *Academy* at the age of nineteen. The American *Forum* published an article, but for years I received back rejected manuscript from every conceivable kind of publication from *Punch* to the *Hibbert Journal.* Recently, there has been evidence of a more benevolent attitude towards me on the part of London editors. A certain magnificent quarterly has published one or two of my essays. . . . I fear, however, the flood-tide has come too late."

In regard to one of the essays, he noted that it called forth flattering comment in *Public Opinion*, but that it did not impress anybody else, even E., his wife, who did not read the critique, although she read twice a pleasant paragraph in the press noticing some drawings of a friend.

It was one of Barbellion's persecutory ideas that he was not appreciated at his full value.

"Ever since I came into the world I have felt an alien in this life, a refugee by reason of some prenatal extradiction. I always felt alien to my father and mother. I was different from them. I knew and was conscious of the detachment. I admired my father's courage and happiness of soul, but we were very far from one another. I loved my mother, but we had little in common."

When his mother warned him that he was in danger of being friendless all his life because of his preference for acerbities to amenities he replied, "I don't want people to like me. I shan't like them. Theirs will be the greater loss."

His family feeling seems to have been concentrated largely on his brother, A. J., who prefixed a brief account of his life and character to "The Last Diary."

Of him Barbellion said,

"He is a most delightful creature and I love him more than anyone else in the wide world. There is an almost feminine tenderness in my love."

There were times when, despite his habitual self-appreciation, Barbellion sold his stock fairly low, and especially after he had been in London for two or three years and realised what little progress he was making in the world and how small the orbit of his activity remained.

"I have more than a suspicion that I am one of those who grow sometimes out of a brilliant boy into a very commonplace man."

In speaking of his personal appearance he said, "I am not handsome, but I look interesting, I hope distinguished"; and at another time,

"If sometimes you saw me in my room by myself, you would say that I was a ridiculous coxcomb. For I walk about, look out of the window, then at the mirror—turning my head sideways perhaps so as to see it in profile. Or I gaze down into my eyes—my eyes always impress me—and wonder what effect I produce upon others. This, I believe, is not so much vanity as curiosity."

Naturally Barbellion's estimate of himself and of his potentialities varied from time to time, but he never rated his abilities lower than the sum total of his accomplishments would seem to justify, save in hours of extreme depression and discouragement. When twenty-one years of age he wrote,

"Sometimes I think I am going mad. I live for days in the mystery and tears of things so that the commonest object, the most familiar face—even my own—becomes ghostly, unreal, enigmatic. I get into an attitude of almost total scepticism, nescience, solipsism even, in a world of dumb, sphinx-like things that cannot explain themselves. The discovery of how I am situated—a sentient being on a globe in space overshadows me. I wish I were just nothing."

A more hopeful note, and one that is of interest in that it foreshadows the plan of publication of the diary, is sounded after he had been working in the museum for less than a year.

"My own life as it unrolls itself day by day is a source of constant amazement, delight and pain. I can think of no more interesting volume than a distilled, intimate, psychological history of my own life. I want a perfect comprehension at least of myself. We are all such egoists that a sorrow or hardship—provided it is great enough—flatters our self-importance."

At the age of twenty-five Barbellion had reached the depth of depression and discouragement.

"I have peered into every aspect of my life and achievement and everything I have seen nauseates me. My life seems to have been a wilderness of futile endeavour. I started wrong from the very beginning. I came into the world in the wrong place and under the wrong conditions. As a boy I was preternaturally absorbed in myself and preternaturally discontented. I harassed myself with merciless cross examinations."

A year later he checked up on such moods and said,

"My sympathy with myself is so unfailing that I don't deserve anybody else's. In many respects, however, this Journal I believe gives the impression that I behave myself in the public gaze much worse than I actually do."

Man is invariably judged finally by his conduct. Opinion is often formed of him from what he says, but the last analysis is a review and estimate of the several activities which together constitute conduct. Conduct is the pursuit of ends. The conduct that is conditioned by taking thought does not by any means embrace all one's activities. The biological discoveries of the latter half of the Nineteenth Century showed conclusively that the ultimate end to which all life is directed and toward which every living being strives is the continuation of the race to which the individual belongs. Life becomes, therefore, a trust, not a gift, and the only way in which the obligation it entails can be discharged is by transmitting life to a new generation. Barbellion had bodily characteristics which permit the biologist to say that his gonadal redex was dominant, and throughout the diary there are frequent entries showing that, despite his shyness, self-consciousness, and lack of "Facility" (using the word in its Scottish sense), the opposite sex made profound appeal to him. His conduct from early youth would seem to indicate that he held with the Divine Poet—

"—In alte dolcezze
Non si puo gioir, se non amando."

But his love was evanescent and he was continually asking himself if it was real or but the figment of desire.

"To me woman is *the* wonderful fact of existence. If there be any next world and it be as I hope it is, a jolly gossiping place with people standing around the mantelpiece and discussing their earthly experiences, I shall thump my fist on the table as my friends turn to me on entering and exclaim in a loud voice, 'Woman!'"

Here and there in the "Journal" there are entries which would indicate that his conduct with women transgressed conventions, though perhaps in harmony with custom. When he was twenty-five he went to see the "Irish Play Boy," and sitting in front of him was a charming little Irish girl, accompanied by a man whose appearance and manner were repulsive. He flirted with her successfully. Later, haunted with the desire to meet her, he sent a personal advertisement to a newspaper hoping that her eye would encounter it. The advertisement and the money were returned, as it was suspected that he was a white slave trafficker. His admiration of the Don Juan type of man is evidenced by an entry in which he referred to his friendship with a bachelor of sixty, a devotee of love and strong drink.

"This man is my devoted friend and truth to tell I get on with him better than I do with most people. I like his gamey flavour, his utter absence of self-consciousness and his doggy loyalty to myself. He may be depraved in his habits, coarse in his language, boorish in his manners, ludicrous in the wrongness of his views, but I like him just because he is so hopeless. If he only dabbled in vice, if he had pale, watery ideas about current literature, if he were genteel, I should quarrel."

The entries that show Barbellion's attitude toward what may be called the minor activities of social life are illuminating. These are the latest activities to be acquired and, in a way, testify to or set forth the individual's development or limitations.

Companionship with one's fellows is necessary to the mental health of man, and it is of prime necessity that he should secure their good opinion. The loss of esteem and the knowledge that he is reprobated and held in contempt and aversion causes a stress that invariably has its baneful effect, particularly upon a sensitive, self-conscious youth.

Barbellion was the type of individual who sits in ready judgment on his fellows, and oftentimes his judgment was violently prejudiced. He had little community feeling. As a youngster he was ostracised by his school fellows because he was different, and he felt alien. He never played games with them, but went off on long solitary rambles after school hours. Nor did he form intimacies with his masters.

"I presented such an invertebrate, sloppy, characterless exterior that no one felt curious enough to probe further into my ways of life. It was the same in London. I was alien to my colleagues. Among them only R. has ventured to approach my life and seek a communion with me. My wife and child seem at a remote distance from me."

In another connection he says,

"A day spent among my fellows goads me to a frenzy by the evening. I am no longer fit for human companionship. People string me up to concert pitch. I develop suspicions of one that he is prying, or of another that he patronises. Others make me horribly anxious to stand well in their eyes and horribly curious to know what they think of me. Others I hate and loathe for no particular reason. There is a man I am acquainted with concerning whom I know nothing at all. I should like to smash his face in. I don't know why."

Barbellion retained many infantile traits in his adult years and these were displayed in his attitude and conduct toward people.

At twenty-six he said,

"I have grown so ridiculously hypercritical and fastidious that I will refuse a man's invitation to dinner because he has watery blue eyes, or hate him for a mannerism or an impediment or affectation in his speech. Some poor devil who has not heard of Turner or Debussy or Dostoievsky I gird at with the arrogance of a knowledgeable youth of seventeen. . . . I suffer from such a savage *amour propre* that I fear to enter the lists with a man I dislike on account of the mental anguish I should suffer if he worsted me. I am therefore bottled up so tight—both my hates and loves . . . if only I had the moral courage to play my part in life—to take the stage and be myself, to enjoy the delightful sensation of making my presence felt, instead of this vapourish mumming. To me self-expression is a necessity of life, and what cannot be expressed one way must be expressed in another. When colossal egotism is driven underground, whether by a steely surface environment or an unworkable temperament or, as in my case, by both, you get a truly remarkable pain—the pain one might say of continuously unsuccessful attempts at parturition."

This may seem adorned and artificial, but to me it is the most illuminating entry in the "Journal" and reveals many of his limitations.

At twenty-eight he made the entry,

"The men I meet accept me as an entomologist and *ipso facto*, an enthusiast in the science. That is all they know of me, and all they want to know of me, or of any man. Surely no man's existence was ever quite such a duplicity as mine. I smile bitterly to myself ten times a day, as I engage in all the dreary technical jargon of professional talk with them. How they would gossip over the facts of my life if they knew! How scandalised they would be over my inner life's activities, how resentful of enthusiasm other than entomological!"

It would have contributed to his peace of mind had he studied more closely the writings of the immortal physician of Norwich, from whom he believed he had spiritual descent:

"No man can justly censure or condemn another; because indeed no man truly knows another. This I perceive in myself; for I am in the dark to all the world; and my nearest friends behold me but in a cloud. Those that know me superficially think less of me than I do of myself; those of my near acquaintance think more; God who truly knows me knows that I am nothing. Further no man can judge another, because no man knows himself; for we censure others but as they disagree from that humour which we fancy laudable in ourselves, and commend others but for that wherein they seem to quadrate and consent with us. So that in conclusion, all is but that we all condemn, self-love."

Self-love, or over-appreciation of self, was Barbellion's most serious stumbling-block. He never got himself in the right perspective with the world, and it is unlikely, even though his brief life had been less tragic, that he would have succeeded in doing so. He was temperamentally unfit.

Barbellion's friends say that he was courteous and soft mannered, but his own estimate of capacity for display of the amenities is so at variance with this that we are forced to believe the manner they saw was veneer.

The following description of Lermontov by Maurice was, he averred, an exact picture of himself:

"He had, except for a few intimate friends, an impossible temperament; he was proud; overbearing, exasperated and exasperating, filled with a savage *amour-propre,* and he took a childish delight in annoying; he cultivated 'le plaisir aristocratique de deplair.' . . . He could not bear not to make himself felt and if he was unsuccessful in this by fair means he resorted to unpleasant ones."

Two years later he expressed much the same opinion of his social characteristics when he described himself as something between a monkey, a chameleon, and a jellyfish and made himself out an intellectual bully. He was honest enough not to omit an invariable trait of the bully—cowardice. He says,

"The humiliating thing is that almost any strong character hypnotises me into complacency, especially if he is a stranger. . . . But by Jove, I wreak vengeance on my familiars, and on those brethren even weaker than myself. They get my concentrated gall, my sulphurous fulminations, and would wonder to read this confession."

In order that any community may exist and thrive each individual must do things for the common welfare. He must regulate his activity so as not to impair or jeopardise the property and self-respect of his neighbours. He must contribute to its existence and development by an active execution of deeds that draw more closely the bonds of fellowship and knit more securely the fabric of society. He must exercise self-restraint in those countless ways by which the conduct of a person in the presence of others is shorn of indulgences which he allows himself when alone, and he must perform those ceremonies and benevolences which constitute politeness and courtesy. The unwritten law which compels these in order that he may have a reputation for "normalcy" is even more inexorable than the written law which compels him to pay taxes and serve on juries and does not permit him to beat carpets or rugs in the open. Although Barbellion seemed to be very keen in participating in the defence of the country against external foes, his diary does not reveal that he had any desire to undertake municipal, political, or social duties. Illness may explain this, but illness did not keep him from recording the desire to do so or the regret that he was prevented from participation in the full life.

Every estimate of Barbellion must take his illness into consideration. Readily might he subscribe to Sir Thomas Browne's statement, "For the world, I count it not as an inn, but an hospital; and a place not to live, but to die in." In the first entries of the diary he speaks of being ill, and although the disease of which he died is not habitually associated with mental or emotional symptoms, it is nevertheless so horribly incapacitating and is accompanied by such distressing evidences of disturbed bodily functions that it invariably tinges the victim's thoughts with despondency and tinctures his emotional activities with despair.

Barbellion capitalised his infirmity to an extraordinary degree. He says we are all such egotists that a sorrow or hardship, provided it is great enough, flatters our self-importance. We feel that a calamity by overtaking us has distinguished us above our fellows. Were it not for his illness his book would never have found a publisher, for it is not a psychological history of his own life—which he believed would make such an interesting volume—but a Pepysian record of his doings, which, taken *in toto,* is fairly drab. It was the display of equanimity, resignation, and courage when confronted with the inevitable, and the record of his thoughts during that time that give the book its value and vogue. He was constantly fighting disease and cognisant of his waning strength.

"I do not fear ill health in itself, but I do fear its possible effect on my mind and character. Already my sympathy with myself is maudlin. As long as I have spirit and buoyancy I don't care what happens, for I know that so long I cannot be counted a failure."

This is one of the keynotes of his character—that he shall not be counted a failure. The other—and it is the same—keynote, is that he shall be a success; that he will make a noise in the world.

The entries after he had got a two-months' sick leave are pathetic. He was on the point of proposing marriage; he had been to see a well-known nerve specialist who said that a positive diagnosis could not be made; he had set out for his holiday at the seaside and had a most depressing time. When he returned to London he was no better; in fact he was much worse, and had thoughts of suicide. After he had found out the nature of his disease he expressed himself with great fortitude, saying,

"My life has become entirely posthumous. I live now in the grave and am busy furnishing it with posthumous joys. I accept my fate with great content, my one-time restless ambition lies asleep now, my one-time furious self-assertiveness is anæsthetised by this great war; the war and the discovery about my health together have plucked out of me that canker of self-obsession . . . for I am almost resigned to the issue in the knowledge that some day, someone will know, perhaps somebody will understand and—immortal powers!—even sympathise, 'the quick heart quickening from the heart that's still.' "

Barbellion's account of his experience with physicians engenders sadness. He went from general practitioner to chest specialists, digestion specialists, ophthalmologists, neurologists, without ever getting the smallest intimation of the nature of his illness, until it had progressed to an advanced stage. For a long time, indeed, it seemed to baffle all the physicians who were consulted. One of the distresses of the diary is that it testifies that doctors are far from omniscient. Nearly always he was advised to go and live on the prairies; and, like all sufferers from incurable diseases, the quacks finally got him.

With the spectre of disease always lurking in the background, when not taking an evident part in the drama of Barbellion's life, it is inevitable that his attitude toward death should colour his thoughts to a very marked degree. As early as 1912, when he was twenty-three years old, he wrote, "As an egoist I hate death because I should cease to be I"; and the next year,

"What embitters me is the humiliation of having to die, to have to be pouring out the precious juices of my life into the dull earth, to be no longer conscious of what goes on, no longer moving abroad upon the earth creating attractions and repulsions, pouring out one's ego in a stream. To think that the women I have loved will be marrying and forget, and that the men I have hated will continue on their way and forget I ever hated them—the ignominy of being dead!"

If this latter entry had been written a few years later, one might suspect the influence of Rupert Brooke. As the date stands, one can only infer that Barbellion, in spite of his much vaunted morbidity, possessed a little of the zest of life which so richly flavoured the genius of that young poet.

The entries in the "Journal" after the nature of his disease had been made known to him express a marked difference in his attitude toward death. In 1917 he said,

"I ask myself; what are my views on death, the next world, God? I look into my mind and discover I am too much of a mannikin to have any. As for death, I am a little bit of trembling jelly of anticipation. I am prepared for anything, but I am the complete agnostic; I simply don't know. To have views, faith, beliefs, one needs a backbone. This great bully of a universe overwhelms me. The stars make me cower. I am intimidated by the immensity surrounding my own littleness. It is futile and presumptuous for me to opine anything about the next world. But I *hope* for something much freer and more satisfying after death, for emancipation of the spirit and, above all, for the obliteration of this puny self, this little, skulking, sharp-witted ferret."

This, one might almost say, shows Barbellion at his best.

A power of fancy which is displayed in few other connections throughout the book made him say, during the same year,

"What a delightful thing the state of death would be if the dead passed their time haunting the places they loved in life and living over again the dear delightful past—if death were one long indulgence in the pleasures of memory! If the disembodied spirit forgot all the pains of its previous existence and remembered only the happiness! Think of me flitting about the orchards and farmyards in——— birdnesting, walking along the coast among the seabirds, climbing Exmoor, bathing in streams and in the sea, haunting all my old loves and passions, cutting open with devouring curiosity Rabbits, Pigeons, Frogs, Dogfish, Amphioxus; think of me, too, at length unwillingly deflected from these cherished pursuits in the raptures of first love, cutting her initials on trees and fences instead of watching birds, day-dreaming over *Parker and Haswell* and then bitterly reproaching myself later for much loss of precious time. How happy I shall be if Death is like this; to be living over again and again all my ecstasies, over first times. . . . My hope is that I may haunt these times again, that I may haunt the places, the books, the bathes, the walks, the desires, the hopes, the first (and last) loves of my life all transfigured and beatified by sovereign Memory."

Nothing in the diaries illustrates more strikingly Barbellion's zest for living than these allusions to death. In the first decade of life, the average person gives no thought as to whether he will live or die; in the second decade he rarely becomes concerned with thoughts of death unless they are forced upon him by painful or persistent illness. In the third decade, when the fear of death is very common, Barbellion knew that he must soon die. This flair for life, which he must have possessed to a marked degree, is evidenced in his love of nature and in his appreciation of beauty and of literature to an immensely greater extent than in contact with his fellows. His pleasure in æsthetics was real and profound, and included an appreciation of sound, colour, and form, both in nature and in art. His capacity for the appreciation of beauty of sound was greater than for the beauty of colour or form. Although apparently he had never studied music, he said of Beethoven's Fifth Symphony that it "always worked me up into an ecstasy"; and after listening to music by Tschaikovsky, Debussy, and others that, "I am chock-full of all this precious stuff and scarcely know what to write."

Whether or not his suspicion that "my growing appreciation of the plastic art is with me only distilled sensuality" was true, the appreciation was unquestionably genuine, as shown by his comment on Rodin's "The Prodigal Son" that it was "Beethoven's Fifth Symphony done in stone. It was only on my second visit that I noticed the small pebble in each hand—a superb touch—what a frenzy of remorse!", and on "The Fallen Angel" that "The legs of the woman droop lifelessly backwards in an intoxicating curve. The eye caresses it—down the thighs and over the calves to the tips of the toes—like the hind legs of some beautiful dead gazelle."

Above his appreciation of æsthetic beauty, however, Barbellion realised, theoretically at least, that the topmost levels of pleasure and pain are constituted of qualities dependent upon achievements of the moral order—of duty well done, of happiness conferred, of services rendered, of benefits bestowed; or of the antithesis, of remorse for abstention and neglect of these or for active misdeeds. He says in "The Last Diary,"

"Under the lens of scientific analysis natural beauty disappears. The emotion of beauty and the spirit of analysis and dissection cannot exist contemporaneously. But just as man's scientific analysis destroys beauty, so his synthetic art creates it. And man creates beauty, nature supplying the raw materials. Because there is beauty in man's own heart, he naïvely assumes its possession by others and so projects it into nature. But he sees in her only the truth and goodness that are in himself. Natural beauty is everyone's mirror."

Barbellion's strong sense of moral values was always coloured by his passion—which was almost a mania for receiving appreciation and applause. Although he denied wanting to be liked, respected, and admired, yet he clamoured for it. He displayed pain upon receiving the marks of disapprobation, and reproof he disliked and despised.

He was singularly free from spontaneous disorder of will; that is, of delay, vacillation, and precipitation. The only evidence he gave of vacillation was about his marriage, and that showed his good judgment. He was much more inclined to precipitation than to vacillation, and for a neurotic individual he was strangely without obsession—that is the morbid desire to do some act which the would-be performer discountenances and struggles not to do.

With all his sensitiveness, Barbellion seemed to have been not without an element of cruelty. This was of the refined, indirect sort and was chiefly noticeable in references to his wife. While he was contemplating a proposal of marriage he made an entry in his diary,

"I tried my best, I have sought every loophole of escape, but I am quite unable to avoid the melancholy fact that her thumbs are lamentable. Poor dear, how I love her! That is why I am so concerned about her thumbs."

In speaking of his fianceé's letters, he once wrote,

"These letters chilled me. In reply I wrote with cold steel short, lifeless, formal notes, for I felt genuinely aggrieved that she should care so little how she wrote to me or how she expressed her love. I became ironical with myself over the prospect of marrying a girl who appeared so little to appreciate my education and mental habits."

Two years later he added to this entry "What a popinjay!" But then two years later he was a confirmed invalid and she was making great sacrifice to take care of him.

In another place he taunted her, after admitting her letters disappointed him with their coldness, and added, "Write as you would speak. You know I am not one to carp about a spelling mistake"; and at another time he recorded,

"My life here has quite changed its orientation. I am no longer an intellectual snob. If I were E. and I would have parted ere now. I never like to take her to the British Museum because there all the values are intellectual."

Of his wife the diaries give a very vague picture. Once he exclaimed, "To think that she of all women, with a past such as hers, should be swept into my vicious orbit!" but no information is given regarding this past. The idea of marriage was in his thoughts for several years, but his attitude was one of doubt and vacillation. In 1914 he wrote:

"I wish I loved more steadily. I am always sidetracking myself. The title of 'husband' scares me."

When he finally recorded his marriage as having taken place at the Registry Office he added,

"It is impossible to set down here all the labyrinthine ambages of my will and feelings in regard to this event. Such incredible vacillations, doubts and fears."

"The function of the private journal is one of observation, experiment, analysis, contemplation; the function of the essay is to provoke reflection," wrote Amiel. Barbellion's observation was of himself and of nature; his experiment how to adjust himself to the world; his analysis almost exclusively of his ego; and his contemplation the mystery of life and death. A "sport" in the biological sense, that is, differing markedly from his immediate ancestors, he fell afoul of infection early in life. From the beginning it scarred and debilitated him.

He was an egotist and proud of it. He did not realise that the ego is a wall which limits the view rising higher with every emotional or intellectual growth. There is a certain degree of greatness from which, when a man reaches it, he can always look over the top of the wall of his egotism. Barbellion never reached it. He was a man above the ordinary, capable of originality and of learning from experience, clever at his profession, apt at forming general ideas, sometimes refined and sometimes gross; a solitary, full of contradictions, ironic or ingenuous by fits, tormented by sexual images and sentimental ideas, and possessed by the desire to become famous, but haunted by the fear that he would not live to see his desire accomplished.

He had the misfortune to be without faith or ability to acquire it, but in compensation he was given to an envious degree immunity to fear, and he endured disease and faced death with courage and resignation. If we contrast his thought and conduct with that of another egotist, Robert Louis Stevenson, after he came to know the number of days that remained for him, as thought and conduct are recorded in the "Vailima Letters," Barbellion suffers from the comparison, for Stevenson was devoid of vanity and selfishness. But the comparison would not be a just one, for euphoria is a feature of the disease with which Stevenson contended, and despair of Barbellion's. Moreover, Stevenson was a Celt and had a sense of humour. Everyone likes to think that his distinguishing characteristic is a sense of humour. Barbellion believed he possessed it tremendously. He may have, but his books do not reveal it.

He forced himself without academic training upon a most conservative institution, a close corporation, archaically conventionalised, and he gave earnest that he could mount the ladder of preferment quickly and gracefully.

He saw himself with the lucidity of genius, but his admirers will not admit that he was the man he said he was. One admirer does.

Would that he had added to his litany: *Defenda me, Dios, de me!*—The Lord deliver me from myself. Had he done so, he would have accomplished to a greater degree the object of life: to be happy and to make others happy.

# CHAPTER IX

## THE PSYCHOLOGY OF THE DIARIST: HENRI-FRÉDÉRIC AMIEL

> "True serenity does not consist in indifference to the
> phenomena of life amongst which we live. It consists
> of judging in an elevated way men and facts. True
> serenity does not reign apart from life. It is in the land
> of the hurricane that it is a grand virtue to know how
> to remain calm. Possibly he who can accomplish this
> will succeed in avoiding its perils, or surmounting its
> consequences. Perhaps it is better to lose one's foothold
> in the waves than it is to prosper in a solitude without
> echo. Only solitude that has been wrought from the
> tumult is precious."—GEORGES DUHAMEL.

NO brief statement ever made applies more fittingly to
Henri-Frédéric Amiel—more widely known now, one
hundred years after his birth, than during his lifetime—than
these words of one of the most promising young men of letters
of France.

Amiel says in his "Journal Intime":

"There remains the question whether the greatest problems
which have ever been guessed on earth had not better have
remained buried in the brain which found the key to them,
and whether the deepest thinkers—those whose hand has been
boldest in drawing aside the veil, and their eye keenest in
fathoming the mystery beyond it—had not better, like the
prophet of Iliom, have kept for Heaven, and for Heaven alone,
secrets and mysteries which human language cannot truly
express nor human intelligence conceive."

"To win true peace, a man needs to feel himself directed,
pardoned, and sustained by a supreme power, to feel himself
in the right road, at the point where God would have him be
—in order with God and the universe. This faith gives
strength and calm. I have not got it. All that is, seems to me
arbitrary and fortuitous. It may as well not be, as be. Noth-

ing in my own circumstances seems to me providential. All appears to me left to my own responsibility, and it is this thought which disgusts me with the government of my own life. I longed to give myself up wholly to some great love, some noble end; I would willingly have lived and died for the ideal—that is to say, for a holy cause. But once the impossibility of this made clear to me, I have never since taken a serious interest in anything, and have, as it were, but amused myself with a destiny of which I was no longer the dupe."

"There is a great affinity in me with the Hindoo genius—that mind, vast, imaginative, loving, dreamy, and speculative, but destitute of ambition, personality, and will. Pantheistic disinterestedness, the effacement of the self in the great whole, womanish gentleness, a horror of slaughter, antipathy to action—these are all present in my nature, in the nature at least which has been developed by years and circumstances. Still the West has also had its part in me. What I have found difficult is to keep up a prejudice in favour of any form, nationality, or individuality whatever. Hence my indifference to my own person, my own usefulness, interest, or opinions of the moment. What does it all matter? *Omnis determinatio est negatio.* Grief localises us, love particularises us, but thought delivers us from personality. . . . To be a man is a poor thing, to be a man is well; to be *the* man—man in essence and in principle—that alone is to be desired." (Written at the age of fifty-four.)

The "Journal Intime," upon which alone Amiel's fame rests, is studded with such expressions, all of which go to prove that he was handicapped with an inability to participate in life. One may call it aboulia, or lack of will power; but it was not lack of will power. That the intellect which could produce such work was not directed into some practical channel during a long and healthy life naturally arouses a question; and this question has been answered by Amiel's admirers and his critics in various ways. The only conclusion, however, to which an unbiassed examination of his life and of his book can lead is the simple one that Amiel was born that way, just

HENRI-FRÉDÉRIC AMIEL

as some people are born Albinos, or, to put it in other words, that he was temperamentally unfit for practical life.

Henri-Frédéric Amiel was born in Geneva September 27, 1821, and died there March 11, 1881. His ancestors were Huguenots who sought refuge in Switzerland after the revocation of the Edict of Nantes. There is no record that any of them achieved greatness or had greatness thrust upon them. Very little has been written of his parents, who died when he was twelve years old, or of his uncle and aunt, in whose house he was brought up apart from his two sisters. All those who have written about Amiel himself are singularly silent about his boyhood, so that we know practically nothing of the formative years of his life save that he was a sensitive, impressionable boy, more delicate than robust, disposed to melancholy, and with a deep interest in religious problems. In school and college he was studious but not brilliant; he had no interest in games or sports and made few intimacies, and these with men older than himself. When he was nineteen he came under the influence of a Genevan philologist and man of letters, Adolphe Picquet, whose lectures answered many a positive question and satisfied many a vague aspiration of this youth already in the meshes of mysticism. They exercised a decisive influence over his thought, filled him with fresh intuitions, and brought near to him the horizons of his dreams.

When he was twenty he went to Italy and stayed more than a year, and while there he wrote several articles on Christian Art, and a criticism of a book by M. Rio. The next four years he spent in Germany, where he studied philosophy, philology, mythology, and history. After this he travelled about the university cities of Central Europe for two years, principally Heidelberg, Munich, and Vienna; and in 1849, when he was twenty-eight years old, he returned to Geneva and secured the appointment of Professor of Moral Philosophy in the Academy there. The appointment was made by the Democratic Party, which had just then come into control of the Government.

The Aristocratic Party, which had had things their own way since the days following the restoration of Geneva's independence in 1814, would have nothing to do with intellectual upstarts, puppets of the Radical Party, so Amiel, by nature and conviction a conservative, found himself in the right pew, but the wrong church; and many of his friends thought that the discouragement which was manifest in his writings and in his conduct may, in a measure at least, have been due to the conflict between his discomfiture and his duty.

He had few friends, but these he impressed enormously by his learning and his knowledge. He made no particular reputation as a professor or as a poet, and had it not been for the "Journal," he would never have been heard of save by his friends and pupils. It is now forty years since the first volume of the book was published at Geneva. It had been put together from the thousands of sheets of diary which had come into the hands of his literary heirs. The Preface to the volume announced that this "Journal" was made up of his psychological observations and impressions produced on him by books. It was the confidant of his private and intimate thoughts; a means whereby the thinker became conscious of his own inner life; a safe shelter wherein his questionings of fate and future, the voice of grief, of self-examination and confession, the soul's cry for inward peace might make themselves freely heard.

It made a great noise in the world and the reverberations of it will not cease.

Some consider that the "Journal Intime" occupies a unique place in literature, not because it is a diary of introspection, but because of the tragedy which attended its production. This is the height of absurdity. There was no tragedy about its production. Amiel lived an unhealthy life, thwarted nature's laws, and nature exacted the penalty. N. J. Symons, in an article in the *Queen's Quarterly*, says, "To be gifted with the qualities of genius, yet to be condemned by some obscure psychosis to perpetual sterility and failure; to live and die in the despairing recognition of this fact; and finally to win posthumous fame by the analysis and confession of one's failure is one of the most puzzling and pathetic of life's anomalies." It would be if it were true. But what were the qualities of genius that Amiel had? And how did he display the obscure psychosis? He discharged the duties of a professor from the time he was twenty-eight until he was sixty. He poetised pleasantly; he communed with nature and got much pleasure from it; and he had very definite social adaptability. His general level of behaviour was high. He was a diligent, methodical worker; he reacted in a normal way to conventional standards; he had few personal biases or peculiarities and none that drew particular attention to him; and he seemed to have adjusted himself without great difficulty to the incidences of life that he encountered.

To say that such a man was the victim of some obscure psychosis is either to speak beyond the facts or to speak from the possession of some knowledge that is denied one familiar with his writings and what has been written about him.

Unique the "Journal Intime" unquestionably is, in that it is the sincere confession of failure, both as a man and as a writer, of a man whose intellectual qualities justified his friends in expecting from him a large measure of success as both. Both admirers and critics agree that Amiel's failure was his refusal or his inability to act. This refusal to act was not the expression of some obscure psychosis, but was entirely consistent with his philosophy of life, which was arrived at through a logical process of thought. "Men's thoughts are made according to their nature," says Bacon. It is to Amiel's nature, or temperament, or personality, that we must look for the answer to the question: To what can his confessed failure be charged?

Any estimate of personality must weigh not only the capacity for dealing with thoughts, but the capacity for dealing with men and with things as well. Intellectual qualities are of value only in relation to the dynamic quality of the mind; emotional qualities must be measured by the reactions to the environment; and the individual, in the last analysis, must take his standing among his fellows upon his acts, not upon his thoughts. In a balanced personality act harmonises with thought, is conditioned and controlled by it. Purely impulsive action carried to the extreme means insanity, and in milder degrees it exhibits itself in all grades and forms of what is known as lack of self-control. Such action is too familiar to call for comment. But there is the opposite type of individual whose impulses are not impelling enough to lead to expression in outward form of either thoughts or emotions. Such thoughts and emotions are turned back upon themselves and, like a dammed-up stream, whirl endlessly around the spring, the ego, until the individual becomes predominantly introspective and egocentric.

Amiel possessed the power of clear logical thought to a high degree, but he limited its expression largely to the introspective musings of the diary. Aside from his daily life, which was narrow but normal and conventional, it is to Amiel's deepest interests and admirations as revealed by his diary that one must look for light upon his emotional make-up. The things with which he occupied himself were extremely few: introspective literature, philosophy and religion, and contemplation of God and the hereafter. The diary covers the years of his life from twenty-seven to sixty, the entire fruitful span of most men's lives. During all of this time his interests showed little or no variation. Nowhere throughout the record do we find any evidence of interest in the developments which were shaping the course of the world's history. Still less do we find any indication of a desire or a conscience to participate in such history. Amiel evidently felt no urge to be an actor in the drama. He was not even a critic or an interested on-looker. Rather did he prefer to withdraw to a sheltered distance and forget the reverberations of the struggle in contemplation of abstractions.

He lived in an era in which the world was revolutionised. The most deforming institution which civilisation has ever tolerated, slavery, was razed and dismantled; yet he never said a word about it. He was a witness of one of the greatest transformations that has ever been wrought, the making of things by machinery rather than by hand; and he never commented on it. His life was contemporaneous with the beginning of discovery in science, such as the origin of species and the general evolutionary doctrine associated with Darwin's name; and it seems only to have excited his scorn.

"The growing triumph of Darwinism—that is to say of materialism, or of force—threatens the conception of justice. But justice will have its turn. The higher human law cannot be the offspring of animality. Justice is the right to the maximum of individual independence compatible with the same liberty for others;—in other words, it is respect for man, for the immature, the small, the feeble; it is the guarantee of those human collectivities, associations, states, nationalities—those voluntary or involuntary unions—the object of which is to increase the sum of happiness, and to satisfy the aspiration of the individual. That some should make use of others for their own purposes is an injury to justice. The right of the stronger is not a right, but a simple fact, which obtains only so long as there is neither protest nor resistance. It is like cold, darkness, weight, which tyrannise over man until he has invented artificial warmth, artificial light, and machinery. Human industry is throughout an emancipation from brute nature, and the advances made by justice are in the same way a series of rebuffs inflicted upon the tyranny of the stronger. As the medical art consists in the conquest of disease, so goodness consists in the conquest of the blind ferocities and untamed appetites of the human animal. I see the same law throughout:—increasing emancipation of the individual, a continuous ascent of being towards life, happiness, justice, and wisdom. Greed and gluttony are the starting-point, intelligence and generosity the goal."

Nor is there anything in the "Journal Intime" to indicate that he had ever heard of Pasteur, or Morton, or Simpson, who laid the foundation of a diseaseless world and a painless world. His diary is a record of his own thoughts, to be sure, but one's thoughts are engendered, in a measure at least, by what is going on in the world. An inhabitant of any other world whose knowledge of this could be obtained only from Amiel's book, would be left with an abysmal ignorance of the subject. He would learn something of the German philosophers and of French littérateurs and of Amiel's ideas of God and of infinity.

Schopenhauer says that

"It is not by the unification of the intellect and the will that man attains to higher truth, but by their dissociation. When the intellect casts off the yoke of the will it rises above the illusion of finite life and attains a vision of transcendent truth. When one can contemplate without will, beyond, when he can dissolve the life instinct in pure thought, then he possesses the field of higher truth, then he is on the avenue that leads to Nirvana."

Higher truth is possible only through the annihilation of the will, and if this annihilation is done after taking thought, that is after planning to do it and determining to do it, the price that one has to pay, or the penalty that is exacted, is an incapacity or diminished capacity for practical life. Amiel was a real mystic, not by choice, perhaps, but by birth. He was proud of it in his youth and early maturity; he questioned it in his late maturity; and regretted it in his senescence. When he was fifty years old he wrote,

"The man who gives himself to contemplation looks on at rather than directs his life, is a spectator rather than an actor, seeks rather to understand than to achieve. Is this mode of existence illegitimate, immoral? Is one bound to act? Is such detachment an idiosyncrasy to be respected or a sin to be fought against? I have always hesitated on this point, and I have wasted years in futile self-reproach and useless fits of activity. My western conscience, penetrated as it is with Christian morality, has always persecuted my Oriental quietism and Buddhist tendencies. I have not dared to approve myself, I have not known how to correct myself. . . . Having early caught a glimpse of the absolute, I have never had the indiscreet effrontery of individualism. What right have I to make a merit of a defect? I have never been able to see any necessity for imposing myself upon others, nor for succeeding. I have seen nothing clearly except my own deficiencies and the superiority of others. . . . With varied aptitudes and a fair intelligence, I had no dominant tendency, no imperious faculty, so that while by virtue of capacity I felt myself free, yet when free I could not discover what was best. Equilibrium produced indecision and indecision has rendered all my faculties barren."

If Amiel had been a real Christian, that is, if he had taken his orientation and orders from Christ, he would have had no doubt whether such a mode of existence was illegitimate and immoral or not. He could have found specific instruction telling him he was bound to act. He was a nominal Christian, but a *de facto* Buddhist.

Next to the output of a man's activity as shown by his work, his selection of recreational outlets for his emotional life is illuminating. What were Amiel's amusements? So far as the diary shows, day dreaming, poetising, fancy, and a contemplation of nature furnished the only outlets for his more organised emotional nature. For play in any form he apparently felt no need.

There is a type of individual whose failure to bring his performance up to the standard which his intelligence would seem to warrant takes the form of inability to face concrete situations. Unable to adjust himself to his environment when realities present difficulties that call for solution, such an individual becomes burdened with a sense of his own inadequacy; and from this he is inclined to seek escape in impersonal abstractions, usually described by him as ideals. Mystic philosophy in some form is the frequent refuge of such tender souls from their own sense of inability to cope with life and its concrete problems.

Throughout the record divergence between ideals and acts stands out. Idealism is everywhere pled as the basis of the hesitation to act. The conscious and foredoomed disparity between conception and realisation is made the excuse for the absence of effort.

"Practical life makes me afraid. And yet, at the same time, it attracts me; I have need of it. Family life, especially, in all its delightfulness, in all its moral depth, appeals to me like a duty. Sometimes I cannot escape from the ideal of it. A companion of my life, of my work, of my thoughts, of my hopes; within, a common worship, towards the world outside, kindness and beneficence; educations to undertake, the thousand and one moral relations which develop round the first— all these ideas intoxicate me sometimes. But I put them aside, because every hope is, as it were, an egg whence a serpent may issue instead of a dove, because every joy missed is a stab, because every seed confided to destiny contains an ear of grief which the future may develop."

"I have never felt any inward assurance of genius, or any presentiment of glory or happiness. I have never seen myself in imagination great or famous, or even a husband, a father, an influential citizen. This indifference to the future, this absolute self-distrust, are, no doubt, to be taken as signs. What dreams I have are vague and indefinite; I ought not to live, for I am now scarcely capable of living.—Recognise your place; let the living live; and you, gather together your thoughts, leave behind you a legacy of feeling and ideas; you will be more useful so. Renounce yourself, accept the cup given you, with its honey and its gall, as it comes. Bring God down into your heart. Embalm your soul in him now, make within you a temple for the Holy Spirit; be diligent in good works, make others happier and better. Put personal ambition away from you, and then you will find consolation in living or in dying, whatever may happen to you."

Complaining of a restless feeling which was not the need for change, he said,

"It is rather the fear of what I love, the mistrust of what charms me, the unrest of happiness. . . . And is there not another reason for all this restlessness, in a certain sense of void—of incessant pursuit of something wanting?—of longing for a truer peace and a more entire satisfaction? Neighbours, friends, relations—I love them all; and so long as these affections are active, they leave in me no room for a sense of want. But yet they do not *fill* my heart; and that is why they have no power to fix it. I am always waiting for the woman and the work which shall be capable of taking entire possession of my soul, and of becoming my end and aim."

Amiel's life was a constant negation. His ideals were all concerned with concepts of perfection, with the absolute, and being sane enough to realise the impossibility of attaining such perfection, he refused compromises. He would not play the game for its own sake, nor for the fine points. If he could not win all the points—and being sane he knew beforehand that he could not—he preferred not to play at all. But he made a virtue of his weakness and called it idealism. Had he possessed the courage to hitch his wagon to a star—and let the star carry him where it would; had he heeded the warning,

> "And the sin I impute to each frustrate ghost
> Is—the unlit lamp and the ungird loin";

or gone the way of thousands of practical idealists who have made their idealism an incentive to action and thereby left the world richer for having passed through it, he would have needed no excuse for his failure to attain perfection. On the contrary, he would have learned with the sureness of a hard-learned lesson that idealism is worth our loyalty only when it becomes an inspiration to living, and that it is worse than futile when it serves merely as a standard for thought or an excuse for failure.

Amiel coddled his sensibilities for fear of rebuff; he hid his intellectuality in the diary lest he should suffer from the clear light of publicity; he denied life out of apprehension that life might bruise his ego. He told himself that he was protecting his idealism. In reality he was protecting his egoism. If he had been the victim of a psychosis he would not have recognised his limitations nor stated them so clearly. It was sanity that enabled him to see the impossibility of attaining the perfection of which he dreamed and wrote. It was cowardice, not a psychosis, which made him refuse to act in the face of this knowledge. Had he been a Roman Catholic, he might have rested upon the conception of absolute perfection offered in the authority of the Church and the life of the cloister. But being a Protestant, both by inheritance and by conscience, he had to think things out for himself; and the more he thought the wider became the breach between his conception of perfection and his hope of realising it. He was tortured by a conscience goading him to action and a temperament paralysing him with the fear that the end would fall short of anticipation. He lacked the moral courage to put his power to the test and be disappointed. He was without the stamina of the man who fights and runs away. He was too much of an egoist to risk a losing game, and in consequence he never tasted the sweet flavour of work well done—even though the end was apparent failure.

The growing sense of inadequacy between the conscience to act and the temperament to deny action is written plainly in these random quotations from the "Journal" during the record of many years. At thirty he wrote,

"He who is silent is forgotten; he who abstains is taken at his word; he who does not advance, falls back; he who stops is overwhelmed, distanced, crushed; he who ceases to grow

greater becomes smaller; he who leaves off gives up; the
stationary condition is the beginning of the end—it is the
terrible symptom which precedes death. To live, is to achieve
a perpetual triumph; it is to assert oneself against destruction,
against sickness, against the annulling and dispersion of one's
physical and moral being. It is to will without ceasing, or
rather to refresh one's will day by day."

Ten years later when the conflict was closing in upon him he
wrote,

"In me an intellect which would fain forget itself in things,
is contradicted by a heart which yearns to live in human beings. The uniting link of the two contradictions is the tendency towards self-abandonment, towards ceasing to will and
exist for oneself, towards laying down one's own personality,
and losing—dissolving—oneself in love and anticipation. What
I lack above all things is character, will, individuality. But,
as always happens, the appearance is exactly the contrary of
the reality, and my outward life the reverse of my true and
deepest aspiration. I whose whole being—heart and intellect—thirsts to absorb itself in reality, in its neighbour man,
in Nature and in God—I, whom solitude devours and destroys—I shut myself up in solitude and seem to delight only
in myself and to be sufficient for myself."

At forty-seven, when most men's work is at the high tide
of realisation, he said,

"I have no more strength left, I wish for nothing; but that is
not what is wanted. I must wish what God wishes; I must
pass from indifference to sacrifice, and from sacrifice to self-
devotion. The cup I would fain put away from me is the
misery of living, the shame of existing and suffering as a
common creature who has missed his vocation; it is the bitter
and increasing humiliation of declining power, of growing old
under the weight of one's own disapproval, and the disappointment of one's friends."

At fifty-four,

"What use have I made of my gifts, of my special circumstances, of my half century of existence? What have I paid

back to my country? . . . Are all the documents I have produced . . . anything better than withered leaves? . . . When all is added up—nothing! And worst of all, it has not been a life used up in the service of some adored object, or sacrificed to any future hope."

Psychology teaches that too much emphasis cannot be laid in education upon the reconciliation of ideals and performance, nor too much effort devoted to the formation of habits of facing concrete situations squarely, reaching definite decisions, and thereby making efforts, however ineffective and crude, to link ideals to action. It has been proved that if natural dispositions are ignored or denied by the repression of normal primary instincts, disassociation of personality is likely to be the result. Amiel's ineffectiveness, his lack of dynamic quality, while in no sense a psychosis, may be considered as a personality defect. How far this defect may have been conditioned by his denial of the basic springs of human action cannot be stated. Neither can it, in any impartial estimate of his life and personality, be ignored. Next to the instinct of self-preservation, the instinct for the preservation of the race to which one belongs is the dominant impulse of the individual. No system of thought, no plan of life can ignore it and not pay the penalty. Amiel's diary is full of such denials, and they frequently carry with them the consciousness that he realised the death sentence to aspiration and realisation which he was reading to himself between the lines.

Amiel was a shy, sensitive, solitary child. We know very little about his adolescent struggles and transition to heterosexual fixation. Indeed we do not know whether it ever came about, and that is where the chief hiatus in our knowledge of Amiel lies. As a youth he became intoxicated with philosophic idealism, and Hegel was for him the fountainhead of all philosophic thought.

There is nothing in the diary to indicate that the normal love-making of healthy youth had any part in his thoughts or his life. Later, his sex consciousness colours the record to a great extent—indeed it might be said to give the colour to the book—but always in the guise of repressions, fears, hesitations, and longings for unattainable perfection, and finally of half-hearted regrets for his own denials.

"I am capable of all the passions, for I bear them all within me. Like a tamer of wild beasts, I keep them caged and lassoed, but I sometimes hear them growling. I have stifled more than one nascent love. Why? Because with that prophetic certainty which belongs to moral intuition, I felt it lacking in true life, and less durable than myself. I choked it down in the name of the supreme affection to come. The loves of sense, of imagination, of sentiment—I have seen through and rejected them all; I sought the love which springs from the central profundities of being. And I still believe in it. I will have none of those passions of straw which dazzle, burn up, and wither; I invoke, I await, and I hope for the love which is great, pure, and earnest, which lives and works in all the fibres and through all the powers of the soul. And even if I go lonely to the end, I would rather my hope and my dream died with me, than that my soul should content itself with any meaner union."

This is the basis of monasticism in the Catholic Church, and it is, in my judgment, the most violent offence to God that can be given. Goethe says that he never wrote a new poem without having a new love affair. Amiel was intrigued by Goethe secondly only to Hegel. If he had copied Goethe more nearly in living, he might have said with him,

> "Wonach soll man am Ende trachten?
> Die Welt zu Kennen und nicht zu Verachten."

There have been books made up of beautiful quotations from Amiel's "Journal Intime," which are supposed to help people live, to mitigate pain, to disperse apprehension, and to assuage misery. They are not a patch on the Bible or on the writings of Socrates.

"The oracle of today drops from his tripod on the morrow," said John Morley. Will this apply to Amiel? Is he a passing fashion? And why has his popularity grown? The best answer to these questions is found in the nature of his audience. To what kind of people does Amiel appeal? To the contemporary purveyors of cloudy stuff; to mystics; to the tender-minded; to those who prefer the contemplation of far horizons to travelling the road just ahead. He does not appeal to anyone with fighting blood, whether he be facing the conflict with the glorious self-confidence of healthy untried youth, the magnetism of past success, the tried measure of his own limitations and powers, the scars of honest defeat, or the pluck of the one who fights a losing fight with more courage and idealism than he would have mustered for a winning one.

Amiel's tragedy was that he outraged nature's unique law and nature exacted the penalty. If the world had a few thousand Amiels and they got the whip hand, it might cease to exist.

# CHAPTER X

THE world is thronged with people who are busying themselves with world ordering. They may be divided into two great groups: those who believe that it is to be brought about by revolution; and those who are convinced that it is to be accomplished by following the instructions given by the Master to the lawyer who asked the question: "Which is *the* great commandment in the law?" The former are called Bolshevists; the latter Pacifists; and both terms are habitually used derisively. Amongst the latter there are few more conspicuous in France than Georges Duhamel, a physician by profession, a littérateur by choice, who at thirty-eight years of age finds himself in a commanding position in French letters.

I have recently had the opportunity of an interview with this brilliant young man, and it occurs to me to present a summary of his aspirations and an estimate of his accomplishments.

His history is brief. Early success, like a happy country, does not furnish history. He was born in Paris in 1884, the son of a physician and the grandson of a farmer. This evolution from farmer to littérateur in three generations Duhamel says is common in France, indeed in all Central Europe. His tastes seem to have been largely influenced, if not formed, by the setting and atmosphere with which his father's profession surrounded his early life. Until he was mobilised in 1914 Duhamel had not practised medicine. Even as a youth he had experienced the literary urge and felt that he would eventually succumb to it. He, however, devoted himself to the sciences and to medicine in the firm belief that such study provides the best preparation for the vocation of literature. In this M. Duhamel is in full accord with another famous theoretical world orderer, Mr. H. G. Wells, but in disagreement with a practical one, Mr. Charles E. Hughes.

"One does not learn life from letters, but from life, through seeing suffering and death," said he when asked to speak of the factors that influenced him to abandon medicine for letters.

In the midst of his studies as a youth he had what he now calls rather a strange adventure.

"I spent much time in the society of friends: writers, painters and sculptors. All of us were seized with a strong desire to shrink from society as it was constituted. Although we were not all Fourierites, we decided to form a phalanstery in which we could live a community life, each one taking part in the work and in the joy of living in an atmosphere adapted to our tastes and our professions. We agreed to make our living by means of manual work, and to abolish the relation of master and servant. We decided to adopt the trade of typography, which would permit us to advance our art. Through mutual economies we bought a printing press and our first books were published by 'L'Abbaye de Creteil,' as our little publishing house was called. The phalanstery was disbanded for financial reasons, but we had a taste of an agreeable life, independent, oftentimes difficult, but in many respects quite ideal."

When asked about his earliest literary productions and why he essayed poetry rather than prose, he replied,

"Generally speaking, all writers begin with poetry and gradually forsake metre. Our little group wanted to initiate a great literary epoch and we believed that this could be done only by creating an atmosphere favourable to intellectual work."

He might have borrowed Socrates' reply when Cebes asked the same question: "For I reflect that a man who means to be a poet has to use fiction and not facts for his poems." M. Duhamel's training had been in facts, and his greatest success

GEORGES DUHAMEL
From a drawing by *Ivan Opffer*
in *THE BOOKMAN*

in letters has been in the recording of facts. His smallest success has been in establishing postulates based upon them.

In 1909 M. Duhamel received his degree in medicine and shortly after appeared the four plays which, with his poetry, "Des Légendes, des Batailles," a collection of verse published by "L'Abbaye" in 1907; "L'Homme en Tête," in 1909; "Selon ma Loi," in 1910; and "Compagnons," in 1912, gave him a definite place in the literary hierarchy. These plays were "La Lumière," which appeared in 1911; "Dans l'Ombre des Statues," in 1912; "Le Combat," a symbolic drama in *vers libres*, in 1912; and "L'Œuvre des Athlètes" in 1920. All of these were produced on the Paris stage and all save the last, have appeared in translations by Sasha Best in *Poet Lore*, Boston, in 1914 and 1915.

These dramas, as well as his early poetry, show the influence of Walt Whitman. His message is conveyed through the medium of symbolism, his method being to create types rather than individual studies, and his purpose to bring art closer to the masses. The result, as might have been expected, is drama of no great popularity.

Almost simultaneously with his work as poet and dramatist M. Duhamel achieved prominence as a critic. For some years he was critic of poetry for *Le Mercure de France*, and his articles contributed to that publication were collected in book form in 1914 under the title of "Les Poètes et la Poésie." His earliest critical work, however, was a collaboration with M. Charles Vildrac, called "Mots sur la Technique Poétique." "Propos Critique," published in 1912, is largely devoted to comments on the efforts of the younger and, at that time, comparatively unknown writers, and it is of special interest that many of these writers are now famous.

"Paul Claudel: le philosophe—le poète—l'ecrivain—le dramaturge," published in 1913, is considered by some of Duhamel's admirers as the best of his critical works, marked as it is by the same gifts of analysis and charm of style which distinguished his briefer critical writings.

It is, however, chiefly of his work since the beginning of the war, and the direction which his ideas and aims have taken under the influence of the war, that this article is concerned.

When the war broke out it found Georges Duhamel—then about thirty years of age—intent upon his literary work: poetry, criticism, interpretation, which had put him in the first rank of littérateurs of his country. Mobilised in the Medical Corps he first went to Verdun and found himself in the thick of the carnage; but he was soon transferred to the Marne where in the comparative quiet of a hospital he was able to make the observations and write the reflections which have carried his name throughout the civilised world. During the four years of the war he produced four remarkable volumes: "Vie des Martyrs" (The New Book of Martyrs), "Civilisation," "Possession du Monde" (The Heart's Domain), and "Entretiens dans le Tumulte" (Interviews in the Tumult), four of the most noteworthy and important books inspired by the war.

Plunged at once into the great war hopper whose purpose was to reduce all human material to a homogeneous mass that would furnish energy for the war machine, Duhamel preserved his perspective and his individual outlook both upon the war and upon life. Nothing illustrates this so strikingly as some of his stories in "Civilisation," gathered from scenes with which he came into contact after he had become a seasoned soldier.

No stronger proof is needed of the essential wholesomeness and strength of Duhamel's make-up than the fact that while these stories, and those of "Vie des Martyrs," were inspired by the horrors of the war, they do not depict horrors, nor do they create an atmosphere of horror. It is not the picture of healthy men in the flower of youth, in the vigour of virility fed to the war machine and left lacerated and broken, that Duhamel impresses upon the imaginations of his readers. It

was thus that he had seen them in the first days of the siege
of Verdun, in an improvised ambulance where from minute to
minute new torments developed to increase their previous torments, while the fragile roof over their heads became a great
resounding board for the projectiles of the siegers and the as-
sieged. He had, however, the vision to see them in another
light, and he was filled with pity and admiration for the French
poilu. It is these two emotions, rather than horror, which
make the atmosphere and colour of the two books of war
stories. He sensed the significance of pain and saw the reactions of strong men to suffering. He saw man in his agony
give the lie to the most misleading of all statements: that man
is born equal. For neither in living nor in dying is there equality. Men are equal, we trust, before God, and they are alleged
to be equal before the law, but after that equality of man does
not exist.

It is this book particularly that makes Duhamel the interpreter of the poor, the obscure, the stupid, the inarticu-
late. With an unerring intuition he reaches the soul. His
sympathies are so large, his understanding so comprehensive,
and his reflection of them so complete, that his readers suffer
with the suffering. It seems impossible to depict the sufferings
of these poor martyrs, sent like droves of cattle to be struck
down for what purpose they knew not, more accurately and
convincingly than he does. With the reader's sympathy
thus awakened, one wonders that the individual can be deprived of his own right to judge whether the cause is great
enough for him to lay down his all; to be crushed by the
chariots of the god of war.

M. Duhamel, in "Vie des Martyrs," has succeeded in making his martyrs immortal. To him has been given in a superlative degree that seeing eye, that understanding heart, that
power of vision which, perhaps more than any other gift,
enriches life, since it enables the fortunate possessor to rid

himself of the trammels of his own narrow existence and live the lives of many.

He has made a contribution to behaviouristic psychology in these little stories, or better said sketches from life, that will endure. He has been able to convey to unenlightened man the difference between the *bon* and the *mauvais blessé* and to show that it is soul difference as well as bodily difference. He has portrayed in simple colours the desire to live, and the determination to live, factors which physicians know are most important in forecasting the chances of recovery of every sick man. And with it all there is tenderness, which the author has had the power to convey through delicacy of style that makes prose poetry of much of his narrative of the thoughts, aspirations, sentiments, and plans of individual men who, from their appearance and position, are the most commonplace of the commonplace. There is no anger, violence, hatred, or despair in any of his pictures. There is sometimes irony, but it is of so gentle a nature that it strengthens the impression of sympathy with his characters, rather than suggesting judgment of them.

"A human being suffers always in his flesh alone, and that is why war is possible," says M. Duhamel in "Civilisation." This is one of those marvellous epitomes of human conduct, of which he has framed many. It is vouchsafed to but few to understand and suffer another's pain. To the majority of mankind it is denied. Were it not so, the fellow-feeling that makes us wondrous kind would displace greed.

There are so many remarkable features of M. Duhamel's war books, such, for instance, as what may be called the thesis of "Vie des Martyrs": that men suffer after their own image and in their own loneliness; or of "Civilisation": that consciousness has outrun life; that it has created for itself reactions and inhibitions so intricate and profound that they cannot be tolerated by life, that I was keen to learn how these attitudes had developed. When questioned, this is what he said:

"I am forced to divide things in the way practiced in the sciences; that is to say, not to confuse the study of facts with conclusions drawn from them. In these two books I showed as faithfully as I could the life and sufferings of soldiers during the war. In the latter two ("The Heart's Domain" and "Interviews in the Tumult") I drew conclusions from the facts established in the first two. This procedure seemed to me the best way to handle anti-war propaganda. The weakness of most books results from the fact that the idea or subject is confused with other, regrettably often sentimental, considerations. The procedure employed in the sciences seems to be more orderly, and therefore more convincing for the exposition of my ideas. These books awoke a great echo, because they corresponded closely to the state of mind of sensible men who are bent on doing everything to make war impossible. Because of this I was looked upon as a Pacifist, and I regard this as an honour. I have never been politically active nor do I belong to any political group. However I am a Pacifist and an Internationalist. I believe that it is only the individual that can be an Internationalist. A nation will never be Internationalist for the reason that Pacifism and Internationalism are indissolubly bound up with individualism."

M. Duhamel's work cannot, therefore, be considered solely in the light of its literary qualities. By his own admission he is a writer with a purpose, and this purpose is the suppression of war. In the interview he stated that this purpose fills all of his work and "will be, I believe, the axis of my work all my life."

Regarding the four war books in this light, a sincere critic can hardly escape the conviction that the author has accomplished the first part of his task with immeasurably greater success than the latter part. Of the convincing appeal of the two books which aim only to present vivid and truthful pictures of the sufferings of the soldiers during the war there can be no question. But of the author's power as a propagandist against war, as expressed in the two latter books, it is by no means easy to form so satisfactory an estimate.

Duhamel does not believe that the war developed a *modus vivendi* for the world. He thinks it left us where it found us, only exhausted. Unless something is devised while this exhaustion is being overcome, the conflict will be taken up again. He believes that a revolution is necessary, but not a revolution in the sense of the term that applies to the affairs of Russia or Ireland.

When Duhamel is read in the light of history, especially of the last one hundred and twenty-five years, one is less hopeful than if he were ignorant of history. If any *ex cathedra* statement is justifiable it would seem to be this: the world war flowed more or less directly from the revolutionary movement which began with the dissemination of the doctrine of the French philosophers, especially Rousseau, toward the end of the Eighteenth Century. His discourse "On the Origin of Inequality Amongst Men" is the fountainhead of modern socialism and the source from which the ferment that brought about the world revolution emanated. Rousseau's thesis was that civilisation had proven itself to be the curse of humanity and that man in his primitive state was free and happy.

"The first time he knew unhappiness was when convention stepped in and said 'you must not do this and you must not do that,' and the State stepped in and said 'this is private property.' The first man who bethought himself of saying 'this is mine,' and found people simple enough to believe him was the real founder of civil society. What crimes, what wars, what murders, what miseries and horrors would he have spared the human race who, snatching away the spade and filling in the ditches, had cried out to his fellows: 'beware of listening to this impostor; you are lost if you forget that the fruits of the earth belong to all and the earth to no one.' "

It was the dissemination of this doctrine and the writings of Voltaire which led to the "Feast of Reason," and the publication of the "Encyclopédie" that led to the world volcanic eruption of 1789, which had its repetition in 1914.

It seems that most of these ideas were to be found in the writings of Adam Weishaupt, an apostate Catholic, who founded the secret society known as the "Illiminati" in 1776. It is interesting to compare some of his statements with Duhamel's aspirations.

"When men united themselves into nations, national love took the place of universal love. With the division of the globe into countries benevolence restricted itself behind boundaries that it was never again to transgress. It became a virtue to spread out at the expense of those who did not happen to be under our dominion. In order to attain this goal it became permissible to despise foreigners and to deceive and offend them. This virtue was called patriotism. Patriotism gave birth to localism, to the family spirit, and finally to egoism. Thus the origin of states or governments of civil society was the seed of discord and patriotism found its punishment in itself. Do away with this love of country, and men will once more learn to know and love each other as men; there will be no more partiality; the ties between hearts will unroll and extend."

Duhamel wants to develop this relationship between men, but he wants to do it in a very different way.

This moral revolution will be accomplished when men love one another, and when they reward good for evil. Even though this had not been shouted from the housetops and whispered through the lattice, in every tongue and in every clime for the past twenty centuries, we should still feel that M. Duhamel is in error, for these precepts are at variance with the teachings of biology, the science for which M. Duhamel has so much respect. You might just as well ask a man who is drowning not to struggle as to ask a man to return good for evil—that is unless he is doing it as a stunt, an artefact, or in redemption of the promise to be saved. It is against nature. First teach him to put a new valuation on life and to get new standards of what makes life worth living. Then M. Duhamel will have a foundation to build upon.

That M. Duhamel is no less earnest than sincere in his purpose is proved by his lectures through Europe during the last few years, as protagonist for the suppression of war; and also by the fact that he was one of the co-founders of "Clarté," so named for the book by Barbusse, which is a group of men who preach anti-militarism, the intellectual solidarity of nations, and the social equality of all citizens.

"Possession du Monde" is by virtue of its title a frank avowal of its aim to set forth the author's idea of finding some satisfactory substitute for the world possession for which the war was fought. It is the effort of a wholesome, buoyant, sympathetic man, after having been brought into contact with the horrors of the war, to find a substitute for orthodox religion; the expression of an emotionally religious man without a creed. M. Duhamel, who was brought up a Catholic, lost all religion, he said, when he was fifteen years old.

The panacea which Duhamel offers in this book for human suffering and world ills is the conscious striving for happiness by means of a sort of "culture of the soul." He puts a personal construction upon happiness and holds that it is and should be the object of all humanity and of the whole world of living things. He quotes Maeterlinck to the effect that "As man is created for health, so was man created for happiness." This soul culture is rather an attitude of feeling toward things than an attitude of thought. There is no attempt to think out any of the problems which have puzzled men for ages. Neither is there any denying of them. He simply says substantially: I am a practical man. Of course I take things as they are—or as they seem to be—but I take the best that is in them. I take the sunshine, the flowers, the wisdom of the ages, the art that has come down to us, the science, human love, the fine qualities of friendship, work, play, my sorrows and adversities, even religion—but I take only what is good out of them all; and I take that temperately, sanely, according to the limitations which nature and circumstances have imposed. And I am happy. You can do likewise and you can be happy.

But can I take poverty and want, and particularly can I take them with equanimity while my neighbour or brother is swaggering with riches, some of which he has robbed me because he is stronger or cleverer than I? Duhamel's formula for achieving happiness, as well as his conception of what constitutes happiness, only fits the average man, and it has been proven countless thousands of times that there is no such person. It is sufficient, perhaps, for people who feel normally and do not think for themselves. So it may be sufficient for the present for a mass of people who want to be led—if they are pious and healthy.

But how about the people who are different, or who are not healthy, or who think they are safer custodians of wealth and power than their so-called brothers? It brings no help to the people who are tortured by an insistent need to think things out for themselves, or else to find something which will answer their questions as to the why. Nor does it tell those who are handicapped, physically, mentally, or even temperamentally, how they can overcome their handicaps so as to, as it were, extract the honey from the flowers. The world is full of people with all degrees of unusualness and abnormality. One may ignore them, but no scheme of things can deny them. Duhamel uses them by preference as a basis for his fiction.

In his conception of happiness Duhamel reads himself and his own emotions into all things. He avers that the algæ growing in a tank of water with nothing but a few grains of dust and sunlight are happy because they subsist and work out their humble joy. Has any sentient soul told him he was happy under parallel circumstances? That is the question. He reads his own philosophy into the algæ. To him to be living as nature intended one to live is to be happy. But who can say? Just here I am reminded of a quotation from Anatole France of which Duhamel makes use in this book: "Men

have cut each others' throats over the meaning of a word."
People might argue forever over the meaning of the word
"happiness" and never get anywhere.

Duhamel says that happiness is the ultimate end of life and
that religion is the search for happiness in a life to come after
this. Everybody wants to be happy in this life and some
people expect to be happy in a life after this—of these two
assertions there can be no doubt. But Duhamel says there
is no life after this, and that the sole object of life is to be
happy in this world. He does, however, speak of "saving the
soul," and he implies his belief in God. He says substantially
that the plants are happy because they are fulfilling their
destiny, or doing what God meant them to do; and implies that
man will be happy if he does the same. Very likely. But
shall he strive to fulfill his destiny—to do what God meant
him to do—merely in order to be happy? Or shall he strive to
fulfill his destiny—and happiness will follow incidentally?
Which should be his conscious end, happiness or the fulfilment
of his destiny? Most religious people would say the latter.
Duhamel says the former. But, for working purposes they
are about the same, except that, for people who are at all
temperamental or who meet with many discouragements,
it is frequently difficult to strive for a happiness which seems
elusive. Whereas, such people, if they are spiritually minded,
can always find a stimulus in trying to do what they were
intended to do. And if they believe in God the stimulus becomes greater. And if they can believe that the soul grows
through every honest effort—that nothing is ever lost, whether
the result appears to be success or failure—and that the limits
of its growth are not bounded by what their senses can tell
them in this life, their capacity for striving becomes sometimes amazing. How else account for the man who expends
ten times the effort in playing a losing game that he would
have spent in one that promised an easy success?

That the soul will find its greatest happiness in the contemplation of itself, is Duhamel's belief. "He is the happiest man who best understands his happiness; for he is of all men most fully aware that it is only the lofty idea, the untiring courageous human idea, that separates gladness from sorrow," he quotes from Maeterlinck. A man should think about his soul at least once every day. But it would be safe to say that for one man who finds happiness in a life of contemplation ten find it in a life of action. The wholesome, sane, average, happy men—of whom Duhamel is an excellent example—are mostly men of action. The very existence of this book is a contradiction of his happiness of contemplation theory as applied to himself. It may well be questioned whether Duhamel would have written "Possession du Monde" if he had not been the kind of man who finds happiness in giving expression to every emotion. Besides self-study is safe only for strong natures. Self-analysis was the undoing of the man in one of Duhamel's best books, "Confession de Minuit."

Finally, what is "happiness"? Is it merely a feeling? Gladness? If that were all, and the ultimate end of life, would not the logical conclusion be that the happiest—and therefore the most successful—man would be the joyful maniac?

The publication of M. Duhamel which has the greatest popularity is the one that his admirers would wish he had not written: "Possession du Monde." It is a protest against the evaluation of life commercially, and a plea for a moral or spiritual standard. This is a topic for an epoch maker, and one who has not a vision or a plan should not essay it. M. Duhamel may have both, but he does not reveal them. He displays only the wish that the world should be better. In the jargon of the Freudian, it is a wish-fulfilment that does not realise. It is neither well done nor convincing, and it has been well and convincingly done by many writers, and still we have not profited by it. Amiel did it; Maeterlinck did it; Karr did it; and "others too numerous to mention." They may have had some effect upon individuals, but the history of the past eight years shows that they had no effect upon the world at large, its evolution, or devolution. Moreover, there is a note of unction and self-satisfaction running through the book that is displeasing, if not offensive. It is quite true, or likely to be true, that "to think about the soul, to think about it at least once in the confusion of every crowded day, is indeed the beginning of salvation," but there is a book in which this is said in a more convincing way than M. Duhamel can ever hope to say it.

Viewed from a literary standpoint alone, the book is in keeping with, if not quite up to, the standard of his other works. His prose is always musical, and he often creates an atmosphere rather than an edifice. He is never emphatic, mandatory, severe, superlative. He is soft, gentle, often ironical, but always human.

Two remarkable pieces of fiction constitute Duhamel's output since the four war books: "Les Hommes Abandonnés" (Abandoned Men) and "Confession de Minuit" (Midnight Confession). The first contains eight histories which try to prove that when men are gathered together in a crowd they are abandoned by the individual soul. It is an illustration on the reverse side in favour of individualism.

"Confession de Minuit" is particularly significant as being named by the author in the interview as his favourite work. "As a human research I believe that it is the one with the most meaning," he said of this novel; and it is, therefore, a matter of self-congratulation on the part of the writer that he found this book to be the one which interpreted to him the author's particular genius in the most convincing and interesting light. The story has its bearing upon the author's theories because it illustrates more clearly than any of his other works a statement made by him in the interview:

"People often reproach me with being interested only in my stories with sick people or with children. Healthy men do not register the motives which govern them. When one studies a sick person one is able to see the relations between moral characteristics which in the healthy man exist, but are hidden." However, I hold that the average man, healthy, typical, scarcely exists in literature, and that the most interesting creations from the human point of view had for their subjects men who were unbalanced—from Hamlet to Leopold Bloom; from Raskolnikov to Dorian Gray.

"Confession de Minuit" is the self-revelation of a man who was decidedly unbalanced. As a bit of art work the book is unique and remarkable. Almost the unity of a short-story is preserved without recourse to any of the usual machinery of the ordinary novel, such as plot, action, or conversation, except a very little of the most casual nature. To a person who reads fiction for character delineation this absence of trappings is a distinct gain.

"Confession de Minuit" is the story of a man than whom a more uninteresting person could hardly be found in life; and yet as told by the man himself, Duhamel sustains the interest of the reader in the recital of pitiful weakness from the first page to the last without one lapse into dryness or loss of sympathy for the character, with whom, in the flesh, it would have been hard to feel any sentiment besides pity. It opens with the incident which causes the man to lose his position as a small clerk in an office through an utterly senseless—although perfectly harmless—performance: yielding to a sudden impulse to touch the ear of his employer just to assure himself that the employer was really made of flesh and blood, as himself. As society, or in this case the employer, is more afraid of an insane person than of a criminal, the reader does not share the man's feeling of injustice because he is first confronted with a revolver and then thrown speedily and bodily out of the office where he had been a faithful worker for several years; although he is able to pity the victim. The story, as told by the man himself, traces his rapid deterioration through progressive stages of self-pity, self-absorption, and inability to get hold of himself, to make an effort to re-establish himself, or even to seek advice or sympathy, until the last night when he pours out his "confession" to a stranger, with the statement that, on account of his failure in every relation in life, he is never going home to his old mother who has supported him with her small income and her needlework— nor is he ever going anywhere else, so far as the reader can see. He does not commit suicide. In fact, the story leaves one with the impression that he is merely "going crazy." Whether or not he is insane when the recital begins with the commission of the insane act is a matter for neither the novelist nor the critic to state.

The great art of the writer lies in his ability to sustain interest at a high level in a pure character study of what is frequently described as a "shut-in personality."

This novel seems to have been written without reference to the author's happiness or "cult of the soul" theory. It might almost be construed as a contradiction of it. One might put a fatalistic construction upon it, if one did not take a material point of view of health and disease. I do not see how anyone could get away from the conviction that the man who makes the "Midnight Confession" of his own pitiful failure in life is a victim of either his own mental limitations, or else of his particular environment, or of both. The only other way in which anyone might account for his utter inability to get hold of life or to stand up against his first discouragement is the refuge of the Radical Socialist—that society gave him no chance, the concrete illustration being the cruel way in which constituted authority, or his employer, treated his first downward step. But if the author had intended to condemn the employer and to excuse the man he would hardly have selected for this step an act which would so readily arouse a question as to the man's sanity, nor would he have followed the incident with a story in which the only development was rapidly increasing loss of touch with the outside world. No philosophy, or religion, or cult could have helped this man, who was handicapped with a nature so weak that it could not resist an impulse which would have been suppressed instantly by any well-balanced person; nor could it have given him the strength to withstand the simple discouragements that are the inevitable lot of all men. He simply was not able to cope with something—define it as one may.

One moral the story teaches. And that is the nobility of sympathy with even the weakest, most despised, and least interesting of human beings.

M. Duhamel consecrates his life to the prevention of war. It is a noble gesture. He is gifted, sane, articulate, and temperamentally adapted and adjusted to the task. Were he a platonist and not a neo-platonist, I am sure greater success would crown his efforts. Twenty-five hundred years ago a man who penetrated the mysteries of life and death more deeply than anyone before or since said to his pupils who had gathered to speed him to the Great Beyond, the ship having returned from Delos and the Eleven having decided to release Socrates from his fetters:

"The body fills us with passions and desires, and fears, and all manner of phantoms and much foolishness; and so, as the saying goes, in very truth we can never think at all for it. It alone and its desires, cause war and factions and battles for the origin of all wars is the pursuit of wealth."

Until that pursuit can be substituted, the labours of M. Duhamel and his co-founders of "Clarté" are likely to be in vain.

# CHAPTER XI

EVEN YET IT CAN'T BE TOLD—THE WHOLE TRUTH ABOUT
D. H. LAWRENCE

ABOUT twenty years ago a brilliant, unbalanced, young Austrian Jew wrote a book, "Sex and Character," whose purpose was to show that woman had played a greater rôle in the world than her possessions warranted, that she was inherently devoid of morality, and that men should cease to procreate. In the autumn of 1903 its author, Otto Weininger, then twenty-three years old, shot and killed himself in the house in Vienna in which Beethoven had died. The author's awful theme and his tragic end caused the book to be widely read and even more widely discussed. Amongst those impressed by it was a boy of humble but uncommon parents, bred in the coal-fields of mid-England where he had led a strenuous life struggling with the sex question, contending with the stream of consciousness as it became swollen with the tributaries of puberty—"Oh, stream of hell which undermined my adolescence." While still a youth he felt the influence of another Austrian mystic of the same faith, Sigmund Freud, who maintains that the unconscious is the real man, that its energiser and director is the libido, and that the conscious is the artificed, the engendered man whose tenant and executive is the ego. By day and by night this exceptionally gifted and burdened boy took his grist to these two mystic millers. To comfort himself, to keep up his courage in the dark on his journeys to the mill and from it, he read the Bible, the poetry of Walt Whitman and Robert Browning, and the prose of Thomas Hardy. From the Old Testament he got an unsurpassed capacity for narrative and metaphor, while the "grey poet" whetted his appetite for worship and exaltation of the human body. Well might he say of Whitman, as Dante said of Virgil:

> "Tu sè'lo mio maèstro e il mio autore
> Tu sè'solo colui, da cui io tòlsi
> Lo bèllo stile che m'à fatto onore."

Thus D. H. Lawrence, like Jeshurun, waxed fat and kicked, forsook God which made him, and lightly esteemed the Rock of his Salvation. And he began to pour forth his protest in a series of books, each a little more lawless than its predecessor, culminating in "The Rainbow." The book was suppressed by the Government of his own country, but the censors of our "free country," who pronounced "Jurgen" a book prejudicial to public morals, allowed "The Rainbow" to be published here. Perhaps that is the reason "Jurgen" has been published in England without molest. After that, when Mr. Lawrence wished to circulate his contributions to world-purification and progress, which many call pornography, he resorted to the camouflage of "published privately for subscribers only."

My information is that Mr. Lawrence is not so widely read in the United States as are many of his contemporaries, Mr. Compton Mackenzie or Mr. Frank Swinnerton, for example. But there is a Lawrence cult here and it is growing, particularly amongst those who like to be called Greenwich Villagers, the breath of whose nostrils is antinomianism, especially sex antinomianism. Moreover, he has a way of interpolating between his salacious romances and erotic poetry books of imagination, observation, and experience, such as "Bay" and "Twilight in Italy," that are couched in language whose swing and go few can withstand. These are replete with descriptions of sense-stirring scenery and analyses of sex-tortured souls, analyses which give lyric expression to the passions of the average man, who finds their lurid and ecstatic depiction diverting. Finally, Mr. Lawrence is striving to say something—something of sex and self which he believes the world should know; indeed, which is of paramount importance to it—and his manner of saying it has been so seductive that there are probably many who, like myself, have been clinging to him, as it were, buying his books and reading him with the hope that eventually he would succeed.

The time limit given him by one of his admirers and well-wishers has expired. In taking leave of him I purpose to set down my reasons for severing the emotional and intellectual thread that has kept us—even though so very loosely, and to him, quite unawaredly—together.

This renders unavoidable a line or two about criticism. I accept Matthew Arnold's estimate of the function of criticism, "to make known the best that is thought and known in the world," providing that the critic also exposes the poor and meretricious which is being palmed off as "just as good," or which is bidding for estimate, high or low. A guide should not only show the traveller upon whose eyes the scales still rest, or who has set out on a journey before the dawn, the right road, but he should also warn him of perilous roads and specify whether the peril is from bandits, broken bridges, or bellowing bulls. It is needless to say that the guide should have travelled the road and should know it and its environment well, and that his information should be recent.

The road that Mr. D. H. Lawrence has been travelling for the past decade and more, and making the basis for descriptions of his trips, is well known to me. I have worked upon it, laughed upon it, cried upon it for more than a quarter of a century. My information of it is recent, for there, even now, I earn my daily bread. It is the road leading from Original Sin to the street called Straight. All must travel it. Some make the journey quickly; some laboriously. Some, those who have morbid sex-consciousness in one form or another, inadequate or deviate genetic endowment, are unable to finish the journey at all.

Mr. Lawrence seems to have learned early that he could not

D. H. LAWRENCE

fulfill his own nature passionally, and he has been struggling all his life to find the way in which fulfilment lies. It is generally believed that "Sons and Lovers" is largely autobiographical and that the writer is to be identified with Paul. In that book he gave ample testimony that he could not fulfill himself because of the conflict between mother-love and uxorial love; for we may venture to catalogue Paul's consortional experiences under that heading, even though he had no marriage lines. He has never been able to define just how he expected to fulfill his nature, but one may legitimately conclude from some of his recent publications that he believes, if the strings of the lyre of sensuality can be made taut enough and twanged savagely enough, the tone produced will constitute not only fulfilment and happiness, but an eternity of ecstasy, a timeless extension of that indescribable exaltation that Dostoievsky was wont to experience in moments preceding his epileptic seizures, which is so vividly described by him and which made such an impression upon his thoughts and so influenced his imagery. Mr. Lawrence apparently believes that fulfilment will be meditated by one "who will touch him at last on the root and quicken his darkness and perish on him as he has perished on her." When this happens,

"We shall be free, freer than angels, ah, perfect";

and,

"After that, there will only remain that all men detach themselves and become unique
Conditioned only by our pure single being, having no laws but the laws of our own being."

Finally:

"Every human being will then be like a flower, untrammelled."

"Ideas and ideals are the machine plan and the machine principles of an automatonised Psyche which has been so prejudicial to human progress and human welfare. We must get rid of them both."

In fact, it is a world without ideals for which Mr. Lawrence is clamouring and which he maintains he is in process of creating. It must be allowed that he is working industriously to do it, but most people, I fancy, will continue to believe that his world will not be a fit place to live in should he be able to finish his task. Meanwhile he is doing much to make the world less livable than it might otherwise be, particularly for those who are not competent to judge whether any of Mr. Lawrence's contentions are tenable or any of his statements in harmony with the evidence of science.

"Psychoanalysis and the Unconscious" contains more misinformation in a small space than almost any recent book save the "Cruise of the Kawa." It may reasonably be expected that anyone who writes upon psychoanalysis and the unconscious today and expects a hearing should know something about biology. But no biologist would accept such dogmatic statements as

"Life begins now, as always, in an individual living creature. In the beginning of the individual living creature is the beginning of life, every time and always. And life has no beginning apart from this. . . . There is no assignable and no logical reason for individuality."

To give such sentences the semblance of truth there should have been added, "so far as I know." It is misleading to follow up such statements by saying, "having established so much," etc. A poet may be permitted to say that "The young bull in the field has a wrinkled and sad face." Indeed, he may abandon all morphology and animal behaviour and make the graceful serpent rest its head upon its shoulder! But the man who invades the field of science should, at least, practise some accuracy of expression, even though he give himself the latitude of poetic license.

"The White Peacock" was Mr. Lawrence's first novel. It was favourably received. Letty, the principal character, is the trial portrait of all his later heroines. Her creator, in his youth and inexperience, did not know how to make her "carry on," but she is the *anlage* for all his female characters, their immoralities and bestialities. Her story is a simple one. Her mother, a lady of fine character, has been put to the acid test by the moral defalcation of her father, a drunkard and wastrel with charm. Leslie, a young man with money and social position, commonplace, emotionally shallow, spiritually inelastic, unimaginative, but intelligent and straightforward, wooes the temperamental, volatile, romantic Letty. The appeal which Leslie did not make to her is made by George. a young farmer "stoutly built, brown-eyed and fair-skinned," whom Letty finds "ruddy, dark and with greatly thrilling eyes" and whom she calls her bull. Meanwhile George and Letty's brother form a friendship which is in dimmest outline the prototype of that extraordinary relationship existing between Gerald Crich and Rupert Birkin in "Women in Love."

The book shows the influence of Thomas Hardy, after whom Lawrence in his early youth sedulously patterned himself. In those days he was concerned with the photographic description of rustic scenes and particularly the lives of farmers and miners —which he knew from experience—and showed a sensitive appreciation of natural beauty. But the interest of the book is in the fact that it contains trial pictures of most of his later characters. George is Tom Brangwen of "The Rainbow"; Leslie, grown up and more arrogant, is Gerald in "Women in Love" and Gerald Barlow in "Touch and Go"; Cyril, more experienced and daring, is called Rupert Birkin when he is introduced again. In all of Lawrence's books the same characters appear. They vary only in having different standards and different degrees of immorality. The environment is always the same—a mining town; a countryside pitted with collieries; farms teeming with evidence of vegetable and animal life which is described with such intensity that the reader feels he is witnessing a new era of creation; mean drab houses; and squalid pubs. Into these and the schoolhouses and churches he puts his sex-tortured men and hyper-sexed women and surges them with chaotic vehemence of invitation and embrace and with the aches, groans, and shrieks of amorous love.

His second novel, "The Trespassers," shows the author to have, in addition to a sensitive and impassioned apprehension of nature, great capacity for describing the feelings of commonplace people. Helena, headstrong, determined, emancipated, self-sufficient, falls in love with her music teacher, Sigmund, a man of forty who had married when seventeen a matter-of-fact young woman who gave him many children which he ill-supported while she slaved and became sour and slatternly. Helena notices that Sigmund is tired and suggests that they spend a few days together in the Isle of Wight. She makes the plans, finds a nice motherly person who will take them into her cottage more for company than money, and, though this seems to be her first adventure, she acts with the certainty which attends experience. The scenery and tools that Mr. Lawrence uses so skilfully are all here: moonlight and its effect to produce ecstasy; bathing and lying naked on the sand or the grass and gazing approvingly at the body; lovely flowers and plants; and above all, a knowledge of the effects of baffled eroticism, of collision between primitive simple passion and artificial fantasying aberrant passion. Like Hermione Roddice of "Women in Love," Helena's genetic instincts are abnormal. She has her Louisa, ten years her senior, whom she treats with indifference, cruelty, or affection, as it pleases her. Early in the history of man the prototype of Helena and Hermione was known. Shuah's second son, it is alleged, was the first example. The Lord slew Onan as soon as he deliberately violated the first and most essential principle of nature, but this drastic measure did not eradicate the biologic aberration, for it has displayed itself in the human species from that day to this, and even today gives more concern to parents and pedagogues than any other instinct deviation. Fortunately novelists, until the advent of Mr. Lawrence, have not featured this infirmity.

Even in these juvenile days, Mr. Lawrence left very little to the imagination. Helena and Sigmund, lying on the cold wet beach in the twilight, enveloped in the Scotch mist (parenthetically it may be said that his heroes and heroines are wholly insensitive to bodily discomfort when they are in the throes of concupiscence) were practising the "Overture to Love,"

"and when Helena drew her lips away she was much exhausted. She belonged to that class of dreaming women with whom passion exhausts itself at the mouth. Her desire was accomplished in a real kiss. She then wanted to go to sleep. She sank away from his caresses, passively, subtly drew back from him."

The next morning Sigmund goes into the sea, and this gives the author opportunity to display the burning passion which the sight and contemplation of the male human body seems to cause in him.

"He glanced at his wholesome maturity, the firm plaiting of his breasts, the full thighs, creatures proud in themselves, and said 'She ought to be rejoiced at me, but she is not. She rejects me as if I were a baboon under my clothing.'"

When Mr. Lawrence convinced himself that he could write a more panoplied description of erotic ecstasy than that with which he afflicted Helena, he wrote the description of Ursula's encounter with the moon in "The Rainbow." Indeed the real motive of "The Trespassers" is a trial portrait of Ursula; and while making up his mind as to the size of the canvas and the colours that he would use in painting that modern Messalina, Mr. Lawrence gave the world "Sons and Lovers," which more than any other of his books, gave him a reputation for an understanding of the strange blood bonds that unite families and human beings, and for having an unusual, almost exquisite discrimination in the use of language.

From boyhood Mr. Lawrence seems to have been possessed of a demon who whispered to him by day and shrieked to him by night, "Be articulate, say it with words," and the agony of his impotence is heartrending, as frustration after frustration attends his efforts. He tries it in prose, then in verse. Gradually, from taking thought, from sex experience and from hasty perusal of scientific and mystic literature, there formulated in his mind a concrete thought, which in time engendered a conviction, finally an obsession. A brief exposition of the mental elaboration and the Laocoon grip that it took on him follows:

The Greeks, fanning the embers of Egyptian civilisation and getting no fire for their torch, said,

"Let there be an ideal to which all mankind shall bow the knee. Let consciousness and all its manifestations be expressed in terms of ideals and ideas or in conduct that expresses them, and finally let everything that tends to hinder such expression, such as the sensual and animal in man be subdued and repressed."

Christianity went a step further and said,

"Not only shall ideals be exalted, but pure spirituality and perfection—man's goal—can only be obtained by the annihilation of what are called Animal Instincts."

Christianity's promoters and well-wishers realised, however, that the continuance of the race depended upon the gratification of these appetites, and so laws and conventions were made under whose operation they could be legitimately indulged, there being small hope that the wish expressed by Sir Thomas Browne, the author of "Religio Medici" and a flock of children, that man might procreate as do the trees, should

D. H. LAWRENCE
From a drawing by *Jan Juta*

ever be gratified. In civilised lands the conquest of the lower self has been objective. Man has moved from a great impulse within himself, the unconscious. Once the conquest has been effected, the conscious mind turns, looks, and marvels:

> "E come quei che con lena affannata
> Uscito fuor del pelago alla riva,
> Si volge all'acqua perigliosa, e guata."

This self-conscious mental provoking of sensation and reaction in the great affective centres is called sentimentalism or sensationalism. The mind returns upon the affective centres and sets up in them a deliberate reaction. These are passions exploited by the mind. Or the passional motive may act directly, and not from the mental provocation, and these reactions may be reflected by a secondary process down into the body. This is the final and most fatal effect of idealism, because it reduces everything to self-consciousness into spuriousness, and it is the madness of the world today. It is this madness that Mr. Lawrence has sworn to cure. He is going to do it by conquering what he calls the lower centres, by submitting the lowest plane to the highest. When this is done there will be nothing more to conquer. Then all is one, all is love, even hate is love, even flesh is spirit. The great oneness, the experience of infirmity, the triumph of the living spirit, which at last includes everything, is then accomplished. Man becomes whole, his knowledge becomes complete, he is united with everything. Mr. Lawrence has mapped out a plan of the sympathetic nervous system and has manipulated what biologists call the tropisms in such a way as to convince himself that he has laid the scientific foundation for his work, but as there is scarcely a page or paragraph in his little book that does not contain statements which are at variance with scientific facts, it is unnecessary to say that his science will not assist him in his propaganda nearly so much as his fiction. Like Weininger, he finally eliminates women. As he puts it:

"Acting from the last and profoundest centres, man acts womanless." It is no longer a question of race continuance. It is a question of sheer ultimate being, the perfection of life nearest to death and yet furthest away from it. Acting from these centres man is an extreme being, the unthinkable warrior, creator, mover, and maker. "And the polarity is between man and man."

That sentence contains to him who can read it aright the whole truth of Mr. D. H. Lawrence. To some that brief statement has the luminousness and significance of the writing on the wall. Anyone who reads Mr. Lawrence's later books attentively—and I appreciate that it is some task to do it—will understand it; and those who, like myself, have devoted themselves to study of aberrations, genesic and mental, as they display themselves in geniuses, psychopaths, and neuropaths, as well as in ordinary men, will sense it correctly.

Mr. Lawrence thinks there are three stages in the life of man: the stage of sexless relations between individuals, families, clans, and nations; the stage of sex relations with an all-embracing passional acceptance, culminating in the eternal orbit of marriage; and finally, the love between comrades, the manly love which only can create a new era of life. One state does not annul the other; it fulfills the other. Such, in brief, is the strange venture in psychopathy Mr. Lawrence is making, and contributions to it up to date are "Women in Love," "Psychoanalysis and the Unconscious," and "Aaron's Rod." "The Prussian Officer," "The Rainbow," "The Lost Girl," "Look, We Have Come Through" were merely efforts to get his propaganda literature into shape.

The Adam and Eve of Mr. Lawrence's new creation are Tom Brangwen and his wife; and to understand their descendants (and no one, not even Mr. Lawrence, can understand them fully) one must study the parents. Tom, the youngest of the Brangwen family, as a boy is rather heavy and stupid intellectually, sensitive to the atmosphere around him, brutal perhaps, but at the same time delicate, very delicate. He does not get on in school, so he leaves precipitously when he is fifteen, after having laid open the master's head with a slate, but not before he has formed a masochistic friendship with a warm clever frail boy. Sex desire begins soon to torment him. His first experience causes his sensibilities to rebel, and the second is a failure because of his self-consciousness and the dominancy of a budding inferiority complex. He is on the way to anæsthetising desire by brandy drinking, to which he periodically gives himself, when one day he meets on the street a demure lady whose curious absorbed flitting motion arrests him and causes a joy of pain to run through him.

"She had felt Tom go by almost as if he had brushed her. She had tingled in body as she had gone up on the road. Her impulse was strong against him because he was not of her sort. But one blind instinct led her to take him, to have him, and then to relinquish herself to him. It would be safety. Also he was young and very fresh."

Her passional reactions are not from the mind. They are spontaneous and know no inhibition. After a second quite casual meeting, Tom goes to the vicarage where she, a Polish lady, is housekeeper since her husband, a doctor obliged to leave his country for political reasons, had died and left her and her baby daughter in dire want. "Good evening," says Tom, "I'll just come in a minute"; and having entered, he continues, "I came up to ask if you'd marry me." He arouses an intensity of passion in her that she cannot, or wishes not, to withstand. But Tom is conventional and so they are married. The description of his marital lust is lurid to the last degree, and finally after one great debauch "he felt that God had passed through the married pair and made Himself known to them." Tom is largely brawn and brute, though he has a vein of sentiment, and finally he yields to drink and meets a violent death, leaving two sons, a namesake who is attracted to his own sex, Fred who suffers the tortures of a mother-sapped spirit, and Anna, his stepdaughter.

Anna hates people who come too near her until she meets Will Brangwen, the son of Tom's brother who had flagrantly offended matrimonial convention. She is fascinated by this æsthetic serious self-satisfied youth with a high-pitched voice, who sings tenor and who is interested in church architecture and ritualism. Anna hurls herself at Will's head and tells him in no uncertain tones of her all-consuming love before he makes any protests. She arranges the wheat shocks in the moonlight so that they will propitiate her purpose, but only passionate caresses and a proposal of marriage result. This disappoints her, but the men of the Brangwen family, though consumed with elemental passion, are sex-slackers compared with the women. Will goes into states of ecstasy sitting motionless and timeless, contemplating stained-glass windows and other religious symbols, and she hates him violently.

"In the gloom and mystery of the church his soul lived and ran free, like some strange, underground thing, abstract. In this spirit he seemed to escape and run free of her."

They are happy only when in the throes of conjugality. She is profoundly fecund and has periods of ecstasy when she thinks God has chosen her to prove the miracle of creation. In her exaltation, big with child as she is, she dances naked in her bedroom, to the Creator to Whom she belongs.

In order to develop the now widely disseminated Freudian ideas about the love of the eldest girl for the father, the antagonism between the mother and daughter, etc., Will falls in love with his oldest child, Ursula. "His heart grew red-hot with passionate feeling for the child" when she is about a year old. "Her father was the dawn wherein her consciousness woke up wide-eyed, unseeing, she was awakened too soon." The writer, master as he is of the mysteries of perversion, uses this sympathy and Will's extrauxorial vagaries and wanderings

to cause, vicariously, a welling-up of passion in Anna. After a
revolting scene with a grisette, Will goes home to his wife who
immediately detects that there is a change in him, that he has
had a new experience. She is excited to wild lubricity, and
"he got an inkling of the vastness of the unknown sensual
store of delight she was." But this is the book of Ursula.
The spontaneous passions of the grandmother and mother are
incidental.

Ursula goes through with the son of the old Polish clergyman
Baron the same sort of experience that her father went through
with the flapper that he picked up at the movie, only not with
such *slancio*. The purpose of this episode is to point out the
intensity of love in the female and her clamour for the dominant male. When Ursula finds that Skrebensky is a slacker,

"She stood filled with the full moon, offering herself. Her two
breasts opened to make way for it, her body opened wide like
a quivering anemone, a soft, dilated invitation touched by the
moon. She wanted the moon to fill into her, she wanted more,
more communion with the moon, consummation."

Since Ursula has not met the one-hundred-per-cent male,
and as "her sexual life flamed into a kind of disease within
her," Mr. Lawrence now brings her into relations with a finely
portrayed Lesbian, Winifred Inger. The description of their
first real contact in the bungalow at night and their night bath
is willfully and purposely erotic. Ursula, tired of Winifred,
plans to marry her to her uncle, Tom. When they meet "he
detected in her a kinship with his own dark corruption. Immediately he knew they were akin." One might safely say that
Mr. Lawrence had before him, or in his mind's eye, when he
penned the description of Tom, the photograph of one of his
fellow-poets of a generation ago whom the English public
found necessary to put in the Reading Gaol.

"His manner was polite, almost foreign, and rather cold. He
still laughed in his curious, animal fashion, suddenly wrinkling

up his wide nose, and showing his sharp teeth. The fine beauty of his skin and his complexion, some almost waxen quality, hid the strange, repellant grossness of him, the slight sense of putrescence, the commonness which revealed itself in his rather fat thighs and loins."

It is in the chapter "The Bitterness of Ecstasy" that Mr. Lawrence takes off the brakes. In London, whither she has gone with Skrebensky, Ursula decides to solve the riddle of the Sphinx. She goes about it in the conventional Brangwen way by biting him, clawing him, and generally tearing him to pieces. It seems good to him and he likes her and wants to marry her. One day, after they have had some tall bouts of love at Richmond, she tells him that she won't marry him and he has a grand crisis of hysteria. She is sorry she has hurt him. She hails a cab and takes the sobbing wooer home, and the lecherous cabby is moved nearly to violence by the radiation of passion from Ursula. She senses danger and persuades Tony to walk. She knows then that he is but a simulacrum of man, and when she has gone home she decides that she will not marry. Finally, however, she gives in and the date is more or less arranged. Then comes the *grande finale* with the scene wonderfully set in the moonlight by the seashore. There she makes an onslaught on him that is tigress-like to the last degree, throws him on the sand, devours him, wrings him like a dirty rag, shows him that he is no good, and hurls him from her, a sucked lemon. He sneaks away and offers himself to his Colonel's daughter, is accepted, and is off to India, leaving "the need of a world of men for her."

Then comes "The Rainbow," a parody of Freud's exposition of the dream of being trampled upon by horses. Ursula finds after a time that the customary result has followed her experiences, so she writes a letter to Skrebensky saying she'll be good and go out and marry him. She goes for a walk in the mist and the rain, into the wood where the trees are all phallic symbols "thrust like stanchions upright between the roaring overhead and the sweeping of the circle underfoot." She begins to hallucinate, to feel her subconsciousness take possession of her, and the sight of a group of horses fills her bestial soul with a hope that she might finally be possessed in such a way as would give her satisfaction, that she might get "some fantastic fulfilment in her life." She goes into a state of delirium and several weeks later, when it has passed, she finds that she has miscarried. This is followed by a mild dementia; she thinks she is moral and will be good, but as she gets strong she sees the rainbow, which is Eros kindling the flames again.

"And she saw in the rainbow the earth's new architecture, the old brittle corruption of houses and factories swept away, the world built up in a living fragment of Truth, fitting to the overarching heaven."

Mr. Lawrence, exhausted with the perpetration of these sensual delights and disappointed with the distrusts of the flesh, turned for a short time to nature to refresh his spirit and bathe his soul. He sensed frustration despite the unleashment of passion; he realised that sublimation had eluded him, and so he turned to primitive life and primitive people, the peasants of Italy. Soon his torments began to creep up again in "Twilight in Italy." The roused physical sensations will not subside. They penetrate pastoral scenes and emanate from sylvan scenery.

After having refreshed himself, he gave the world "The Lost Girl," whose genesic aberrations are comparatively mild, and whose antics with the half-gipsy, half-circus folk are rather amusing. Some of Mr. Lawrence's early admirers were encouraged to look for his reformation, especially after the appearance of a thin book of poems entitled "Bay." Even in this, here and there, the inhibited and mother-sapped spirit crops out, as in the poem called "The Little Town in the Evening," but for the most part the verses are founded on sane ideas, even ideals, truths, and morality. Most of them are poems of the war, wonderful pen pictures and silhouettes, such as "Town," a London transformed by the war as no picture or prose description could render it, ending,

> "It is well,
> That London, lair of sudden
> Male and female darknesses
> Has broken her spell."

In previous volumes of poems, particularly in "Amores" and in "Look, We Have Come Through," he had published verse which was highly appraised by competent critics, and hailed by a small group steeped in preciosity, as epoch-making. However, if most of his poems have any central or dominant idea, he is unable to express it. They are the verbal manifestations of moods expressed symbolically, allegorically; of sensuous desires, satisfactions, and satieties "seeking polarity," to borrow his favourite expression. Nearly everything is passion with Mr. Lawrence, or suggestive of passion. The pure lily is a phallic symbol, the bee sucking honey from a flower is a ravisher of innocence, the earth itself bursts asunder periodically in the throes of secret sensuality. Only the sea is free from the trammels of lust, and it is

> "Sworn to a high and splendid purposelessness
> Of brooding and delighting in the secret of life's going."

"New Poems," published in this country in 1920, did not fame or defame him, although "Piano," "Intime," "Sickness," and "Twenty Years Ago" might well have done the former, and "Seven Seals" the latter.

The lull did not last long, and it was only a lull before a storm, a hurricane, a tornado which spent its force and destruction upon the author and made him the outlaw, if not the outcast, of English literature. "Women in Love" is the adventure of two sisters, Ursula and Gudrun Brangwen, the Brangwens whose frightful passions we have now known for three generations, and two men of breeding, wealth, and culture, Gerald Crich, a Sadist by inheritance and natural inclination, and Rupert Birkin, an intellectual, apparently male, but contradicted in this by his instinct and by his conduct, whose purpose and ambition is to fall into the long African process of purely sensual understanding.

The portrait of Rupert Birkin is superb. No excerpt could convey Mr. Lawrence's capacity for characterisation as well as the paragraph which describes him:

"He was thin, pale and ill-looking. His figure was narrow but nicely made. He went with a slight trail of one foot, which came only from self-consciousness. His nature was clever and separate. He did not fit at all in the conventional occasion. He affected to be quite ordinary, perfectly and marvellously commonplace. And he did it so well, taking the tone of his surroundings, adjusting himself quickly to his interlocutor and his circumstance, that he achieved a verisimilitude of ordinary commonplaceness that usually propitiated his onlookers for a moment, disarmed them from attacking his singleness. He did not believe in any standards of behaviour though they are necessary for the common ruck. Anyone who is anything can be just himself and do as he likes. One should act spontaneously on one's impulses—it's the only gentlemanly thing to do, provided you are fit to do it."

Hermione Roddice, daughter of a Derbyshire baron, a tall slow reluctant woman, with a weight of fair hair and pale long face that she carries lifted up in the Rosetti fashion, and that seems almost drugged as if a strange mass of thoughts coil in the darkness within her allowing her no escape, is in love with him. "She needed conjunction with Rupert Birkin to make her whole and, she believed, happy. But the more she strove to bring him to her, the more he battled her back."

Gerald Crich, whose gleaming beauty and maleness is like a young good-natured smiling wolf, flashes upon Gudrun Brangwen and she succumbs at once, just as the Polish lady did when Gudrun's grandfather got sight of her from the tail of his eye. The first time Gerald and Rupert meet "There was a pause of strange enmity between the two men that was very near to love." Going up in the train to London together, they have a talk about ideals, the object and aim of life. This gives Rupert time to formulate his thought that Humanity does not embody the utterance of the incomprehensible any more. Humanity is a dead letter. There will be a new embodiment in a new way. Let humanity disappear as quickly as possible. They are introduced into bohemia; that is, the haunts of the semi-abandoned and the perverted. Birkin shares a flat with Halliday, a degenerate "with a moving beauty of his own," and his friends. Just how far this group expresses Mr. Lawrence's own views of art and philosophy, in their discussion of wood carvings of the primitive negroes of West Africa, we need not attempt to estimate, but that need not deter us from saying that the description of a gathering around the fireplace in a state of complete nudity is indecent and disgusting, even though Mr. Lawrence thinks this kind of thing marks a milestone on the way to that which he calls "Allness."

A large portion of the book is, in my judgment, obscene, deliberately, studiously, incessantly obscene. Obscenity, like everything else, has its gradations, its intensities, its variations, and the author of this book knows how to ring the changes upon obscenity in a way that would make Aretino green with envy. For instance, the so-called wrestling scene between Rupert and Gerald is the most obscene narrative that I have encountered in the English language—obscene in the etymological sense, for it is ill-omened, hence repulsive; and in the legal sense, for it tends to corrupt the mind and to subvert respect for decency and morality. The major part of Hermione's conduct with Rupert is in the realm of perversion, and Rupert in his speech to her conveys by innuendo what Mr. Lawrence knows the laws of his country would not permit him to say directly. The Marquis de Sade was a mere novice in depicting the transports of lust that result from inflicting injury or causing humiliation compared with Mr. Lawrence; and as for Sacher-Masoch, who worked on the other side of the shield, he merely staked out the claim for a young Britisher to cultivate.

Hermione says that if we could only realise that in the spirit we are all one, all equal in spirit, all brothers there, the rest would not matter. There would then be no more struggle for power and prestige, the things which now destroy. This drives Rupert to violence. He denies it savagely. We are alike in everything *save* spirit. In the spirit he is as separate as one star from another; as different in quality and quantity. Establish a state on that. This destroys the last vestige of Hermione's restraint and facilitates the consummation of voluptuous ecstasy at last. With a beautiful ball of lapis lazuli, a paper weight, she smashes his skull while he is sitting in her boudoir.

A second blow would have broken his neck had he not shied it with a volume of Thucydides (a deft touch to make the immortal Greek save the prototype of the Superman that Mr. Lawrence is introducing while he buries Greek idealism).

"She must smash it, it must be smashed before her ecstasy was consummated, fulfilled forever. A thousand lives, a thousand deaths matters nothing now, only the fulfilment of this perfect ecstasy."

But he gets away from her.

"Then she staggered to the couch, and lay down, and went heavily to sleep"; and he wanders into the wet hillside that is overgrown and obscure with bushes and flowers. Here Mr. Lawrence gives a classic description of masochistic lust.

"He took off his clothes and sat down naked among the primroses . . . but they were too soft. He went through the long grass to a clump of young fir trees, that were no higher than a man. The soft-sharp boughs beat upon him, as he moved in keen pangs against them, threw little cold showers of drops on his belly, and beat his loins with their clusters of soft-sharp needles. There was a thistle which pricked him vividly, but not too much, because all his movements were discriminate and soft. To lie down and roll in the sticky young hyacinths, to lie on one's belly and cover one's back with handfuls of fine wet grass, soft as a breath, softer and more delicate and more beautiful than the touch of any woman; and then to sting one's thighs against the living dark bristles of the fir-boughs; and then to feel the light whip of the hazel on one's shoulders, stinging, and then to clasp the silvery birch trunk against one's breast, its smoothness, its hardness, its vital knots and ridges—this was good, this was all very good, very satisfying."

And this is the man who Mr. Lawrence would have us believe was Inspector of Schools in England in the beginning of the Twentieth Century! The idea that he wants a woman is now absurd. This is his idea of bliss. He knows where to plant himself, his seed: along with the trees in the folds of the delicious fresh-growing leaves. This is his place, his marriage place.

It may interest Mr. Lawrence to know that this procreative idea of Birkin's is not original with him. Many years ago I encountered a man in the Kings Park State Hospital who was of the same belief and addicted to the same practice.

It would not be convincing if only æsthetes, intelligentsia, artists, and the like had revolutionary ideas. Gerald, a man of business, an executive, a coal baron, aggressive, capable, also had them, inherited from his mother, acquired from Birkin and "made in Germany" where he had been sent to school. He makes love to Ursula by expounding his theories of life:

"If only man was swept off the face of the earth, creation would go on so marvellously, with a new start, non-human. Man is one of the mistakes of creation—like the ichthyosauri. If only we were gone again, think what lovely things would come out of the liberated days; things straight out of the fire."

He wants her without contract, understood or stated:

"There is a final me which is stark and impersonal and beyond responsibility. So there is a final you. And it is there I should want to meet you—not in the emotional, loving plane—but there beyond, where there is no speech and no terms of agreement. There we are two stark, unknown beings, two utterly strange creatures. I should want to approach you and you me.—And there could be no obligation, because there is no standard for action there, because no understanding has been reaped from that plane. It is quite inhuman—so there can be no calling to book, in any form whatsoever—because one is outside the pale of all that is accepted, and nothing known applies. One can only follow the impulse, take that which lies in front, and responsible for nothing, asked for nothing, giving nothing, only each taking according to the primal desire."

In other words, sheer savagery, and the worst African variety at that!

One of Mr. Lawrence's obsessions is that he can distinguish between the sexual writhings of his characters, depending upon the environment in which they writhe and the immediate exciting cause. This justifies him in describing the same writhe over and over with a different setting. Of the five hundred pages, at least one hundred are devoted to descriptions of the sensations that precede and accompany ecstasy provoked and induced by some form of unhealthy sexual awareness.

It is impossible to give even a brief synopsis of "Women in Love." One chapter, however, must be mentioned, for in a way it is the crux of the book. For some time Birkin has been trying to state his case to Ursula and stave off her clamour for consummation. He wants sex to revert to the level of the other appetites, to be regarded as a functional process, not as fulfilment. He wants her to give him her spirit.

"He knew he did not want further sensual experience, he thought. His mind reverted to the African statues in Halliday's rooms. They displayed their thousand upon thousand of years of sensual knowledge, purely unspiritual. Thousands of years ago that which was imminent in himself must have taken place in these Africans. This is what was imminent in him; the goodness, the holiness, the desire for creation and productive happiness must have lapsed, leaving the single impulse for knowledge in one sort, mindless, progressive knowledge through the senses, knowledge arrested and ending in the senses, mystic knowledge in disintegration and dissolution. Is the day of our creative life finished or are we not ready for the sensual understanding, the knowledge in the mystery of dissolution? The man Ursula would take must be quaffed to the dregs by her, he must render himself up to her. She believed that love surpassed the individual. She believed in an absolute surrender to love. He didn't."

They then have a violent verbal altercation in which Ursula tells him what she thinks of his obscenity and perverseness in words that admit of no misunderstanding. She then leaves him in a state of wrath and resentment after having thrown the topaz engagement ring, bought from a second-hand dealer, in his face. But her ardour conquers her righteousness and she goes back to him, saying, "See what a flower I found you." And then it is settled quietly and as if they were normal humans. They go to a hotel and there they have supercorporeal contact that beggars description. As far as can be made out, there is no consortion in the ordinary sense. It is neither love nor passion.

"She had established a rich new circuit, a new current of passional electric energy, between the two of them released from the darkest poles of the body and established in perfect circuit, and she had done this in some mysterious ways by tracing the back of his thighs with her sensitive fingertips, his mysterious loins and his thighs. Something more mystically-physically satisfying than anything she had imagined or known —though she had had some experience—was realised. She had thought that there was no source deeper than the phallic source, but now from the strange marvellous flanks and thighs came the flood of ineffable darkness and ineffable riches."

They laughed and went to the meal provided. And this is what they had:

"There was a venison pasty, of all things, a large broad-faced cut ham, eggs and cresses, and red beet root, and medlars and apple tart, and tea."

There is a deep, dark significance in this meal, which the Freudian will understand perfectly, but which to the uninitiated will seem quite meaningless, even after Ursula says, "What *good* things.   How noble it looks."

There is a lot more about the full mystic knowledge that she gets from his suave loins of darkness, the strange, magical current of force in his back and his loins, that fills with nausea. They finish by driving to Sherwood Forest, taking all their clothes off and beginning anew their effort for fulfilment.

"She was to him what he was to her, the immemorial magnificence of mystic, palpable, real utterance."

I have neither the strength nor the inclination to follow Gudrun in her search for her amatory *Glückeritter*, or to hear further exposition of the *credo* of the strange freak of nature that Mr. Lawrence strives to apotheosise.   Suffice it to say that the precious quartette go off to the Tyrol, Ursula and Birkin having gone through the formality of marriage; Gudrun and Gerald dispensing with it.   And there Gudrun begins writhings which are designed to put all the others in the shade.   And in a way they do, because Gerald's violent death is required to facilitate her supreme moment.   They introduce a super-degenerate Loerke, a sculptor, who represents the rock bottom of all life to Gudrun.

"There was the look of a little wastrel about him that intrigued her, and an old man's look, that interested her, and then, besides this, an uncanny singleness, that marked out an artist to her.   He had come up from a street Arab.   He was twenty-six, had thieved, sounded every depth.   He saw in Gudrun his soul-mate.   He knew her with a sub-conscious, sinister knowledge, devoid of illusions and hopes.   The degradation of his early life also attracted her.   He seemed to be the very stuff of the underworld of life. There was no going beyond him. Birkin understood why they should like him, the little obscene monster of the darkness that he is. He is a Jew who lives like a rat, in the river of corruption."

Birkin and Ursula come back for Gerald's funeral. Birkin does some soliloquising, the burden of which is "He should have loved me. I offered him." He is sure Gerald would have been happy if he had accepted. When Ursula wants to know if she is not enough for him, he says,

"No, to make life complete, really complete, I wanted eternal union with a man too, another kind of love."
"It is a perversity," she said.
"Well——," he said.
"You can't have two kinds of love. Why should you?" she said.
"It seems as if I can't," he said. "Yet I wanted it."
"You can't have it because it's wrong, impossible," she said.
"I don't believe that," he answered.

And that is the unvarying and final answer of the advocates of the enigmatic aberration whose doctrines Mr. Lawrence is trying to foist upon an unsuspecting English-reading public.

In "Aaron's Rod" Mr. Lawrence returns to the theme of "The Rainbow" and "Women in Love." His ardour, fortunately, has cooled somewhat, but his psychology is more at variance with facts and his philosophy more mystic than in either of these. Aaron Sisson, a miner's checkweighman, with a talent for music, marries when twenty, an oversexed young woman of better social position than himself. Though he soon betrays her, they manage to live, with their three children, an average family life for twelve years. He then determines that he will not be the instrument and furnisher of any woman. He rebels against the sacrament by which we live today; namely, that man is the giver, woman the receiver. He can not and will not tolerate the life centrality of woman. Man's contact with woman should be for procreational purposes, but man should blend his spirit with man: "Born in him was a spirit which could not worship woman, and would not."

So he sets up the Christmas tree for the children, goes out to buy candles for it, and never returns. Instead, he falls in with a family group of inverts which the little mining towns always seem to have—a man of perverted type; his fiancée, a Lesbian, the daughter of a promiscuous Hermione and her complaisant husband; and several others—and they proceed to have a mild orgy in the ugly midland mining town, "in which it is remarkable how many odd or extraordinary people there are to be found." Aaron gets a position as flutist in an orchestra, and at the opera he meets Mr. Lilly, who, though married, is by nature of inverted genesic instinct. He is Aaron's downfall.

It is to be noted that there is a deep symbolism in the names that Mr. Lawrence selects for his heroes and heroines. Aaron is sure that he never wanted to surrender himself to his wife, nor to his mother, nor to anybody. But he falls ill, and Lilly cares for him and nurses him like a mother, and then goes off to Italy—Aaron after him like a hound after the scent. We are introduced to a choice lot of males in Florence, all portraits of exiled Britishers who find it suits their tastes, which their country calls their infirmities, to live there, and easily recognisable by anyone who has lived in Florence. We are regaled with their philosophy and with Mr. Lawrence's reflections on art and Sixteenth Century music. Finally, to show Aaron's charm and concupiscense, the author throws a modern brooding Cleopatra—Anthony-less—across his path. She is an American woman from the Southern States whose father was once Ambassador to France. Aaron capitulates at the second interview and then despises himself. But again he falls a few days later, and then he realises that there is nothing left for him but flight, flight to Lilly and abandonment of the love idea and the love motive. Life submission is his duty now, and when he looks up into Lilly's face, at the moment resembling a Byzantine Eikon, and asks, "And to whom shall I submit?" the reply comes, "Your soul will tell you."

And my soul tells me that he who submits himself to reading the doctrines promulgated by D. H. Lawrence deserves his punishment. Moreover, I maintain that, both from the artistic and the psychological standpoints, Mr. Lawrence's performances are those of a neophyte and a duffer. He can make words roar and sing and murmur, and by so doing he can make moral, poised, God-fearing, sentiment-valuing man creep and shudder, indeed, almost welcome the obscurity of the grave, so that he will not have to meet his fellow again in the flesh. He libels and he bears false witness against man. There are persons in the world such as Mr. Lawrence describes. So are there lepers and lunatics. We do not talk about them as if the whole world were made up of them; and we do not confidently look for world reformers or world orderers among them.

Mr. Lawrence is a self-appointed crusader who is going to destroy European civilisation and at the same time revivify that of six thousand and more years ago. He is the most shining avatar of mysticism the Twentieth Century has yet produced, and the most daring champion of atavism in twenty centuries. He is using a medium to facilitate his manifestations and embodiments of which he is a consummate master, viz., fiction. But his statements, both when he uses the language of science, and when he uses that of fiction, are at variance with truth and fact; and he has not furnished, nor can he furnish, a particle of evidence to substantiate his thesis: enhancement of the awareness and potency "of that other basic mind, the deepest physical mind" by sensuous satisfaction or through sexual ecstasy. His "broodings and delightings in the secret of life's goings" are anathema.

During the past decade biology has accumulated a convincing amount of evidence to show that sex integrades, or imperfect sex separation and differentiation frequently exist, and furthermore it may be produced experimentally. These facts justify the belief that individuals with the convictions and conduct of Birkin result from a definite developmental condition, which is the fundamental cause of the peculiar sex reactions. Such persons are actually different from fully expressed males or females, and their peculiar condition is permanent, present from childhood to old age, and uninfluenceable by any measures; pedagogy or punishment, mandate or medicine.

My experience as a psychologist and alienist has taught me that pornographic literature is created by individuals whose genesic endowment is subnormal *ab initio,* or exhausted from one cause or another before nature intended that it should be, and that those who would aid God and nature in the ordering of creation are sterile, or approximately so. This is a dispensation for which we cannot be too grateful.

There are two ways of contemplating Mr. Lawrence's effort. Has he a fairly clear idea of what he is trying to say, of what he is trying to put over; or is he a poetic mystic groping in abysmal darkness? I am one of those who is convinced that he knows just what he wants to accomplish, and that he could make a statement of it in language that anyone could understand, did the censor permit him. Public opinion is adequate to deal with the infractions of taste and ethics that he has perpetrated, and it is quite safe to leave him finally to that judiciary.

Mr. Lawrence once wrote, "The Americans are not worthy of their Whitman. Miracle that they have not annihilated every word of him." To which I would make rejoinder, "The Britishers have not deserved D. H. Lawrence. Pity it is that they do not annihilate every trace of him."

Ten years have gone since Henry James, walking up and down the charming garden of his picturesque villa in Rye, discussing the most promising successors of Hardy, Meredith, and Conrad, said to me, "The world is sure to hear from a young man, D. H. Lawrence." It has heard from him. He has sown in glory and raised in corruption. He has triumphed, and his triumph has stained English literature. He has debased an unusual talent and devoted his splendid endowment of artistry to spoking the wheel of evolutionary progress, even to spinning it in a reverse direction. He has arrived, and in arriving has brought with him a sweltering, suffocating South African atmosphere, difficult and dangerous for one of his former admirers to breathe, who as he withdraws from it ventures to call the attention of others to its noxiousness.

# CHAPTER XII

## THE JOY OF LIVING—AND WRITING ABOUT IT:
## JOHN ST. LOE STRACHEY

TWENTY-FIVE years ago, browsing among the second-hand book-shops of Shaftesbury Avenue, my attention was arrested by a sombre volume entitled "From Grave to Gay," by J. St. Loe Strachey.

Until then I had not heard of Mr. Strachey, and though I admit it with reluctance, I had not even heard of his famous cousin, Henry Strachey, who was private secretary to Lord Clive. But the subtitle of his book: "Concerned with Certain Subjects of Serious Interest, with the Puritans, with Literature and with the Humours of Life, Now for the First Time Collected and Arranged," intrigued me. Those were the very subjects, I had convinced myself, with which I was concerned, for did they not give spice to life and make for surcease of its burdens? "Now for the First Time Collected and Arranged" I construed to be a belief on the part of the writer that from time to time he could substitute for the word "first" the other numerals in progressive order. Whether or not he has been able to do so, I have not determined, but every one knows that he became "editor and sole proprietor" of the London *Spectator* and has occupied a conspicuous place in journalism for the past quarter of a century. And now he recounts his life, or such parts of it as seem to him will permit others to understand how and why he has carried on, and he calls it "The Adventure of Living: A Subjective Autobiography," stressing "the influences that have affected my life and for good or evil made me what I am." He emphasises that the interesting thing about a human being is not what he is, but how he came to be what he is, which naturally includes what he does and why he does it.

Mr. Strachey came to be what he is from his heredity, aided and guided—after it had formulated itself in the organism to which, a few months later, the name John St. Loe was given—by Mrs. Salome Leaker, the family nurse. Once the reader gets her name out of the realm of risibility, he falls in love with her. A face radiant with a vivid intelligence, a nature eager and active, a fiery temper—reserved almost entirely for grown-ups—an appreciation for good literature and art, which, although she had been brought up in illiteracy, she had developed by self-education and "threw quotations from the English classics around her in a kind of hailstorm," supplemented a genuine love of children and abounding common sense.

"There was no nonsense in her nursery as to over-exciting our minds or emotions, or that sort of thing. She was quite prepared to read us to sleep with the witches in 'Macbeth' or the death scene in 'Othello.' I can see her now, with her wrinkled, brown face, her cap with white streamers awry over her black hair beginning to turn grey. In front of her was a book, propped up against the rim of a tin candlestick shaped like a small basin. In it was a dip candle with a pair of snuffers. That was how nursery light was provided in the later 'sixties and even in the 'seventies. As she sat bent forward, declaiming the most soul-shaking things in Shakespeare between nine and ten at night, we lay in our beds with our chins on the counterpane, silent, scared, but intensely happy. We loved every word and slept quite well when the play was over."

The pen picture of Mrs. Salome Leaker, and the photograph, are of the book's best. It is not unlikely that Mr. Strachey owes his worldly success and pleasure quite as much to his nurse as to "the famous men, and our fathers who begat us," of whom his father, "though without a trace of anything approaching pride, was never tired of talking."

In his early childhood he was subject to occasional experi-

J. ST. LOE STRACHEY
From a drawing by *W. Rothenstein*

ences—a sense of spiritual isolation with poignancy amounting
to awe. Although he devotes several pages to them he does
not succeed in describing his sensations, but in characterising
them. One day while standing in a passage he suddenly had a
sensation of being alone, not merely in the house, but in the
world, the universe. With this came a sense of exaltation and
magnification of personality so ample that it was difficult to
describe. He felt then, though he was only six, that his soul
had become naked. The effect on him was intensely awe-
inspiring, so much so as to be disturbing in a high degree.
Though not terrified, he experienced a kind of rawness and
sensitiveness of soul, such as when a supersensitive mucous
membrane is touched roughly by a hand or instrument. In
addition to this awe and sensitiveness, was a sudden realisation
of the appalling greatness of the issues of living, not only of
the imminence but of the ineffable greatness of the whole
of which he was a part. He felt that what he was "in for"
as a sentient human being was immeasurably great. It was
thence that the sense of awe came, thence the extraordinary
sensitiveness, thence the painful exhilaration, the spiritual
sublimation. "As a human being I was not only immortal
but *capax imperii,*—a creature worthy of a heritage so tremendous."

Mr. Strachey defines his state as one of *isolement,* and further defines it as ecstasy. The latter term has probably been
borrowed from current psychoanalytic terminology. It is
purely a subjective term, and as this is a subjective autobiography, satisfies his needs, though it puts us only a little
way on the road to understanding.

No objective description of this state has been worked out.
A scheme for it would be elaborate and require more patience
than the behaviourists have so far displayed. They know some
things in an exact way about organic reactions to simplified
laboratory situations. They have never followed out the life
history of any of the reactions they describe, either exactly or

in tentative descriptive terms. Autobiographic writings furnish rich material for an objective psychologist. Mr. Strachey, for instance, has an unusual memory, has never suffered any serious breaks in his reaction system, and would seem not to be subject to any wealth of parallel reactions. The objective psychologists may, in the not distant future, work out a description of *isolement* in terms of organic reactions, and their life histories in terms of organic memory. I do not see how a highly organised intelligence in such a setting—reminiscent father, tradition-ladened background, cultivated and uncultivated mysticism of his nurse—could have failed to develop some such moments.

It is quite likely that the main outlines of Mr. Strachey's intelligence as a working mechanism had been laid down, even at this early age. It was said of him that when a little more than two and a half years old, when his family was starting on a long journey to Pau, he insisted that his father should take with him Spenser's "Faerie Queene!" He must have had in late childhood a rich freight of memories. An elaborate and delicate set of reaction mechanism, spontaneously called forth these definite movements of detachment in the interests of further internal organisation. Moreover, it seems to me entirely a normal experience, in view of the fact that there was so much incentive to fantasy and so little progress beyond mere normal ecstasy.

It is a fearsome thing to contemplate how little fruit the arrival of powers of abstraction bring with them. Immediately Mr. Strachey was plunged into the artificial region of letters and politics, he made no effective contacts with scientific and social thinking of his period. His whole mental career from this standpoint was a gradually elaborated detachment, significant mainly for its richness, brilliancy, and generally prevailing consistency.

One other psychic experience he records, a dream during an afternoon nap: His wife came to him with a telegram in her hand which related that his son had been killed in a hunting accident in France.   The incident of this telepathic dream from the objective standpoint is not very significant.   The dreamer had plenty of reasons for apprehension over the welfare of his son, who was in a country where hazards were of frequent enough occurrence to make some time identity between dream and occurrence possible.   The form of the hazard in the dream could probably have been traced at the time to some recent event or hearsay, and was gratuitously attached to the state of apprehension which came to the surface in the dream state.

The story of one who for a third of a century has been in British journalism while the world was being recast and remoulded must of necessity be rich in the raw material of "human interest," as well as of history and politics.   But it is not this material which the author of the subjective autobiography has chosen to present.   It is with the adventure of his own life that he would interest the reader.   He says,

"Every life is an adventure, and if a sense of this adventure cannot become communicated to the reader, any one may feel sure that it is the fault of the writer, not of the facts."

He quotes Sir Thomas Browne's advice to a son about to write an account of his travels in Hungary

"not to trouble about methods of extracting iron and copper from the ores, or with a multitude of facts and statistics, but not to forget to give a full description of the 'Roman alabaster tomb in the barber's shop at Pesth.' "

The alabaster tomb in the barber's shop, rather than high politics or even high literature, is the goal which he has set before him in writing this book.   The test by which he invites judgment of it is the power to enthrall the imagination of the reader with the sense of adventure.

The "supreme good luck to be born the second son of a Somersetshire squire and to be brought up in a Somersetshire country-house" was reinforced by the influence of parents to whose qualities he pays tribute in a chapter devoted to memories of his parents, and in another devoted to the stories told him as a child by his father. These stories serve to cloak the genealogical facts that always flavour so keenly, to the adventurer himself, the zest of his adventure. In this case they leave the reader free to trace, should he possess a relish for such a trail, through the rattling rust of ancient armour, the spell of great country houses and other symbols of authority. One may also trace Mr. Strachey's hereditary urge for literature, for there was a certain ancestor who "almost certainly knew Shakespeare" and "had a considerable amount of book-writing to his credit," including "two or three pamphlets written by him and published as what we should now call "Virginia Company propaganda.'" No light is thrown upon the heritage, guardian angel, or kind fate which was responsible for providing the adventurer at the outset of his journey with the most fortunate of all possessions, the temperament to "take the good the gods provide," and for relieving him of all encumbrances in the way of "inferiority" and other complexes, which have become so fashionable a part of the modern adventurer's equipment.

If, indeed, anything in the way of good fortune was wanting in the gifts of fate to the author of the autobiography, he was more than compensated by a disposition which made it easy for him to appreciate the good qualities of others, even of his mother-in-law—that usually most unappreciated of all human relations—and to live in unimpaired serenity in her family. Of her we are told that

"she was an admirable talker and full of clear and interesting memories. I had no sooner entered the Simpson house and family than I found that there were a hundred points of sympathy between us. She had known everybody in London who was worth knowing . . . and had visited most of the political country houses in England on the Whig side, and most of the neutral strongholds."

Aside from the chapters on his parents and old nurse, only a few glimpses are given of a normal and happy childhood passed in the good old days when ladies still had time to cultivate the art of correspondence—of which he says, "I have no time to dwell on my mother's most intimate friendship with Lady Waldegrave and with their habit of writing daily letters to each other." The salient point of his childhood seems to be that he was saturated with precocity and filial piety. He was not quite so strong as other boys and was not sent to public school, and "the irony of accident," he says, "had designed my mental equipment to be of a kind perfectly useless for the purposes of the preliminary Oxford examinations." Knowledge of literature, a power of writing, a not inconsiderable reading in modern history, and a commendable grasp of mathematics were of no use whatever for the purpose of matriculation. So the youthful Strachey turned to Latin and Greek and finally entered Balliol as an unattached student. The first discord in the harmony of his relations with life was sounded when he became a student at Balliol, where he did not get on well with the Dons.

"I can say truthfully that I never received a word of encouragement, of kindly direction, or of sympathy of any sort or kind from any of them in regard to work or anything else. The reason, I now feel sure, was that they believed that to take notice of me would have only made me more uppish."

His recollections of Jowett, the Master of Balliol, are tempered by the successes and the good fortune that have come to him in the intervening forty years, but he remains convinced that "the Master of Balliol evidently felt the Stracheyphobia very strongly, or perhaps I should say felt it his duty to express it very strongly." The sarcasm that Jowett poured upon him on his return to Balliol after his first year as an unattached student still rankles. But in those early days there must have been an atmosphere of self-sufficiency, complacency, possibly one might be justified in saying conceit, that dissolved the testy Master's inhibitions.

Mr. Strachey is never tired of emphasising the good fortune of his friendships.

"I have no doubt I was considered odd by most of my contemporaries, but this oddness and also my inability to play football or cricket never seemed to create, as far as I could see, any prejudice. Indeed I think that my friends were quite discerning enough and quite free enough from convention to be amused and interested by a companion who was not built up in accordance with the sealed pattern."

Nothing better illustrates his mental endowment and his cultural equipment as estimated by himself than this statement:

"In my day we would talk about anything, from the Greek feeling about landscape to the principles the Romans would have taken as the basis of actuarial tables, if they had had them. We unsphered Plato, we speculated as to what Euripides would have thought of Henry James, or whether Sophocles would have enjoyed Miss ——'s acting, and felt that it was of vital import to decide these matters."

Good old days, indeed! We can imagine what the fate of the student at Harvard, let us say, would be today if he shaped his talk to indicate that "the most important thing in the world" was talk of this kind.

At an early age Mr. Strachey yielded to the urge of poetry writing, and even had a book of verses printed by a local publisher, of which he says:

"The thing that strikes me most, on looking back at my little volume of verse, is its uncanny competence, not merely from the point of view of prosody, but of phraseology and what I may almost term scholarship."

*Omne ignotum pro magni-* (or *miri*)*fico.* In spite of this he felt no great desire to adopt poetry-making as his profession.

"Possibly I thought the trade was a bad one for a second son who must support himself. It is more probable that I instinctively felt that although it was so great a source of joy to me, poetry was not my true vocation. Perhaps, also, I had already begun to note the voice of pessimism raised by the poets of the seventies, and to feel that they did not believe in themselves."

"The pivot of my life has been *The Spectator,* and so *The Spectator* must be the pivot of my book." His connection with it began when he was about twenty-six, after he had settled in London to study for the Bar. The book opens with an account of the spectacular success of his first adventure of writing for this journal. Armed with a formal introduction from his father, who had been a friend of the joint editors, Mr. Hutton and Mr. Townsend, and a frequent contributor to the paper, Mr. Strachey called at *The Spectator* office in Wellington Street and listened to the well-worn story—no less true thirty years ago than it is today—of "more outside reviewers than they could possibly find work for," and received, out of friendship for his father alone, the choice of five volumes to notice. One of them was an edition of "Gulliver's Travels," and it was destined to play a leading rôle in the adventure of John St. Loe Strachey. Nothing daunted by the indifferent encouragement, he promptly despatched the completed reviews, and in due time again presented himself at the office for the sole purpose of returning the books. Great was his amazement when, instead of a lukewarm reception, he was immediately asked to select anything he would like to review, from a new pile of books. When he protested that he had not come to ask for more books to review, he learned that the position of the editors had been entirely changed by the review of "Gulliver's Travels," and "they hoped very much that I should be able to do regular work for *The Spectator.* I was actually hailed as 'a writer and critic of the first force.' " Even a stronger head might have been turned by such praise from such a source.

This, however, was only the first chapter of his successful adventure with *The Spectator*. Shortly afterwards, he received a letter from Mr. Hutton asking him to write a couple of leaders a week and some notes while Mr. Townsend was away for a holiday. His first leader brought a delighted response from Mr. Townsend, who requested him to remain as his assistant while Mr. Hutton was away, and soon afterward suggested,

"with a swift generosity that still warms my heart, that if I liked to give up the Bar, for which I was still supposing myself to be reading, I could have a permanent place at *The Spectator*, and even, if I remember rightly, hinted that I might look forward to succeeding the first of the two partners who died or retired, and so to becoming joint editor or joint proprietor."

His second political leader, entitled the "Privy Council and the Colonies," brought down even bigger game than the first. Fate, always the ally of Mr. Strachey, so arranged that Lord Granville, then Colonial Secretary, had been prevented by a fit of gout from preparing a speech which he was to deliver when he received the Agents-General of the self-governing Colonies, and he supplied the hiatus by beginning his speech with the words: "In a very remarkable article which appeared in this week's *Spectator*"—and then going on "to use the article as the foundation of his speech," with the result that Mr. Hutton was "greatly delighted, and almost said in so many words that it wasn't every day that the editors of *The Spectator* could draw Cabinet Ministers to advertise their paper."

So the "first two leaders had done the trick." Still, as the young adventurer was soon to learn, it was possible for an aspirant to success to get by both editors, and even a Cabinet Minister, and still fail of entire recognition from the most critical member of *The Spectator* staff. Even this distinction, however, Mr. Strachey was destined promptly to achieve. "The last, the complete rite of initiation at *The Spectator* office," occurred one day as he was talking over articles, when

"a large, consequential, not to say stout black tom-cat slowly entered the room, walked around me, sniffed at my legs in a suspicious manner, and then, to my intense amazement and amusement, hurled himself from the floor with some difficulty and alighted upon my shoulder. . . . The sagacious beast had realised that there was a new element in the office, and had come to inspect it and see whether he could give it his approval. When that approval was given, it was conceded by all concerned that the appointment had received its consecration."

And so, having received the unqualified endorsement of the office cat, the future "editor and sole proprietor" of *The Spectator*, within a few weeks of his introduction to the office, had his career mapped out for him. That Mr. Strachey has been content with that career this subjective autobiography is likely to convince the most sceptical.

Two chapters are devoted to an estimate of Meredith Townsend, who was successively his chief, his partner, and later—after Mr. Strachey became "sole proprietor and editor-in-chief"—merely leader-writer for *The Spectator*. The sketch of Mr. Townsend, which will undoubtedly appeal more to British than to American readers, is vivid and sympathetic, bringing into high relief the rather picturesque side of an altogether lovable and thoroughly practical personality—although any weak points which he may have displayed as leader-writer are not blurred over. His fairness, both toward his junior partner and toward those who differed with him, is emphasised, as well as his sound philosophy, his wit, his capacity for felicitous epigram, and his mental directness and forcefulness.

Mr. Strachey has the same pleasure in recalling his early

days with *The Spectator* that the aged courtesan is alleged to have in telling of her youthful *amours*.

"When an occasion like this makes me turn back to my old articles, I am glad to say that my attitude, far from being one of shame, is more like that of the Duke of Wellington. When quite an old man, somebody brought him his Indian dispatches to look over. As he read, he is recorded to have muttered: 'Damned good! I don't know how the devil I ever managed to write 'em.' "

When Mr. Strachey became "proprietor, editor, general manager, leader-writer, and reviewer" of *The Spectator* he naturally asked himself: "What is the journalist's function in the State, and how am I to carry it out?" After reflection and deliberation he decided that the journalist must be the watch-dog of society, and this in full recognition of the fact that the watch-dog is generally disliked, often misunderstood, and burdened with a disagreeable job, even with its compensations. He defends the watch-dog for barking,

"in a loud and raucous way, even for biting occasionally. It is good for the dog and it is good for the one who is barked at or bitten, though the latter, like the boy who is being flogged for his good, neither sees it nor admits it."

Mr. Strachey recites a specific instance of his watch-dog methods in dealing with Cecil Rhodes, whose methods of expanding the British Empire seemed to *The Spectator* dangerous and inconsistent with the sense of national honour and good faith. He therefore

"warned the British public that Rhodes, if not watched, would secretly buy policies behind their backs and that the party machine, when in want of money, would with equal secrecy sell them. And I proved my point, incredible as it may seem."

Mr. Strachey says that he could, of course, mention other examples of the way in which this particular watch-dog gave trouble and got himself heartily disliked, but recounting them would touch living people. Mr. Strachey does not bow the knee to archaic conventions like *"De mortuis nil nisi bonum."* Next to the watch-dog function of the journalist is that of publicity. Publicity is one of the pillars of society, and while this has long been recognised in America, Mr. Strachey says, it is only very recently that it has come to be thoroughly appreciated in his country. Publicity is as important a thing as the collection and preservation of evidence at a trial, but it is not the whole of journalism. Comment is an important part, and infinitely more important apparently in Britain than in this country. The journalism of comment may be divided into two parts: judicial, and the journalism of advocacy. It is the former that Mr. Strachey has practised or that he has meant to practise.

On the ethics of newspaper proprietorship he thinks that it makes for soundness that newspaper proprietors should be pecuniarily independent. It is also most important that they should be men whose money is derived from their newspapers, and not from other sources. A great newspaper in the hands of a man who does not look to it for profit, but owns it for external reasons, is a source of danger. In view of this opinion, it is interesting to recall that the control of the greatest newspaper in the world has recently passed, in great part, into the hands of a man who possesses a considerable portion of one of America's greatest fortunes.

The chapters of Mr. Strachey's book which should have been most interesting are those entitled "Five Great Men," in which he discusses Lord Cromer, John Hay, Theodore Roosevelt, Cecil Rhodes, and Joseph Chamberlain. Many will find them the most disappointing, particularly those who knew in the flesh any of these great men. They would be less disappointing, perhaps, if they were not so palpably self-laudatory. Mr. Strachey had a profound admiration for Lord Cromer and he shared it with thousands of his countrymen and Egyptian well-wishers the world over. Recalling a visit to Lord Cromer in Cairo, he says:

"Inexperienced as I then was in public affairs, it was a matter of no small pleasure and of no small amount of pride to find my own special opinions, views, and theories as to political action plainly endorsed by an authority so great. In not a single case was I disappointed or disillusioned either with what had been my own views or with what were Lord Cromer's."

This reminds strangely of Mr. Strachey's opinion of the Dons in his youthful days at Oxford. Future biographers of Lord Cromer will have to note the fact that "he was, with the single exception of my cousin, Lytton Strachey, the most competent reviewer I ever had," and that "he wrote a review every week for *The Spectator* on some important book," also that "he took an immense amount of trouble to realise and understand *The Spectator* view, and to commit me to nothing which he thought I might dislike."

In the same way, Mr. Strachey tells with great relish how he won the approval of Roosevelt with his tact and discretion when the President invited him to be present at one of his Cabinet meetings, and of Roosevelt's admiration when Mr. Strachey went with him in floods of rain for a ride on a dark November evening. In curious contrast to his statement that on this occasion he was mounted on a superb Kentucky horse procured from the cavalry barracks, "a creature whose strength and speed proved how well deserved is the reputation of that famous breed," is the photograph of Mr. Strachey on his pony at the end of the chapter, from which one would not readily gather that he had been selected by Mr. Roosevelt to accompany him "on these afternoon winter rides" as a test of men.

Mr. Strachey says that the bed-rock of his political opinions is a whole-hearted belief in the principles of democracy, and he defines his conception of democracy as being "not devotion to certain abstract principles or views of communal life which have the label 'democratic' placed upon them, but a belief in the justice, convenience and necessity of ascertaining and abiding by the lawfully and constitutionally expressed Will of the Majority of the People."

He states his belief in the referendum

"in order to free us from the evils of log-rolling and other exigencies of the kind which Walt Whitman grouped under the general formula of 'the insolence of elected persons.' "

He admits, however, that a whole-hearted belief in the democratic principles need not prevent one from having strong views on special points of policy, and one of his special points of policy is in regard to Ireland.

"I objected to Home Rule as bad for the Empire, bad for the United Kingdom, and bad in an even extremer degree for Ireland herself. If, however, it should be determined that some measure of Home Rule must be passed, then the existence of the two Irelands must be recognised in any action which should be determined upon. When, therefore, the support which the Unionist party decided on giving to Mr. Lloyd George at the end of the war made some form of Home Rule seem almost inevitable, I strongly advocated the division of Ireland as the only way of avoiding a civil war in which the merits would be with Northern Ireland."

One who comes to this delightful narrative as an admirer of the author may feel, on taking leave of it, that what Mr. Strachey has said of a famous fellow editor, William T. Stead, might also be said of him:

"Stead, though a man of honest intent, and very great ability, was also a man of many failings, many ineptitudes, many prejudices and injustices. Further, there was an element of commonness in his mental attitude, as in his style."

Yet this would not be quite fair or accurate. Mr. Strachey is a man of honest intent and very great ability, but there is no element of "commonness" in his mental attitude. His admirers would not admit that he is a man of many failings and many injustices. The word "some" should be substituted for "many," in any case. But then there are his pronunciamentos on Ireland and his recollections of Cecil Rhodes.

# CHAPTER XIII

FOR one who has devoted a considerable portion of his life to a study of the human mind in dissolution there are few things more diverting than popular disquisitions on the subject of insanity. If popular comments and interpretations regarding other subjects—world politics, for instance—are as apropos and penetrating as are those on mental disorder, the less readers are guided by them the more instructed they may expect to be.

I have recently read in an important magazine an article entitled "Up from Insanity" which has all the qualities that a contribution intended to be instructive and helpful should not have. It reeks with misinformation, not only misstatement of facts, but unwarranted inferences and unjustifiable and illogical conclusions.

The Editor of that distinguished and dignified periodical says: "It is a revealing narrative, genuine down to the latest detail." And so it is. It reveals the writer's incapacity to grasp the fundamental principles of psychology, established experimentally and empirically, and which have taken their place amongst the eternal truths of the world; and it reveals that the writer, whether because of his previous mental disorder, or willfully, is quite ignorant of what has been accomplished by countless students and innumerable workers in the field of psychiatry by way of throwing some light upon the mysteries of the normal mind.

"I am almost a pioneer in the field of written experience of insanity," he writes; and yet Mr. Clifford Beers' book, "A Mind that Found Itself," and "The Autobiography of a

Paranoic," two comparatively recent works that are most illuminating and have had a great effect in concentrating the attention of the public on insanity as a social problem, must have been known to him.

"It is a privilege conferred upon few men in the world to return from the dark and weird adventure [meaning insanity] to live a normal life."

Considering that upward of one-third of all insane individuals recover, there is no other interpretation to be put upon this statement than that the writer of it does not know whereof he speaks.

"A friend of mine lost his mind from thinking too much about his income tax."

This may be an attempt at facetiousness on the part of the writer. No physician who has dealt with the insane has ever encountered an individual made insane by "thinking too much." If so, he has been silent about it.

"I suppose, first of all, you would like to know how it feels to be insane. Well, it is indeed a melancholy situation."

It is, indeed, a melancholy situation if you have melancholia, but if you have mania, and especially if you have certain forms in which your self-appreciation is enhanced and your belief in your potencies and possessions quickened to an immeasurable degree, it is far from being a melancholy sensation. It is a sensation of power and possession which renders its possessor incapable of believing that any such thing as depression exists in the world.

"Lately a movement has arisen to change the name of insane asylums to 'mental hospitals.' We now recognise former madmen as merely sick people. We used to think of insane people as wild-eyed humans gnawing at prison bars or raving in a straight-jacket."

The casual reader might infer from this that "lately" means within the past few years, and yet three generations have come and gone since Conolly, Hack, Tuke and others initiated the movement which accomplished this.

"It was inconceivable to a well-known New York publisher that an insane man could play golf, go to Africa, or talk about his experiences."

The mental and emotional make-up of "well-known New York publishers" is enigmatic. There is general agreement on that point, but if there is one amongst them who believes that an insane man cannot play golf, he could readily divorce himself from the conviction by driving past any hospital for the insane. There he will see a golf course and some of the patients playing, though he will not be able to distinguish them from "regular" golfers. As for an insane man talking about his golf or his experiences in Africa, no New York publisher, well-known or otherwise, would need proof to convince him that an insane man can do that.

"On my way through New York I called on a celebrated specialist who told me that I had only six months to live and told me to go out and hunt, roam the world and make the best of the passing hours. Six months later that great physician died insane."

It is to be assumed that the celebrated specialist was a specialist in diseases of the mind. If that is so, the writer is in error. No celebrated alienist of New York has died insane within the past quarter of a century. In the second place, there has never been a celebrated alienist in New York who would fit the description,

"forty, rich, famous, living in an elegant home amid exquisite surroundings on University Heights with his wife, one of the most beautiful women I ever looked upon, a statuesque blonde of astounding loveliness," save in the last qualification. Each one of them has had a beautiful wife, but none "a statuesque blonde of astounding loveliness."

· If the writer consulted a physician who made that statement to him, he had the misfortune not only to be insane himself but to seek the counsel of a physician who was also insane.

The writer of the article says that he will attempt seriously to show that the centre of the will is distinct from the centre of the mind, and is a separately functioning organ; but in the stress of relating his experiences he forgot to do so. In fact, there would be no more satisfactory way of estimating his mental possessions and equilibrium than from an examination of this written document.

Those who are experienced with the insane give great diagnostic weight to their writings, not only the orthography and the syntax, but the sequence of thought, the rhythm of expression, the continuity of narrative, the pertinency of reference, the credibility of citation or example, the discursiveness of the narrative, and the way in which the writer develops and finally presents the central thought or idea. All these and other features of the written document are evidences to which he gives great weight. "Up from Insanity" is neither sequential in thought nor in narrative. Nearly every paragraph furnishes evidence of the distractibility of the writer's mind, and the discursiveness of the entire article amounts almost to rambling. It is marked with journalese jargon which reminds me of the newspaper accounts of the kidnapping or spiriting from Cuba of Señorita Cisneros.

The pith of the human document that we are discussing is that "every man's strength wells up from some centre deeper in him than the brain." It does. A man's personality at any moment is the sum total of all the reactions of every cell or physiological unit in his body; but acceptance of this fact does not alter the universally accepted belief that the brain is

the organ of mind.  To have it said by a psychopathic individual that his restoration to a normal mental state came after
he had observed "that a double nerve centre at the base of the
spine had been aroused and the function of these centres
brought balance and poise and strength, which was instantly
reflected in every movement and thought, and that these basic
nerve centres are the centre of the will," neither proves that
there is such a centre nor makes it at all probable that it
exists.

Why such humanistic and scientific puerilities as these
should have been taken seriously is not easy to understand.

Our knowledge concerning the human mind is not by any
means complete or satisfactory, but there are certain things
about it which we know.  For instance, we know that there
is a conscious mind and a subconscious mind.  The discovery
in 1866 of the "subliminal consciousness" of the psychologist
(the "unconscious mind" of the psychoanalyst), was called
by William James the greatest discovery in modern psychology.  We know that the person the individual thinks he is
is the equivalent of his conscious mind.  The man that he
really is is the man his unconscious mind makes him.  The
face that he sees when he looks in the glass is the face that
goes with his conscious mind.  The face that others see is the
one that fits his unconscious mind.  Anyone who would observe the revelations of that unconscious mind in literature
can readily gratify his wish by reading the "Portrait of the
Artist as a Young Man," that remarkable presentation by
James Joyce.

Many believe today that a man's ego or individuality is the
equivalent of this unconscious mind; that therein lies the
power of genius, the source of vision, the springs of inspiration that gush forth in prophecy, in artistic creation, in in-
vention.

We are now engaged in investigating this subliminal consciousness, or unconscious mind, with every means at our

disposal, and year by year we are making headway. Our progress is not adequate, perhaps, to satisfy the impatient and the impulsive, but with each succeeding decade there is a distinct achievement. Nevertheless, in the half-century during which we have been working at the matter in a methodical—perhaps one might almost say a scientific—way, we have discovered things about the mind which are truly epoch-making.

It is evident that the writer of the article, "Up from Insanity," has never been insane. He is a psychopathic individual who has had distressing episodes. At times these episodes have parallelled with considerable closeness the features of definite mental diseases such as manic depressive insanity, at other times they seem to have resembled the features of dementia præcox; but he never was the victim of either one. He inherited an unstable nervous system which displayed itself in youth as a shut-in, markedly sensitive, anti-social personality. Like the majority of individuals so burdened, he was subject to periods of excitation, at which times he did things at top speed. Neurologists call this a "hypo-manic state," that is, a state that resembles mania in miniature. Such states would be followed by periods of inadequacy, of retardation of mental and physical activity, and of depression.

After a severe attack which he suffered when he was twenty-one, he had what is called in polite circles a "nervous breakdown," the chief symptoms being abortive delusions of reference. He thought that certain parts of his body had changed so materially that it was necessary to hide them from the gaze of onlookers. It made him sick to look at his own face. He had to wear coloured glasses in order that others might not read his secret from his eyes, and his sense of relationship with everything constituting the external world was disordered disagreeably. Accompanying this there were a series of symptoms which constitute "feeling badly," and all the functions of the body that were concerned with nutrition were disordered, so that he became weak and lost flesh. Oftentimes his depression of spirits was so great that he convinced himself he wanted to die, but he did not embrace a good opportunity to accomplish this end when it was offered to him. In fact, he struggled so valiantly with the run-away horse that he checked him and "slid from his back ingloriously," physically exhausted. It would be interesting to know why sliding off the back of a horse who has run away and whose frenzy has been subdued by the rider should be an inglorious dismounting. Of course it might be more glorious to tame him to such a degree that his master could stand upon his back and direct his capriciousness with a glance or a silken cord, but surely there is nothing inglorious about *any* kind of dismount from the back of a horse who has been transformed from a gentle to a wild animal.

Nevertheless, the experience was a beneficial one. When he reviewed his prowess he realised that he had imposed his will-power, mediated by muscle, upon the animal, and it occurred to him, a victim of aboulia like the majority of psychopathic individuals, that to impose a similar will-power upon himself would be a salutary procedure. With this discernment came other revelations. One was that he had always been lacking in concentration and was easily distracted —psychopathic hallmarks which can be effaced to a remarkable degree, in many instances, by training. The first fruit of his labour in this direction was the discovery that Dr. Cook had been understudying Ananias, Munchausen, *et al.*

In another part of his article he says, with consummate familiarity, "You are from Missouri when it comes to asking you to accept new thoughts." He may be assured that one of his readers is not. New thoughts are as acceptable to this reader as breath to his nostrils; but he would claim citizenship in that State if asked to accept it as an indication of perspicacity to have discovered that Dr. Cook was a fake.

Despite the fact that the writer of the article had "developed the sixth sense to a startling degree," which assured him success as a journalist, he was chafing under his impotencies when he met a former medium who "had given up that life since her marriage." Unlike the celebrated specialist's wife, who was the most beautiful creature he had ever seen up to the time he met his own wife, this one was "the most insignificant little woman I ever saw." Whether it was her experience gained as a medium, or as the wife of a rich lumberman of the Middle West, that prompted her to shy the alleged lunatic, fearing he would bore her with a narrative of his troubles, or whether she did not want to rake up her past, cannot be gathered from the meagre narrative. However, he got from her this nugget of wisdom:

"To be really successful you must get in touch with the great reservoir of experience."

From "one of the country's greatest physicians," the like of which are his personal friends, he got a paraphrase of the Scripture:

"Learn a lesson from the flowers of the field, be humble and modest, be natural and play a man's part."

It was then that calm repose settled upon him, and his nervous energy returned to the old channels and nourished him.

If Mr. E. J. had only appended a few of his dreams to his human document, there would be very little difficulty in pointing out the emotional repression that was at the bottom of all his mental symptoms. That he conforms to a certain well-known type of psychic fixation there is very little doubt. He has always been bereft, because he has a feeling of being spiritually or mentally alone. He never learned to be independent in mind, but always looked for an uncritical, soothing, maternal sort of love from people who were not ready or willing to give it. He has not changed materially. Now that his so-called recovery has come, and being unable to find what he demands, he takes refuge in the next best thing, and plays at obtaining it vicariously; he convinces himself that he is going to devote himself to doing for others "all the little kindnesses that life offers."

The layman who would get some knowledge of insanity should avoid such confessions as that of E. J. If he would make acquaintance with the self-coddling of a neurotic individual who delights in self-analysis, self-pity, and exaggeration of his symptoms, and who is a fairly typical example of juvenile fixation, his purpose will be accomplished by reading this and similar articles. There is, however, a safer and more satisfactory way of securing such information, and that is by reading the writings of Pierre Janet. There he will find the obsessed, the hysteric, the aboulic, the neurasthenic individual discussed in masterly fashion, and he will find the presentation unmixed with mediæval mysticism and puerile platitudes, unflavoured with specious "uplift" sentiment and psychological balderdash.

On the other hand, he may get real enlightenment from "The Jungle of the Mind," published recently in the same magazine, providing he closes his eyes to the editorial comment and refuses to read the letter "of a physician of reputation" which sets forth that "according to all our text-book symptoms of dementia præcox she was surely that."

The purpose of such editorial comment must be either to suggest that the enigmatic dissolution of the mind to which Schule gave the name "precocious dementia" may eventuate in recovery, or to show that doctors make mistakes. If it is the former, it needs a lot of proof; if the latter, none whatsoever. Though students of mental pathology know little or nothing of the causes of the mental disorders of hereditarily predisposed individuals who get wrecked on the cliffs of puberty, or of the alterations and structure of the tissues that subserve the mind, they know, as they know the temperaments of their better halves, the display, the types, the paradigms of the disease. And the lady who has recently contributed some notes on a disfranchisement from the state of *non compos mentis* to the *Atlantic Monthly* with such subtle display of proficiency in the literary art, may be assured that the doctors who averred she had dementia præcox added one more error to a list already countless. With the daring of one who hazards nothing by venturing an opinion, I suggest that she merely made a journey into a wild country from whose bourne nearly all travellers return. The country is called "Manic-Depressive Insanity."

A young woman of gentle birth develops, while earning her bread in uplift work, "nervous prostration," that coverer of a multitude of ills. Her sister's home, to which she goes, brings neither coherence nor tranquillity. In fact, she gathers confusion rapidly there, and seeks to get surcease of it in oblivion. After three attempts at suicide, she is sent to a sanitarium. Six months of that exhausts her financial resources. This, with increasing incoherency and fading actuality, necessitate transfer to a state hospital, and there she remains three years, going through the stages of violence, indifference, tranquillity, resignation, and finally the test of work and recreation, culminating happily in probational discharge and resumption of previous work.

This is the record of thousands in this country and in every civilised country. The variety of insanity which she had (and it is the commonest of all the insanities) nearly always terminates in recovery—that is, from the single attack. There is, of course, the likelihood of recurrence. How to avoid that is what we are keen to learn from mental hygienists and from those taught by experience. If this disenfranchised lady will tell us ten years hence what she has done to keep well and how her orientation has differed from that of the ten years following puberty, she will make a human document of value intellectually, not emotionally, as this one is. Meanwhile, should she be disposed to do something for future psychopaths, she may record the experiences of her life from childhood to the period of full development, and particularly of the decade following her fifth year. If she will do this with the truthfulness of James Joyce, the chasteness of Dorothy M. Richardson, and the fullness of Marie Bashkirtseff, it may be said of her: "Out of the mouths of babes and sucklings thou hast perfected praise."

It may be literature to describe one's fellow inmates of a psychopathic hospital, to portray their adult infantilisms, to delineate their schizophrenias, to recount their organised imageries, but it does not contribute an iota to our knowledge of insanity, how to prevent it, and how to cure it.

We need intrepid souls who will bare their psychic breasts and will tell us, without fear or shame, of their conventionalised and primitive minds: how the edifice was constructed, the secrets of the architect, and of the builder. If Dostoievsky had been insane, not epileptic, the literature of psychiatry would today be vastly more comprehensive.

THE END